Forbes Taylor was Head of Documentaries at Anglia Television, the ITV regional broadcaster for East Anglia and the East Midlands, for nearly twenty years from its first days.

He wrote and directed the first pictures that appeared on its screen in 1959, and produced Anglia's flagship documentary series on archaeology.

He has also been an artist, carrying out portrait commissions, a soldier, producing the Edinburgh Military Tattoo at the tender age of twenty-six, a journalist on the magazine *Picture Post,* and film-maker in Britain's pioneering days, directing action sequences on *The Adventures of Robin Hood.*

He lives in Southwold, Suffolk, with his former actress and batik artist wife, Mary.

TOY TOWN TELLY

Forbes Taylor

TOY TOWN TELLY

and
Stone Age Filming

A Memoir

Vanguard Press

VANGUARD PAPERBACK

© Copyright 2013
Forbes Taylor

The right of Forbes Taylor to be identified as author of this work has been asserted by him in accordance with the Copyright, Designs and Patents Act 1988.

All Rights Reserved

No reproduction, copy or transmission of this publication may be made without written permission.
No paragraph of this publication may be reproduced, copied or transmitted save with the written permission of the publisher, or in accordance with the provisions of the Copyright Act 1956 (as amended).

Any person who commits any unauthorised act in relation to this publication may be liable to criminal prosecution and civil claims for damages.

A CIP catalogue record for this title is available from the British Library.

ISBN 9781 84386 762 3

Vanguard Press is an imprint of
Pegasus Elliot MacKenzie Publishers Ltd.

www.pegasuspublishers.com

First Published in 2013

Vanguard Press
Sheraton House Castle Park
Cambridge England
Printed and bound in Great Britain

*To Roddy, Frank, Bernadette,
Thelma, Brian, Ian and Harry,
and all those other friends who
"played with the train set" with me,
and who have preceded me to
The Great Studio in the sky.*

Are you sitting comfortably? Then I'll begin...

THERE WAS once a jolly farmer who stood on the edge of his field watching his men harvesting his corn. He had brought his *magic* camera along because he had *a very important task* to perform. The jolly farmer's landlord up at the *CASTLE* (well, the hall) had been awarded a licence to broadcast *television*, and his trusty tenant, he knew, made home movies. He was – was he not? – all that was needed to provide the programmes.

His lordship had broached the subject one morning in the yard behind the stately hall. 'But I haven't got a television set,' the jolly farmer had pointed out.

'Neither have I,' said his lordship, 'but my butler has.'

As the farmer began filming, the driver of the *GIANT* combine harvester stopped his juggernaut, climbed down and crossed the field to confront his master.

'What's that you're a-doin, squire?' he demanded suspiciously.

'I'm photographin',' the farmer replied.

'Oh,' said the worker, '– could Oi ha' one er them when that come out?'

'No,' the farmer explained. 'That's a cine-camera. That doesn't make photographs.'

'Well, will that be on at the Central, Fakenham?' the man persisted.

'No,' the farmer continued patiently, 'that's for the new television. Anglia Television.'

The man considered for a few moments. Then:

'Well yor'll ha' er tell me when that's gor'n to be orn – an' Oi won't watch it!'

Commercial television had come to Norfolk.

I finally decided that I would have to make the move from film to television a week before my thirty-third birthday.

I was in the dubbing theatre in Merton Park Film Studios – in those days at Wimbledon in West London – directing two films about nuclear warfare for the Home Office. The phone caller said he was with a new regional broadcasting company called Anglia Television – was I still interested in a job as Head of Films?

I remembered that, several months earlier my wife had seen an advertisement in a Sunday newspaper inviting applications for top jobs in this company. I had turned my back on television on more than one occasion – making pictures for a tiny, fuzzy black-and-white screen in the corner of the living room seemed a poor alternative to the big screen, Technicolor and Cinema Scope. But we had talked about this one. Cinemas seemed to be closing wherever one looked, film studios experiencing the latest of their habitual recessions. One could not escape the conclusion that television was likely to come out on top in this contest. Might be the future as far as careers were concerned. Anglia Television was one of the last two commercial TV stations to start up – this might well be the final opportunity to move from what seemed to be a dying industry to a burgeoning one. I had sent off a CV – but received no reply and forgot about it.

I learned the truth about that, and something of the ways of sunrise commercial television companies, when I met the caller that evening. Michael Seligman was a heavily built young man with a disconcerting nervous tic. He told me that none of the people in the group that had won the East Anglia licence had any experience of running a television service. Seligman was production manager of an advertising agency that made "commercials", and had been loaned to the new company to bring some professional experience to the start-up operation. This included sifting through the job applications, which had piled up in an "in" tray. Most of those for the job I had applied for were from cinema projectionists – nearly all the existing broadcasters had recruited such people, because they assumed the only use a "Head of Films" could be put to was seeing that the filmed "commercials" were joined together in the right order (anyone could *make* films!). I had naively supposed that a "Head of Films" would manage the production of filmed programmes and my application had described my career as a film director.

It had caught Seligman's eye. Anglia intended to be "different" from the other regional companies. (I was to hear that word many times in the future – in Norfolk *patois* it is "du different" and it says all you need to know about Norfolk attitudes.) One of Anglia's principal owners was the film production company, Romulus Films, and there were ambitious plans for drama productions for the national network.

I was not entirely won over by what Seligman told me, but accepted his invitation to go to Anglia's office in Park Lane to meet the board of directors.

The following afternoon I was ushered into an elegant room overlooking Hyde Park – at one time it had been Lord Mountbatten's flat. Two men were sitting behind a desk, and Seligman murmured the name, Lord Townshend. The other name I did not catch. A very tall man in his early forties welcomed me with a smile and asked me to sit down. This was the company's chairman, Marquess Townshend of Raynham. He seemed warm and human and I instantly liked him.

It always helps at a job interview if you don't really care whether you get the job or not, and in answer to his question, I said I thought Anglia Television should find its staff as far as possible from the local area. This seemed to please my interviewers.

The shorter man then took up the questioning. This was the new company's Chief Executive, Donald Stephenson, a former BBC "mandarin".

'What do you know about 16-millimetre film?' he enquired. 'The BBC and the network companies use 35mm. They say that 16mm is no good.'

I was able to answer, truthfully, that I had rather a good knowledge of 16mm, having "pioneered" some aspects of the professional use of what was then a chiefly amateur medium. I said I thought 16mm should be quite adequate for television. This was clearly what my interviewers wanted to hear.

All the same, what struck me was that no one present seemed to have the necessary knowledge or expertise to choose the right person for the job in question. They might well have had reservations about me, for I knew absolutely nothing about television. However, at the end of the interview it seemed I had been offered the job, at a salary of

£2,000 a year, provided I was prepared to demonstrate my goodwill by accepting £250 less for the first six months while the infant company was getting on its feet. It was all delightfully – and as I was to find, typically – muddled and unclear.

I waited outside the room for Seligman, and when he emerged a moment later, he said I should return in a day or two for Anglia's Programme Controller, Stephen McCormack, to look me over. I was surprised he had not been present at the interview.

'Have I got the job or not?' I asked.

'You've got the job,' Seligman assured me. And next morning a letter arrived, formally confirming my appointment.

Two days later I returned to Park Lane to meet Stephen McCormack. I was shown into an office jam-packed with people. McCormack, a slim, wiry man of indeterminate age, was on the phone shouting to someone that he "had the Dagenham Girl Pipers" in the office. I could see no sign of girl pipers, so presumed he meant us.

When he hung up I introduced myself. He seemed bemused by my presence, so I told him that I *thought* I had been engaged as Head of Films – provided he liked the look of me.

'I've fallen in love with you, dear boy,' he retorted.

At this moment the new "Head of Drama" came into the room, and I was surprised to recognise an old friend. George More O'Ferrall and I had worked on a film together. He had gone on to win a high reputation, directing one or two major films for Korda. George was also a legendary figure in the history of television, having been the first person in the world to produce a play on television back in the early 1930s. It seemed that Anglia intended to be a quality company.

Before I left the office, McCormack had words of advice for a novice entering a new life in television and I waited to hear the essence of profound wisdom distilled from his years of experience.

'Never sleep with your *own* PA,' he said.

Part One

A Fortune Of War

1

IF THERE had not been a war my life would have been utterly different. I would not have been in the army. And if I had not been in the army I would not have been given the amazing and unexpected opportunity that led to my career as a film-maker.

Everyone I meet nowadays seems to have made a film! It is strange to think there was a time when filmmaking was a great mystery, carried on within buildings that were strictly "off limits" to the uninitiated. It was rare to meet anyone who worked in a film studio. If you were one of that priesthood, the question you were almost always asked, with something approaching awe, was 'How did you get into films?' Probably no two answers were the same. Mine was almost certainly among the most unlikely. I had been *ordered* to be a film director when I was in the army.

I like to say that I began my film career as Carol Reed's Assistant Director. I was nine at the time.

There was a film studio not far from my childhood home. In later years it became famous as "Ealing Studios", but at that time it was known as "ATP" – Associated Talking Pictures. The films being made there usually starred the Lancashire comedienne Gracie Fields, who was said to cross the road in the lunch hour plastered with bright yellow make-up, to drink in the Red Lion pub. Perhaps it was true – early films were photographed with blue-sensitive orthochromatic film which made flesh tones unnaturally dark. European film actors (or "Caucasian" as the Americans mysteriously call them) were daubed with yellow grease-paint to stop them looking like Indians.

The studio backs on to Walpole Park, where my school friends and I played on summer days. One day we spotted something big being constructed, high up on scaffolding on the other side of the park fence. Day by day it grew until it was recognisable as the hull of an eighteenth-century man-of-war. We were puzzled. Quite obviously it was nowhere near any water. Word went round that it was for a film called *Midshipman Easy*, starring the boy wonder Hughie Green. We all knew him from his radio programme, *Hughie Green And His Gang*.

Eventually filming began. We were not near enough to catch a glimpse of Hughie and soon began to marvel at how boring filming appeared to be. The same bit was done over and over again with no apparent connection with anything that went before or came after. A man with a megaphone kept shouting 'Cut!' We juvenile delinquents got the idea and shouted it for him, to his growing fury. Eventually a park keeper arrived and told us to shut up.

Many years later I learned that the young man with the megaphone was Carol Reed, directing his first film. He went on to become one of the world's greatest directors, of films like *The Third Man* and *Oliver!*

So there you are – I began my career working with Carol Reed.

Actually, I never met him. But I did direct a film myself when I was twenty-one – and was "hailed as a genius" in what may be the most fanciful headline the *Sunday Express* ever printed. I worked for Alexander Korda's London Films when Carol Reed was there making *The Third Man*. I was an action director on the television series *The Adventure Of Robin Hood* (where my boss and drinking companion was the film editor of *Midshipman Easy*, Sidney Cole). As a television producer-director I pioneered ITV's archaeology programmes. I wrote for the magazine *Picture Post*, produced the Edinburgh Tattoo when I was twenty-six, and even made a brief appearance on ITN's *News At Ten* as an involuntary war correspondent reporting from an Arab-Israeli battle. At the height of my career I led "a glittering consortium" (as the press described it) that attempted to win an ITV contract, and was among the first British producers to experiment with UK-US co-productions.

High fame and fortune eluded me, however. Like most people who spent their lives in the film and television industries, it was just a job, a way of paying the rent. But I did see some interesting things and met some remarkable people.

The family I was born into, in the small hours of 15th August 1926, had migrated to London at the end of the nineteenth century from Scotland. My ancestors had lived for centuries in a tiny *clachan* called Kilspindie, which stands at the foot of the hills known as the Braes Of The Carse about eight miles east of Perth. My forefathers were millwrights – they designed and built watermills along the streams that flowed through the village to the river Tay below, a way of life that was brought to an end with the introduction of steam-power, fuelled by the coal brought up the Tay estuary to Dundee. My great-grandfather moved with his family to that smoky "city of the three Js" – jute, jam and journalism (and one "A" – alcohol – it was described in Parliament as the alcoholic capital of Europe).

It must have been a culture shock. Life in Dundee in the 1860s may not have been shorter than many other places in Britain but it was certainly nasty and brutish. My grandfather's life was gentlemanly, however. He was General Manager of the photographic and picture postcard company, Valentines, which employed over a thousand people. It was founded by pioneer photographer James Valentine in 1825. The firm's catalogues advertised work by photographers in Norway, and my grandfather travelled to Scandinavia – I believe to set up that side of the business. I do not know why he moved his large family to Ealing, West London, though the presence of a leading photographic company – next door to the film studios – may have had something to do with it.

All but one of the close-knit Taylor family settled in Ealing, which in those days was known as "the Queen of Suburbs". My genteel aunts and uncles were typically "suburban", respectable and conservative – probably with a capital "C", though I can't be sure. They were Victorians, and propriety and respectability were paramount. The family history was not spoken about. One reason for reticence was that my parents had divorced. I was about three when it happened. My father then set up home in a pleasant house in a leafy road in Ealing with his older unmarried sister, and she effectively became my "mother". She certainly thought of herself as such, and I loved her dearly. She was a lovely, and much loved person, and a talented artist who worked as a photographic re-toucher, removing lines and wrinkles from people's portraits.

It was both my fortune and misfortune that my father was different from the rest of the family. In his young days he was always into something unusual, exciting – and sometimes alarming to his sisters. But at least he wasn't boring – anything new was a source of immediate and total attention, and he was enthusiastic about nothing so much as the cinema.

Like him, I was always mad about films. I remember with absolute clarity the first film he took me to – in 1933 or 34, when I was about seven. It was *Ben Hur*, the epic of Ancient Rome – the silent version (some small cinemas had still not installed sound equipment) with a musical accompaniment from a piano below the screen (someone thought Lizst's *Hungarian Rhapsody* a suitably Roman choice – Rome – Hungary – both foreign, aren't they?). I can still hear the gasps of *Ooooh!* when the screen blossomed into gaudy colour for a few seconds, during the brief hand-tinted scenes. Yes – hand tinted! Assembly lines of 1920s artistic ladies had dabbed coloured dye on the strips of celluloid as they passed along a bench before them.

The Saturday afternoon trip to "the pictures" (only Americans used the baby word "movies") was unfailingly regular in those pre-television days. Cinemas were described, not unjustifiably, as "picture palaces". They had vast ornate foyers, grand staircases and imposing Art Deco auditoria. "Brand loyalty" to a particular cinema was the rule – never mind that a better film was on at the other place, you went to your familiar local. The only exception was when a British film was shown. We avoided them like the plague. They were either adaptations of stage plays, featuring incredibly plain actresses with cut-glass accents, and actors with brilliantined hair in white tie and tails, or brainless "North Coontray" so-called comedies starring George Formby and his ukulele. Only Gracie Fields was tolerated. She punctuated stories of cheery hardship with songs sung in a hideous soprano that could break wine glasses.

The usual programme lasted up to four hours and consisted of a "first feature", a "second feature", a fifteen-minute newsreel, and trailers for the following week's films. Sometimes there was a recital from a gaudily lit organ that appeared from somewhere in the lower reaches below the plush crimson curtains. The performances were continuous, and you went to the pictures at whatever time suited you, usually arriving in the middle of a film and seeing the programme round till it reached the point where you came in. Amazingly we seemed to have no trouble picking up the threads of the story. Oblivious to regular disturbances caused by people squeezing past on their way to or from their seats, I seemed to "pass through" the screen, like Alice through her looking glass, to join the characters in their adventures. I rode beside George Arliss as *The Iron Duke* at the Battle of Waterloo, sailed to Tahiti with the Bounty mutineers, marched through the Khyber Pass with Laurel and Hardy in *Bonnie Scotland*, and was scared out of my skin by Peter Lorre, playing a mad surgeon who sewed back the heads of guillotined murderers in *Hands of Orlac*. I think I was taken to that one by mistake – I was not allowed to see Frankenstein or Dracula. It was entertainment of course, but "the pictures" taught us about Abraham Lincoln, Queen Victoria, Louis Pasteur and Emile Zola. We also saw adaptations of the classics: *David Copperfield*, *A Christmas Carol*, and Max Reinhardt's

Midsummer Night's Dream – we went to that two or three times.

I was fascinated by what seemed like magic in films. I wondered why no camera was visible when the point of view switched so that we were looking over the shoulder of an actor we had just been seeing full-face. One day, with a tiny thrill, I figured out how it was done. *The scenes had been photographed twice, with the camera in reversed positions,* and the pieces had then been joined together. What a conjuring trick! Very nearly magic. Not bad for a nine-year-old – in those unsophisticated times, the rest of the audience believed they were watching a continuous scene, as in the theatre.

This regular exposure at an early age must, I suppose, have set the course for what became my life's work. Even then I thought how marvellous it would be to be *in* films! There was a legendary place across the ocean on everyone's tongue. *Hollywood!* There dwelt gods and goddesses known as *film stars*. Gary Cooper. Wallace Beery. Greta Garbo. Jean Harlow. Fred Astaire and Ginger Rogers. How wonderful to join them, to *become* different characters having exciting adventures in colourful places! But one did not nurse impossible ambitions. Instead I decided to become an artist. Artistic talent ran in the family, after all.

The war that broke out in 1939 disrupted my education, but I eventually found myself at art school in Ealing (coincidentally just across the road from the film studio). I discovered the joy of painting in oils and had an instinct for perspective and composition. I made progress in figure and portrait work – and in poster art, which was held in high regard at the time.

I cannot remember my father showing interest in my paintings. I certainly do not recall his ever studying one, or remarking on it. All the same, it was he who spotted an advertisement in the newspaper one morning in 1943, when I was seventeen. It invited applicants for a job as commercial artist in a small, newly-formed advertising and printing business.

'You could do that,' he told me, exhibiting the confidence born out of sheer ignorance that I would marvel at on a further occasion, far in the future.

I replied to the advertisement and to my surprise was invited to an interview. Mister Reeves, and distinguished-looking Mister de Solla (I suspect his real name was Solomon), had fitted out a studio in an empty house in Maida Vale, where they intended to produce advertisements by the "silk-screen" process. Because of the wartime "blackout", illuminated signs were not allowed. Reeves and de Solla planned to beat the ban by using fluorescent paint, which could be made to glow in the dark when illuminated by ultra-violet light.

The day's second surprise was that I got the job. Probably it was because every other potential candidate was away fighting Hitler. Or it may have been because the salary my father had told me to ask for – three pounds, ten shillings a week – was readily acceptable. I thought I caught an exchange of glances between my prospective employers out of the corner of my eye. I thought it seemed an enormous amount, and a cheek to ask for (it would be about £130 in today's money).

So I started my first work as a professional artist. Mister Reeves showed me how to cut stencils, using the tricky "Profilm", while continuously sighing as though tired of life. I must have pleased him, because at the end of the second week I was asked if I was satisfied with my salary. I heard myself replying that I could do with some more. Whereupon Reeves announced that my salary would henceforth be raised to five pounds. Riches! I was among the ranks of the higher wage earners. Two or three weeks later, the firm went bust.

It was discovered that ultra-violet light was as visible to enemy aircraft as the conventional kind and that scuppered the business. I was nominally out of work.

2

A FRIEND gave me an introduction to someone he knew who managed the animation department at Merton Park Film Studios, which was making military instruction films. Perhaps I could become a trainee animation artist? I made enquiries but there were no immediate vacancies. I was, however, invited to leave my address (years later I learned that teenage Roger Moore was beavering away at a drawing board in a similar studio).

With paper hard to come by and a world not yet dominated by advertising, there were few jobs going for commercial artists. In any case, the prospect of being "called up" for military service in little more than a year's time made it rather irrelevant to be worrying about a career. Everyone had to do war work of some kind, and a job was found for me on the staff of the forces' entertainment organisation, ENSA. It was housed in Drury Lane Theatre, which had taken a bomb through the dress circle one night during the *Blitz* and was closed for shows.

ENSA – it meant Entertainments National Service Association (or alternatively, Every Night Something Awful) – was both famous and notorious. The wags called it "Hitler's Secret Weapon" – the tatty and talent-starved shows were produced by enemy agents to demoralise our troops. Other wags argued that it was a brilliant government plan. The shows were deliberately horrendous, so the enemy would not seem so bad by comparison. All this was monstrously unfair, of course. Although feeble comedians and faded chorus girls did gyrate before the suffering servicemen, many excellent shows went out from "The Lane" to distant theatres of war, at no small risk to the performers and conducting staff. There was an ambitious drama department, run by veteran actor Henry Oscar. This side of the operation caught my interest, and I took to remaining behind after my time to go home to watch rehearsals, which went on late into the night, and help when asked. One of the more ambitious productions was Shaw's *Arms And The Man*, which had a Hollywood film-star in it – Richard Greene. I was to meet him again, many years later.

I had been at Drury Lane only a couple of weeks when I received a letter from Merton Park Studios saying that there was now a job for me in the animation department. I politely refused it – I had been seduced by "show biz".

That summer of 1944 was a particularly gorgeous one.

How to conjure up a vision of those times?

Everywhere uniforms. Khaki, navy, air force blue. Leaden skies dotted with silver barrage-balloons, gently swinging on their cables. The streets empty of cars. Rain drizzling into large circular tanks at street corners – "Static Water Tanks" for fighting incendiary bomb fires. The "blackout" – total, velvety blackness, shuffling and groping, hands in front like a blind person. Painful collisions with lampposts and pillar boxes. "Pea soup" London fogs. Creepy. But no muggers or rapists, that we've ever heard of. *There's a war on* is the explanation for every hardship.

"BE LIKE DAD – KEEP MUM"

Instructs the security poster. Spies, apparently, are everywhere. Another exhortation, in the Underground trains. From "Billy Brown of London Town". Cartoon figure Billy is politely correcting a misguided passenger who is attempting to peel off the netting glued to the train's windows to protect the passengers from blast:

"I trust you'll pardon my correction
That stuff is there for your protection"

Graffiti scrawled underneath:

*I thank you for your information
But I can't see the bloody station*

Moaning air raid sirens, though not heard so often in 1944, because the "alert" is in operation all the time – no one can tell when a V1 flying bomb will evade the East Coast anti-aircraft guns and explode in the centre of London. And Londoners have just become aware of a new, *uncanny* sound – more sinister even than the rumble of the doodle bugs. A massive explosion, *followed* by a rushing roar. The signature of a V2 rocket arriving, *faster* than the speed of sound! At least, as the optimists say – 'If you hear the bang, you know you're still alive'.

London, 1944...

Another world...

No television aerials. No supermarkets. No McDonalds.

No jet airliners overhead. No tourists. No black faces, except among the Americans.

No "Nite Spots" – for the working class, anyway. No students. No "binge-drinkers". No drugs. No policemen toting machine guns. And we've never <u>heard</u> of "homosexuals".

A world that has entirely disappeared.

But unforgettable – as fresh in my mind as yesterday as I write this.

With the Allies advancing across Europe, and the German army in full retreat in Russia, London had not suffered a concentrated attack by the Luftwaffe for some time. The battery of heavy anti-aircraft guns positioned in a field about a quarter of a mile from our house occasionally opened up, with Wagnerian thunder, on a bomber that appeared overhead to remind London that the war had not yet been won. I got used to the racket and I managed to sleep through it.

It became easy to believe that the worst of the war was over. Until – that is – one night in mid-June. I was tucked up in my bed, as usual oblivious to the cacophony from the anti-aircraft guns, when I returned to consciousness to find my father frantically shaking me. The guns were slamming away like the hammers of hell.

'Get up!' my father shouted. 'Something different's happening!' Then I heard, through the racket of the guns, a strange pop-popping rumble. The sound of some sort of engine. I joined the family downstairs and a moment or two later there was a loud explosion which made the house judder. The guns suddenly ceased and there was an eerie silence. We waited for half an hour or so, then crept back to bed.

The following Saturday morning the BBC news informed us that, on the preceding Tuesday, the 13th of June, a new weapon had been used on Britain. Some kind of pilotless aircraft. A *flying* bomb. A house in South London had been destroyed and three people had been killed.

The bulletin had hardly ended when we heard the ominous sound again. We ran into the garden, and were treated to an extraordinary spectacle. A "VI" flying bomb was streaking low overhead, flame shooting from its tailpipe. A Spitfire was attempting to intercept it, but falling further and further behind – outstripped by the weapon's jet-propulsion engine. The display disappeared into the far distance, from where we eventually heard a dull thud. Later we learned not to run out and watch the "doodlebugs". They killed thousands of people in the first weeks they were used.

Although the anti-aircraft defences on the south-east coast became increasingly effective in shooting down the flying bombs, they continued to get through to London. It was impossible to predict when this might happen, and sirens were no longer any use. Life could not come to a standstill, so a more immediate warning system had to be improvised. Bush House in Aldwych, the overseas headquarters of the BBC, had communication with air defence. It was arranged that on the approach of a flying-bomb, a red flag would be as run up on its roof to warn lookouts in the buildings round about. Drury Lane's staff took turns on the roof of the theatre as "spotters". On the appearance of the red flag a button was pressed, bells would sound in the theatre, and everyone was supposed to go to the safest place – under the stage.

People became blasé however and began to ignore the warning.

Friday, the thirtieth of June, dawned bright and sunny. As usual I set out for work on the Piccadilly Line train from Park Royal. Standing room only, wedged beside one of the doors. Shatterproof netting glued to the windows left a small diamond-shaped clear space in the centre to allow passengers to identify stations. The first part of the journey ran on the surface, and I peered out at the outskirts of London flashing by. We were at full speed on the non-stop stretch between Acton Town and Hammersmith, near Ravenscourt Park Station, when I suddenly saw a flying bomb in the air about half a mile away. The sound of its engine was drowned by the noise of the train. The robot craft was swooping down towards a large Victorian school building, and as I watched, the school disintegrated in a flash of flame and black smoke. The force of the blast struck the train, making it sway wildly. For a moment, it seemed it might topple, then it managed to recover and careered on its way. Seconds later the horrifying scene was far behind us. I looked at my watch. It was not quite half-past eight. With luck, none of the children would have arrived at the school. I never knew the truth. We were not told things like that during the war.

At Covent Garden station, I went up in the lift to street level and the hazards of wartime London.

Drury Lane's "paint-shop" is a lofty cavern of a place behind the stage, with a glass roof far overhead, reinforced with chicken-wire. There worked the beautiful Pat Batchelor, her sole shortcoming, as far as I was concerned, her tender years. It did not stop me spending my lunch hours with her. I was painting furiously at the time, she was a talented artist, and we had a lot to talk about. We stood in the centre of the vast space discussing a painting I had brought in to show her. An older scene-painter worked away in a far corner.

We ignored the warning bell. The next thing we were aware of was a dark shadow that seemed to flick across the space above us. There was a blinding flash, and an ear-splitting BANG!

For a split second we exchanged frightened glances.

Far overhead, there was the tinkling sound of glass shattering.

'Run for the door!' bawled the elderly scene painter.

We covered only a couple of steps before the roof was upon us. The thought flashed through my head that men should throw themselves over girls to protect them. But there was no time for that. We bent over, clutching each other around the waist as the entire glass roof crashed down on us, thumping on our backs, neck and head. Dust blinded us.

It was over in a matter of seconds. As the dust settled, we straightened up and stared at the floor. Glass covered every inch of it, to knee height. Miraculously we were not even scratched! I picked up a piece that had bounced off my back. It was shaped like a long dagger.

The streets outside had been crowded. It was a brilliant summer's day and office workers in bright summer dresses had been taking the air and dawdling round the shops during the lunch break. The bomb had glided in silently and hit the road right in the centre of Aldwych, exploding close to the side of Ad Astral House, the Air Ministry building (in later years it was the headquarters of the

London ITV station Rediffusion, and then the Public Record Office of Births, Marriages and Deaths).

Crowds of pedestrians were blown to bits, together with the passengers in a wrecked bus. Lots of girls, most in the WAAF, had been sunbathing on the roof and they were killed along with others who were sucked out of shattered windows by the vacuum caused by the blast. The record lists 198 deaths, but there were almost certainly many more, as some of the casualties were government officials whose identity was covered by the Official Secrets Act. By any standards it was a catastrophe of epic proportions, and I was lucky to have escaped such a close-run thing. I was 150 yards from the point of impact.

That summer of 1944, 2,419 flying bombs hit Britain, killing over 8,000 people.

3

THE WAR had been in progress for nearly five years, and I was approaching eighteen, the age when young lads were "called up". As the time approached, it became increasingly impossible to contemplate prospects of a proper career. On my way to Drury Lane one morning, frustrated and impatient to get the suspense over with, I made up my mind to volunteer. I had no idea what war was really like, and the thought of flying in a bomber or serving in a submarine did not fill me with terror. I *could* imagine a bayonet charge, however, and did not like the thought of that. The army, I decided, was not for me. I assumed I'd be eagerly snapped up by the navy or the RAF.

The RAF recruiting officer told me that they had enough fliers, and anyway my sight disqualified me for aircrew, so I went along to the Navy, where I received even shorter shrift. The war at sea was thought to be past its climax. No more sailors were needed.

It had to be the army, then.

Walking through Duke Street, Westminster, a building across the road caught my eye. A sign said it was the headquarters of "The Artists Rifles". That seemed to be *me,* right down to the ground. I went inside. A senior NCO at the desk eyed me with suspicion – as well he might, for unknown to me and most other people, this was no longer the Artists Rifles' drill hall but the London headquarters of another unit – a highly secret one. The SAS.

The NCO said he was not a recruiting officer, but made a note of the purpose of my visit, and said I should hear more in a week or two. Whether the SAS ever knew of my generous offer of help, I do not know, but a month or so later the army sent for me. I was summoned to present myself in Edinburgh.

I discovered, somewhat to my surprise, that I liked being a soldier. I liked being in Scotland too. I could not explain it, but I had an overwhelming feeling that I'd come home.

Redford Barracks was at Colinton, a rather gentrified suburb of Edinburgh nestling below the Pentland hills. "Auld Reekie" – Edinburgh – a *bracing* place at the best of times – was, though, unfortunately in the grip of a bitter white winter. We thought our instructors were having fun with us when they made us lie in the snow to learn the "leopard crawl". It was our initiation in the mad world of the military.

After a week or two square bashing and finding one end of a rifle from the other, we were paraded in front of a wooden hut and one by one we were sent in. I found myself facing an elderly officer with scarlet patches on his lapels seated behind a trestle table. He asked me, in a surprisingly kindly manner, about my past life.

When I told him of my time as a commercial artist in Maida Vale, he chuckled.

'Isn't that's where all the tarts are?' he asked.

My expression must have told him that my years were too tender to know things like that.

He changed the subject. If I were offered promotion, would I accept it?

Surprised, I said I would.

'And if you were offered a commission?'

The question floored me – that anyone with such an unimpressive physique, not to mention inadequate education, could be an army officer seemed to me rather far-fetched. But...

'Yes,' I answered.

And that is what happened. After some more training and an appearance at a selection board they sent me on a crash course to Sandhurst and in February 1946 commissioned me in my forefathers' local regiment, the Black Watch. The war had come to an end the previous August (on my birthday, the 15th, to be precise, and I was tossed in a blanket in celebration). I was sent to Greece, where I joined a strange regiment called The Lovat Scouts, which was there to "rattle sabres" and discourage the communist partisan force operating in the mountains, during the civil war that heralded the beginning of the Cold War.

Before going abroad I went on embarkation leave. Spring 1946 was bright with new hope and enthusiasm. London was still crammed with uniforms, but everything seemed strange and not quite right after so many years of wartime conditions. For the first time since I had become an adult there were lights in the streets and shop windows. I spent an evening or two at the Stage Door Canteen in Piccadilly, and at the Nuffield Centre in the repaired Café de Paris, which had been bombed early in the war with heavy loss of life. These places were exclusive to members of the forces, and stage and film stars gave their services free. Some were "unknowns" getting their first public engagements. I saw Harry Secombe, Michael Bentine and Jimmy Edwards. The commercial theatre was also coming to life again. In *Starlight Roof* at the Hippodrome I saw a little girl in a party frock with a loud voice named Julie Andrews. She looked all of ten. I went to a revue called *Sauce Tartare* at the London Casino, where I could not take my eyes off a glowingly pretty girl in the chorus. One could forgive her appalling dancing. The programme said her name was Audrey Hepburn.

I travelled to Greece in an extraordinarily complicated way. Across the Channel from Dover to Calais, and then by slow train on the military "Medloc" route south through a war-wrecked France to Toulon, where I boarded a troopship to Port Said. I then had three or four weeks' "holiday" in Cairo, visiting the sites of antiquity, before re-boarding a troopship to be taken across the Mediterranean to Athens. On arriving, I was treated to another few days' holiday, during which I shared the Acropolis with one other person, before riding on the open back of a 15 cwt truck to Chalcis on the island of Euboia, where the Lovat Scouts were based.

I was immediately despatched into the mountains, to join a squadron patrolling a region which was largely in the hands of the communist "ELAS" guerrillas. My unit was commanded by a handsome twenty-six-year-old major named Peter Glass. He had joined the army straight from the Royal Academy of Dramatic Art, and was itching to get home to resume his career as an actor, and we became firm friends. We enjoyed a few "Schoolboy's Own" adventures pretending to sniff out the communists, until the regiment was moved down to Athens to help rattle a more political sabre under the nose of the corrupt government there.

Christmas came, and as part of our celebrations we put on a show – *"The Lovat Scouts Christmas Follies"*. Peter and I named ourselves producers. We formed a band of sorts from troopers who could tinker away at the piano, an accordion, drums – even, amazingly, a saxophone. We called at the ATS women's camp, in search of girls who could sing and high kick. Their portly lady commanding officer looked aghast when Peter informed her that we had come in search of girls (he was given to stuttering at such moments). When our mission had been explained, and she had recovered her composure, she paraded her glamorous army. We selected two lovelies, Sergeant Joyce Lawrence and Corporal Dot Smith.

From Peter, I began to learn about performing and holding an audience, and I wrote and produced some revue sketches, poking fun at issues of the day. I suppose it was inevitable that I would choose feeble British films – with *Margaret Lockwood, Phyllis Calvert, Stewart Granger* – and me as *James Mason* in the role of *Lord Barsteward*. I suppose you could call that side of the show "satire".

The "Follies" opened to wild applause. The girls executed nimble tap dances in their fishnet tights. Two sergeants did a comic double act, and a Trooper led a "singalong" with his accordion. The show ended with "a surprise address by Field Marshal Montgomery". This was me, wearing an authentic uniform, complete with the legendary black beret and two badges. I used the words Monty himself had uttered, with his characteristic lisp, when he had addressed us during a visit to Athens a few weeks before:

'Some of you will be wund'vin when you are leavin' Gveece... Not yet!'

The troops roared and jeered, and it went down marvellously – until one night I looked across the footlights and saw the victor of Alamein himself in the front row. He was *not* laughing, and did not come round to the dressing rooms to congratulate us afterwards.

(The Lovats' commander was a famously naughty Scots Guards officer who adored a jolly jape. The officers' mess was in a requisitioned mansion house on the coast road out of Athens. One lunchtime he ordered me to put on the Monty uniform and stand with him on the terrace in front of the mess, waving to passing cars. Probably some Greeks still tell their grandchildren they had a glimpse of the great war leader.)

The show had been intended just for the Lovats, but guests from other regiments liked it so much that we received orders to give performances in front of all the units stationed in Athens. Everywhere we gave the show we received tumultuous ovations – and increasingly extravagant mess parties after the show, by way of thanks.

It was after one of these that disaster struck. Peter Glass and I were returning from Brigade Headquarters, based along the coast from Athens at Glifadha. The coast road in those days was undeveloped and in the pitch darkness. Our Jeep driver gave no sign of being drunk (although, to be fair, Peter and I were in no condition to judge). Suddenly, we saw in our headlights, a vehicle – a taxi – well out in the road, jacked up and changing a wheel with its occupants standing around it. Our driver made no effort to stop, or even swerve.

I can still see that obstruction racing towards us. We hit it full tilt, square on. I was perched on the back seat of the Jeep and took off. My head connected with the steel frame of the roof canopy. Somehow I scrambled out of the smoking wreck, with something wet trickling down my face. Peter was in the front seat, motionless. His face had gone through the windscreen. In front of the wrecked Jeep was a screaming group of people. The taxi had only been knocked off its jacks and no one had been hurt, but they were horrified by what had happened to us. I realised that blood was streaming down my face.

It was some relief to see that Peter was coming round. But his face was a ghastly mess. I do not recall how we got to hospital, or who took us there. I just remember sitting in a chair while an army medical officer poured whisky over my wound – it seemed he could not find the antiseptic. The stitching that followed was without anaesthetic.

I went to see Peter. He was in a hospital bed, his face covered with bandages. Our driver, I learned, had escaped without a scratch. The military police found that he was drunk, and arrested him.

The disaster did not *quite* put an end to *"The Lovat Scouts Christmas Follies"*. We had been booked for a final show at one of the headquarters units – they must not be disappointed. Peter was unable to appear, of course, but with re-arrangement "the show" managed "to go on". I filled in with an off-the-cuff stand-up comic act, and to my considerable amazement and relief "brought the house down", though – as with the anaesthetic, nitrous oxide – it was the impurities that caused the laughter (a memorable line from my future employers, Launder and Gilliat's, film *Green For Danger*). It was quite a "farewell performance".

Far from home as carefree young soldiers, and taking little interest in serious matters, it passed us by that our country was almost bankrupt, bankrupted by the war we had fought – as we thought – to save the world. The Labour government was struggling to stave off economic collapse against a worldwide shortage of raw materials to supply industry. An enormous number of Britons were still under arms all over the world, and drastic reductions in military commitments were necessary. Britain would have to pull out of Greece.

The Lovat Scouts had only been mobilised for the war in any case, and on the 5th of January 1947, the regiment "Stood Down", in a moving ceremony. We saw Peter Glass off to England and a return to his acting career. He had the bandages off, but a broken nose permanently marred his former good looks. For most of the officers and troopers it did not mean the end of service overseas, and new postings were found for them. In my case, my "theatrical background" caught up with me.

At the end of the war, ENSA had been closed down (Drury Lane Theatre had re-opened with Rodgers and Hammerstein's *Oklahoma*). The armed forces still needed entertainment, so a military organisation called Combined Services Entertainment was formed. I was despatched to Palestine to run a unit.

My immediate task on arrival in Jerusalem was to manage the tour of a concert party that had just come out from England. It was called *"The Bunny Doyle Show"* – the eponymous star was a Yorkshire comedian who specialised in playing pantomime "Dames". The most striking member of the cast was Kim Kendall, six feet two tall and lusciously beautiful. Her sister was a rising film actress named Kay.

Kim's only problem was that she couldn't sing, and when she danced her weight shook the stage.

The show's first engagement was at the military hospital in Jerusalem. I assembled the cast in CSE's single-deck bus and gave the standard briefing:

'We will be passing through unsecured districts. The driver and I are armed and you will be quite safe. However, there are some precautions I'd like you to observe. If we come under attack from terrorists get down on the floor. I am sure the gentlemen will want to protect the ladies, so would they please occupy the window seats during the journey?'

All the men changed places with the girls. Except for Bunny Doyle. He sat tight, staring straight in front of him, with Kim Kendall wedged in the window seat – providing, no doubt, a formidable shield.

I thought he may not have heard so I said, 'Mr Doyle, would you like to change places with Miss Kendall?'

He went very red, then snapped:

'I'm star of show! *She's* got no talent!'

The terrorists left us alone on that occasion, for once missing a deserving target.

I was in Palestine for just over four months, during which there was a steady escalation in the terrorist activity that would end in the withdrawal of British forces the following year. I had been overseas for more than the time that qualified me for UK leave, and at the beginning of September I boarded the troopship *Alcantara*, to sail under a cloudless sky across a Mediterranean as calm as a millpond. I shared the job of ship's entertainments officer with a twenty-one-year-old subaltern in the Grenadier Guards named Lord Montagu of Beaulieu. In fact, we had nothing to do except enjoy a delightful cruise, past the Pillars of Hercules, into the Bay of Biscay and home to good old Blighty.

On the last day I got up early and went on deck to catch a first sight of English greenery. As the ship passed through the Solent, Edward Montagu joined me at the rail.

'My home is there,' he said, pointing in the direction of some distant trees.

'A nice place to return to,' I observed, thinking of my own modest home.

He smiled wryly.

'No one will ever afford to live in houses like mine again,' he said.

There was a Labour government, and I did not doubt that he was right. How innocent we were. (Edward did, of course, manage to live in that house. After wisely serving an apprenticeship in a public relations company and thoroughly learning his trade, he exploited his father's collection of vintage motorcars and made Palace House, Beaulieu, a money-making public attraction.)

I had a month's leave at home during which I did some thinking about the future. It was now a peacetime army I had found myself in and I would soon have to make up my mind whether I wanted to make it my career.

Much was being said and written about the British film industry, which was enjoying a golden period. American films had been in short supply during the war because of shipping priorities, creating an opportunity for British filmmakers, which they seized with enthusiasm – demonstrating, with "documentary"-based films made to support the nation's war-effort, a creative leap forward from the dire products of the thirties. Nineteen forty-six had been a great year, beginning with films like David Lean's *Brief Encounter* and Launder and Gilliat's I *See A Dark Stranger* and ending with Lean's *Great Expectations*. Powell and Pressburger's *A Matter Of Life And Death*, with its pretentious speechifying, was less highly regarded. (It amazes me that this, and the same team's later travesty *The Red Shoes*, are declared masterpieces today by the artsy intellectuals who decide such things. I remember the distinguished critic Richard Winnington pouring scorn on me when I praised Jack Cardiff's photography, with the words: 'Anyone who thinks there is anything to admire in *The Red Shoes* is artistically blind'. And indeed there is little to admire in the Mills & Boon story, or Michael Powell's curious idea of what ballet is all about – or in the casting, with Marius Goring looking every bit of his forty-one years as a teenage student – or most memorably of all, in the scene near the end when "Diaghilev" Anton Walbrook brings the film's partiality for ham-acting to its high point with that embarrassing curtain speech following the ballerina's suicide.)

Ambitious production continued in 1947, and the industry, led by the Rank Organisation at Pinewood Studios, seemed headed for a prosperous, assured future.

My father said he thought I should get into films. 'You could be an art director,' he said – as usual without the faintest idea of the qualifications necessary for such a job. However, it planted a thought in my head that recurred more and more frequently during the following months.

For the moment, it was a posting to Glasgow to train the lads who were still being called up. As it turned out, this proved to be the turning point in my life.

4

MARYHILL BARRACKS in Glasgow was the headquarters of the Highland Light Infantry, the notorious "HLI", the "poison dwarfs" from the Gorbals. It was my first taste of life in the peacetime army, albeit not in my own regiment. Every Wednesday was "Mess Night". We dressed in our best uniform and sat far into the night round a great mahogany table crammed with regimental silver gleaming in the candlelight, while the regimental band played in an adjoining room. The mess president sat at the head of the table, and at the end of the meal he would raise his glass and call, 'Mister Vice, the King'. At the other end, the junior officer taking his turn as vice-president, would get to his feet and declare very loudly, 'Gentlemen – the King!' Everyone would then stand and repeat 'The King', before downing a good measure of whatever the mess waiters had put in his glass. The door would burst open and a parade of pipers would march in, the sound deafening as they circled the table. The Pipe Major would halt at the head of the table, and a small shallow cup, called a *quaich*, full of whisky would be handed to him. He would hold it aloft and declare in Gaelic, 'Health to the King. Good health'. He would then knock the dram back in one.

A word in these "healths" was soon to change, though we could not know that at the time. In November, our future *female* monarch was married to a young naval lieutenant, Prince Philip of Greece.

Sometimes, if an important guest was present, a general or local dignitary, there would be "requests". The callow young vice-president would have to approach the colonel, sitting at the centre of the table with the guests on either side, and ask 'Requests, sir, please.' We dreaded this, because by this time we would be blind drunk. On one occasion, when the ordeal came my way, the visiting general muttered something that sounded like *Tulloch Ard*. A brigadier beside him added *Caber Feidh*. And the Lord Provost of Glasgow grunted *The High Road To Gairloch*. By now I could not even remember the first one. Asking them to repeat their requests was not an option. I would have been eaten alive. In the army, you just 'bloody well get on with it!'

I staggered from the room. The Pipe Major was waiting outside.

'Sorry, Pipe Major,' I blurted, 'I haven't the faintest idea what they asked for.'

He nodded solemnly.

'Never mind, sir,' he said, 'I'll play anything at all. They'll never know the difference.'

The evening always ended with Highland dancing in the anteroom. The senior officers were "the men" and the subalterns were "the ladies", making it a rather weird event. Many years later, I read the memoirs of one of the senior officers, Maurice Willoughby – *Echo Of A Distant Drum*. In the 1930s in India, he wrote, the ladies of the Raj believed the HLI officers' mess was 100% homosexual. No one there ever made a pass at me, I hasten to say.

When 1947 came to an icy end, there began a series of unforeseen (and extremely unlikely) events that was to set me on the road to my lifetime's work. Just after Hogmanay the barracks received a visit from *a very important person*. "Malcolm of Poltalloch" was the grandiose title of a retired Argyll and Sutherland Highlanders colonel. He was the grandson of Edwardian actress Lily Langtry, and it was whispered (no doubt fancifully) that he might be a grandchild of "Jersey Lily's" lover King Edward VII. Malcolm announced that he was organising a recruiting display in Glasgow's Kelvin Hall, similar to London's prestigious Royal Tournament. *"Services Cavalcade"*, as he called it, would have marching and counter-marching by military bands and pipes and drums, demonstrations of Highland dancing, and some sort of pageant. It was of *great importance* and he required help. Because of my CSE episode, I was believed to possess theatrical expertise, so without further ado I was nominated producer. Never mind that I was only a lowly subaltern, or that I was just twenty-one years old – or, for that matter, that I had never produced a show before.

I decided – *of course* – to produce something spectacular. I devised a series of acted scenes depicting the HLI's history, using historic uniforms in the regimental museum and set to music played by the regimental band – King George III granting the commission to raise the regiment – the Highlanders recruiting in a Highland village – battles in India, the Peninsular, Waterloo et cetera...

I did not think that soldier "amateur actors" would be up to playing speaking parts in front of a paying audience, and we went in search of professionals. An ancient, fruity-voiced thespian with the ponderous name Duff

McCullough was persuaded to take time out from Glasgow Citizen's Theatre to play King George III. I brought an actor I had met in Palestine from London to play the important role of the HLI's founder, Lord Macleod. His "star" salary was £15 plus his keep for the run of the show – one week!

For the grand finale I had a squad of men dressed in the scarlet uniforms of the Boer War march across the arena singing the Victorian song *We're The Soldiers Of The Queen M'lads*. As they got midway, a second squad in Great War puttees and tin hats entered from the opposite corner of the arena with the music mingling into *It's A Long Way To Tipperary*. Both squads then interwove with a third squad in World War II battledress singing *Roll Out The Barrel*, and a fourth contingent in tropical kit – "Desert Rats" – whistling *Lili Marlene*. The entire assembly came to rest in the form of a cross – the Saltire – to the emotive strains of *Scotland The Brave*. It was an unapologetic appeal to the sentimentality of the time.

On the opening night the whole of Glasgow seemed to have flocked in to see the show. There wasn't an empty seat in the house. My finale raised the roof. The moment the spotlights hit the Boer War uniforms the audience went wild – they knew that the lads in front of them were the real thing; many of them had all too recently been in battle in the Western Desert and Europe. I shall never forget the almost hysterical roar that greeted the last two squads when they marched on. A shiver passed through me as the music rose to a crescendo. Like the audience, I could not help but be deeply moved.

I felt another emotion as well. I had heard the roar of an audience, the thunder of applause, for something I had done. For the first time I had tasted success.

The morning after the final performance I stood in the upper gallery of the empty Kelvin Hall looking down on the "squaddies" as they cleared up. Standing beside me was the HLI's depot commander, a veteran officer named Leckie Ewing.

'It was a marvellous show,' the major said. 'What a pity there's no permanent record. A film or something.'

'If someone had a cine camera maybe we could stage it again – on the barrack square,' I suggested.

The major thought it an interesting idea. I believe now that for the next few days he thought of little else. One evening over dinner in the mess he returned to the subject. He knew I was undecided about my future and that I talked a lot about the film industry. My fascination was not accompanied by any knowledge of film production, however, which made the major's next question hard to answer.

'How much would it cost to make a film? It should be in colour. And with sound, of course.'

I used the metaphorical "back of an envelope" to calculate my first film budget. Five hundred pounds I thought – principally for the purchase of a cine camera, which we could sell after we'd finished with it.

'The bits that are supposed to be happening out of doors – the Battle of Waterloo, et cetera – we can do up at Fort George, where there's lots of open country, rather than the barrack square,' Leckie Ewing suggested.

I caught the mood.

'Well why not film the entire history of the regiment?' I suggested. Cecil B. DeMille talking...

'Why not?' smiled Major Leckie Ewing. (Sam Goldwyn talking.)

We had progressed far beyond the idea of simply filming the Kelvin Hall pageant. Before the week was out, the barrack square photographic record had grown into a plan for a full-length film, to be shot on location in the country around Fort George in Morayshire with the proverbial "cast of thousands". But the budget was still five hundred pounds.

Leckie Ewing assumed the role of film producer, and I was ordered to go to work and make a film which would be shown to all new recruits on joining the army to instil regimental pride. We decided on a title – *Proud Heritage.*

In an age when most people have seen a television crew at work, when countless people have seen themselves on the screen, when almost every youngster one meets has made a film for Channel Four, it is hard to imagine a time when films were a sort of magic, practised in a closed never-never-land called "film-studios". The secrets of the arts and technology of filmmaking were known to only a handful of professionals.

It was astonishing at that time, therefore, that a group of soldiers should think they could make a film. And not just a film. An epic.

Just as astonishing was that I was to be the director. I accepted the role without a doubt in my head. I knew nothing whatever about film direction, cine photography or scriptwriting but in the army of those days you were told to do a job and you bloody well got on with it. Success was presumed. I was on the brink of realising a dream. Less than five years before I had been one of the crowd flocking to the local Odeon to gape at "the pictures". Now, in what seemed very little time, I was on the brink of realising a dream. It was almost too much to take in.

Five hundred pounds was a substantial sum to find – around £20,000 in today's money. Leckie Ewing went to see the Colonel of the Regiment. Retired Major-General Alec Telfer-Smollett lived in an imposing house on the banks of Loch Lomond (it is now an hotel). The general was a film fan, as I learned years later, when I read David Niven's autobiography, *Bring On The Empty Horses*. "Telfer" had been the commanding officer who was so sympathetic to Niven, arranging his extrication from an unsuitable career in the pre-war HLI for a Hollywood one. The general found the necessary finance from defunct regimental social funds.

In those days only the most lavish of films were shot in colour. The sole professional process was Technicolor, which used a special camera running three rolls of film simultaneously – it was so huge and heavy that a crane was needed to mount it on its tripod. For us the only feasible choice was 16-millimetre Kodachrome. There was also the little matter of sound. Magnetic recording had not been invented, and the optical recording machines were so unportable that "talking pictures" had to be made inside the studios. Exterior scenes were mostly shot silent, and sound, including speech, was added later. I had only a vague idea how this was done but left that problem for later.

I had never seen, let alone handled, a cine-camera. The major and I went in search of a photo shop which might have such a rare object. We found a second-hand Bell & Howell, with lenses, for £25 – a large sum by present day standards. Something like £800. There was no instruction book, but the shopkeeper showed me how to put film in and which button to press. He sold us a slim little book, called *Color* [sic] *Movies For The Beginner*, which told me how to cope with mysteries like exposure, and "colour-temperature", measured in "degrees Kelvin", whatever that meant. That was my "film school". The shopkeeper also threw in another piece of information, unanticipated and unwelcome. We would not be able to buy colour film. Kodachrome was only made in the USA, and had been unobtainable since the beginning of the war. I was confident that we would somehow find a way to overcome this problem along with everything else. I tried a letter to the Kodak company, and to our delight they agreed to ask their American parent company to send over a supply of "Kodachrome". We were now ready to turn the first feet of our "epic".

Before we could begin shooting we had to have a script and I pored over monumental histories of the army (very Victorian in sentiment) and leafed through musty volumes of *The HLI Journal*. Eventually I had produced a "shooting script", with battle scenes, cavalry charges, a troopship sinking and lots of dialogue sequences. I was too inexperienced to know that it was a plan for a film that would have run for nine or ten hours if we had shot everything in it.

Leckie Ewing and I became firm friends, though he was in his forties and much senior to me in rank. I discovered that his first name was Rhoderick – Roddy. He was generally known in the mess as "Old Leckie" because of his elderly appearance. He was a tallish, loose-limbed man with thinning sandy hair and a ragged moustache, rarely seen without his pipe, sucked empty or burning. He did not enjoy the best of health, and it had blighted his army career, barring him from the high rank he would otherwise have achieved. During the Western Desert campaign he had been "Town Major" of Cairo, with responsibility for handing over the city to Rommel if Montgomery had failed at Alamein.

We flattered ourselves by thinking of our movie as a "professional" production, and decided that a professional actor would be needed once again, to play the key role of the founder of the regiment, Lord Macleod, who would be seen progressing through the highlands of Scotland making stirring speeches to drum up recruits. Our budget to pay this "star" ran to £20 or so and I left for London on a talent-scouting trip. The actor who had played the part in the Glasgow show was now earning real money, and politely declined the opportunity to compete for an Oscar, but recommended someone he had met on a film set.

'He's a friend of the film director Frank Launder,' he added.

I knew that name. Frank Launder was a celebrated film producer, one half of the talented and successful Launder and Gilliat team. He was currently in Fiji, filming Jean Simmons in *The Blue Lagoon*.

I called on Paul Connell at his flat above the disused Royal Court Theatre in Sloane Square, where he lived with his lady friend, a film editor named Thelma Myers, and Thelma's actress friend Bernadette O'Farrell, who was Frank Launder's fiancée. Connell was in his very early twenties and blond and therefore a rather unlikely casting for Lord Macleod, who must have been at least forty-five in 1777. He was also rather conspicuously Irish. However he was probably the only actor prepared to accept my less than bountiful offer. Of such chance encounters are careers – and history – made...

Shooting the first scenes of *Proud Heritage* has a dream-like quality in my memory. The sequence depicted King George III in St James's Palace granting a commission to raise the 73rd Highlanders. Roddy Leckie Ewing had persuaded the Lord Provost of Glasgow to let us film it in the sumptuous marble and mahogany halls of the City Chambers in George Square. The "actors" – officers and soldiers ordered to "volunteer" by Roddy – put on knee breeches and powdered wigs hired from a local theatrical costumier, and the totally green director, who was also the cameraman, tried to make it look authentic. The camera and tripod were mounted on a homemade "dolly" so we could do "tracking shots" – it was going to have an authentic "Hollywood" look if I had anything to do with it! I switched on the lighting, three or four feeble photofloods, and they brightened a corner of the great room. My exposure meter hardly registered. Kodachrome in those days required ten times more light than modern colour film.

For people who had little idea what they were doing it all went remarkably smoothly. A week later the first rolls of film came back from processing and we viewed "the rushes" – as the big boys called them – on an ancient War Office projector. It was a pleasant surprise. The colour was far better than I had expected and the interior of the City Chambers glowed with a luminous beauty. We thought we were justified in believing that we were not totally mad.

With our "blockbuster" now well under way, Paul Connell arrived in Glasgow, and on a gorgeous August day we set out for the Trossachs, about thirty miles from Glasgow, to film Lord Macleod recruiting men for his regiment. In the village of Gartmore we found an unspoilt little square and terrace of eighteenth-century cottages. The owner of a hotel in nearby Aberfoyle provided horses for Lord Macleod and his lieutenant. We dressed two or three score enthusiastic National Servicemen as eighteenth-century "Highland villagers" – and another dozen in skirts and shawls as their wives! They thought it better than army training. They raised a cheer, as "Lord Macleod" – Paul Connell astride a chestnut mare – exhorted them to join his new regiment. By today's standards the speech seems trite and naïve, but I think I took it from the actual record. Bearing in mind that he was recruiting people to crush dissident colonists during the American War of Independence, it is odd to hear him speak of fighting for "freedom and its preservation"! What may seem even stranger to today's readers is that we simple 1940s folk didn't see anything anachronistic in it.

"Oo joins 'is Lordship?' bawled Company Sergeant Major Ray, who disconcertingly turned out to be a cockney (he was subsequently dubbed as a gravelly highlander).

'Ah wull!' answered a reassuring Gorbals voice, followed by another and another.

Ray got them fallen in, as Regimental Sergeant Major Donald Maclean, a former Pipe Major and native of Lewis, played the *piobaireachd*, Mackenzie *Gathering*. The drones began to moan as he pumped his bag, and the ragged little army trooped off down the street to the skirl of *The Mackenzie Highlander*.

I photographed the scene from a high angle perched on the back of an army truck. My art experience gave me an instinctive feel for composition and I knew to shoot "complementary close-ups" with the characters looking out of the correct side of the frame so as not to "cross the line" – unforgivable sin for professionals...

The production now transferred to the far north, where the large body of troops that we needed were stationed at Fort George. The countryside around Inverness and the Moray Firth would provide spectacular backgrounds for battle scenes. It was the first time I had seen the central highlands, and *en route* in Roddy's pre-war Wolseley we stopped off beside Loch Ness and in Glencoe to film "establishing shots". I had learned to "pan" the camera smoothly, and made sweeping panoramas of the magnificent landscape, which was remote and empty in those pre-tourist times.

In the back of Roddy's car we carried hampers of "period uniform", run-up by a Glasgow theatrical costumier. They consisted of thin cotton tunics dyed a watery red, with white canvas crossbands serving as webbing equipment. Trousers had to be modern battledress denims. Topping all in most of the scenes was a "shako", which was really a paper party-hat, shiny black with a piece of red and white diced paper glued round the brim. From a distance, it was all just about acceptable. Roddy said everything could be "excused" because the norm in eighteenth-century regiments, in contradiction to the gorgeous finery seen in military prints, was raggedness and squalor. Soldiers were clothed at their colonels' private expense and colonels looked after their pennies. Raggedness and squalor we were certainly able to reproduce!

Cheap and cheerful though these costumes were, they still accounted for the major part of our budget, along with the meagre collection of early 19th-century "Brown Bess" flintlock muskets supplied by specialist film armourers in London. At least we did not have to pay the "crowd artistes", or feed and accommodate them – HM government unknowingly did.

5

WE BEGAN filming in the hope that this year the traditional Scottish wet summer would not hamper us. Alas, we were frequently rained off, and on all too many days there was a depressing overcast. For an apprentice cameraman it made assessing exposure extremely difficult. No "automatic" camera then! On several occasions we were compelled to suspend shooting and return to Glasgow for a few days. Mostly, however, we managed to keep going, using the ramparts of the fort and the countryside all around to stage scenes from the regiment's battles, principally in India and Spain. Fort George's massive walls, built by Napoleonic prisoners of war and eleven metres thick, figured in the Peninsular War sequences. The surrender of Tippoo Sahib, after the second Battle of Seringapatam, was also filmed below the brooding ramparts. I tried rudimentary "trick photography" to simulate lightning during the storm that took place during the incident.

Apart from Paul Connell's "Lord Macleod", Roddy decided that for obvious financial reasons all parts could be played by service people. Fort George's constantly changing establishment, however – due to demobilisation, postings and new arrivals – meant that some people had to play more than one role. On one unfortunate occasion a character who had "died" rather conspicuously earlier on reappeared in good health playing someone else. For similar reasons, some notable historic characters ended up being played by more than one person. In the "Battle of Waterloo", the Duke of Wellington was played by Captain John Slim of the Argyll and Sutherland Highlanders, the son of Field Marshal Slim, commander of the 14th Army in Burma (he subsequently achieved high rank as a colonel in the legendary SAS). By the time we got round to filming another battle commanded by Wellington, Slim had moved on. The part had to be played by a national serviceman, Private Reynolds, who happened to be a good horseman (strange how life imitates art – Reynolds went on to become a general).

The most ambitious sequence was a cavalry charge, an incident in the 1803 battle of Assaye in India. We recruited a local riding school to carry out the charge. Borrowing more than an idea or two from Laurence Olivier's *Henry V*, I clambered onto a trolley that carried targets on a disused anti-tank firing range, and held on for dear life as we tracked alongside the charge pushed by a team of sweating "volunteers" – they had a hard time keeping up with the horses. The riding-school girls were in heaven. They "blacked up" with Leichner greasepaint and went at it like mad things, galloping their ponies full tilt into the ranks of the national servicemen. It's a wonder no one was killed.

The 16mm camera was very light and portable and I found myself not bothering to mount it on the tripod. I shot much of the battle footage "hand held", anticipating a trend that has become standard practice – albeit with the aid of stabilisers – today. It was something that never happened in film making at the time.

The Culbin Sands, an incredible stretch of Sahara-like desert along the Morayshire coast, provided the background for the 1882 battle of Tel el-Kebir. For once, we were blessed with an electric blue sky, which created a passable illusion of Egypt. We found more sand – a seaside holiday beach – at Irvine in Ayrshire, a popular resort for Glaswegians. It became the Western Desert, for an incident in World War II during the Battle of Mersa Matruh, when a handful of HLI soldiers made a suicide charge at an overwhelming force of Germans disguised as British soldiers. The holidaymakers and townspeople were amazed when Royal Artillery 25-pounder field-guns appeared on the beach and "Waffen SS" piled out of three-ton trucks. Amazement turned to mirth when the guns got bogged down in the sand, and had to be winched off, with some amount of bad humour on the part of the Anti-Tank Regiment we had persuaded to take part.

We had shot a great deal of film and, as the cost mounted alarmingly, so did our enthusiasm. Roddy appeared to have friends and contacts everywhere, and there was nothing it seemed he was incapable of arranging. I had only to ask, 'Where on earth are we to find eighteenth-century cannon for the Battle of Assaye?' for him to remember a cousin who was an officer at the Navy's boy training establishment at *HMS Ganges*, in Shotley, Essex. I would find then myself filming the youngsters, their faces blacked to look like Indians, firing quaint little guns under the supervision of naval officers dressed as Frenchmen. When I protested, 'How can we possibly stage the wreck of the troopship *Birkenhead*?' Roddy persuaded British Rail to lend us their Clyde paddle steamer, "Jeanie

Deans", for a day. He even got us into Buckingham Palace, as I shall explain.

Trying to reconstruct the sinking of the troopship "Birkenhead", which went down off the Cape of Good Hope in 1852 with the loss of nearly everyone aboard, proved to be a little too ambitious. We obviously could not sink the *Jeanie Deans*, and worse – could not even have the ship in motion. I simulated the vessel striking the rocks by violently shaking the camera. Maryhill's commanding officer, Lieutenant Colonel "Old Titus" Oatts, splendidly authentic in a *real* historic uniform from the regimental museum and sporting mutton-chop side-whiskers, stuck on with spirit gum (to his great pleasure, by a gorgeous drama student named Rosemary Sutherland), rushed on to the bridge brandishing his sabre. Threatening the troops with instant execution, he commanded them not to jump overboard and endanger the few lifeboats carrying the wives to safety.

We included a few scenes of modern warfare. The Parachute Regiment Demonstration Platoon, based at RAF Netheravon in Hampshire, helped suggest the Battle of Arnhem, which was commanded by an HLI officer, General Roy Urquhart. Roddy and I went aloft in the Dakota and I squeezed myself out of a small escape hatch on to the wing of the aircraft, so that the parachutists could fall past me. Roddy hung on to my feet to prevent my being sucked out. Choosing to wear my kilt that day was not the most sensible of decisions.

I did not wear my kilt when I appeared in the film myself. Roddy had ruled that everyone must be in the film somewhere, so I "did a Hitchcock", and appeared as a

Great War platoon commander rather inefficiently firing a signal pistol and leading an attack "over the top".

As summer ended I returned to Glasgow to sort out all the film we had shot. I had learned a very great deal about film making. I had learned how to "break down" a shooting script, work out shooting schedules, and issue workmanlike "call sheets" so that the right people and resources were there at the right time. I had also discovered to my cost the traps that lay in wait for a cameraman, like "hairs in the gate" and running out on a shot. Most importantly, I discovered how hard it was to direct adequately while operating a camera – a lesson that is being relearned in television documentary making today.

I wanted *Proud Heritage* to have a specially created musical score performed by the HLI's superb military band. The bandmaster, Archie Wilson, discovered a young National Servicemen named Private Thompson in his band who had spectacular talent. He composed a stirring piece of music to accompany the cavalry charge and a moving theme-tune, reminiscent of Walton's *Crown Imperial*, to give the film an emotional climax. What became of Thompson in later life I never heard – in my view he was an embryo genius. I thought the score and the performance was quite wonderful. Roddy Leckie-Ewing persuaded the BBC to record it for us in the Scottish Symphony Orchestra's studio. The tracks were cut into soft wax discs that then had to be handled with the utmost care.

The notion of a bunch of soldiers trying to emulate Hollywood attracted a lot of interest from the newspapers, national as well local. The film had the proverbial "cast of thousands" after all, which always looked good on a page. We received as much press coverage as any professional film made that year – the year of Ealing's *Whisky Galore*, made on the Hebridean island of Barra, and the disastrous *Bonnie Prince Charlie*, starring the HLI's own David Niven. *The Scotsman* gave *Proud Heritage* its entire front page, complete with photographs.

Most of the press blurbs highlighted the twenty-one-year-old officer who was in charge of the epic, and I came in for a lot of ribbing in the mess. The BBC commissioned a newspaperman named Jack Gourlay to put together a broadcast about us. He worked on the Scottish *Daily Express*, but also freelanced, publishing a monthly film magazine. He was a few years older than me, tall, handsome and suave. We struck up a friendship and he suggested that we team up to write screenplays. It began a collaboration that would become an important part of my life.

Robin Russell Steele, who had provided the horses when we were filming in the Trossachs, also became a close friend and I spent most weekends at the hotel he owned in the village of Aberfoyle. Robin had worked in an Edinburgh bank before the war, during which he became a glider pilot in the airborne forces. He was a natural adventurer, game for any amusing caper, and had no intention of returning to the bank when he was "demobbed". He bought the run-down inn with his wartime savings and built up a thriving business, putting Aberfoyle on the map as the centre of tourism in the Trossachs. The Covenanter's Inn became celebrated in later years when it was revealed that the Coronation Stone was secreted there after it was stolen from Westminster Abbey.

Paul Connell also spent as much time as he could there and brought his lady friend Thelma and Frank Launder's fiancée Bernadette for a short holiday. Bernadette O'Farrell was a statuesque Irish beauty with chestnut hair, a beautiful mouth and large green eyes. She spoke with a soft Irish accent that perfectly expressed her fey and innocent persona. Thelma was some years older than Paul. She was rather unusual to look at, very thin with a pronounced aquiline nose and straw-coloured hair. She had a delightful, bawdy sense of humour. At thirty-six, she was one of the country's most successful film editors, having begun her career with David Lean. She spoke several languages, some fluently, and was a talented artist.

The group had met during the filming of Frank Launder's Irish drama *Captain Boycott*. Launder had invited members of the public to take part, and medical student Paul and bank secretary Bernadette were among the eager volunteers. Both were keen amateur actors. They caught Launder's eye and he had given them small speaking parts. As time went on, Frank had fallen for Bernadette, and Paul with film editor Thelma Myers. When the film finished shooting Paul and Bernadette decided on acting careers and moved to London.

I was told that the Frank Launder was to stop by in Aberfoyle for a day or two during a break in filming *The Blue Lagoon*. I viewed the prospect of meeting the celebrated director with some excitement. Who could know? – He might well turn out to be very important for my future.

He turned out to be a rather strange-looking man, small and wiry, with sharp features, jet-black hair balding at the front, and spectacular eyebrows jutting over penetrating dark eyes. He had a boyish sense of humour and to my delight we took an instant liking to each other. It was the beginning of a friendship that was to grow ever stronger over many years until Frank's death.

I had been relieved of my military duties, but my "cast" had other duties to perform, so I had time on my hands. I thought that, if I could write a screenplay for *Proud Heritage*, I ought to be able to write about something else. I tried a wartime espionage thriller set in the Greece that I knew. I also tried my hand at (illegally) adapting a best-selling novel. Jack Gourlay knew what I was doing and told me of his own ambitions to write screenplays. As a newspaper reporter he had covered every kind of story, from weddings to murders, and had all the background material he would ever need.

He suggested that if I left the army we could form a team, and it was another development that seemed to be nudging me in along a certain pathway. We kicked off our tentative collaboration on a script inspired by a murder that had occurred not long before on Glasgow's underground railway. As the setting would be a newspaper office we gave it the title *Dead Line* – a play on the newspaper and the railway term. I found that Jack's partiality was to pepper dialogue with what he called "cracks" – wise cracks, the stuff American films were full of. I soon found out, as well, that he was chronically late for meetings and would take any opportunity to avoid work.

All this inevitably led to further contemplation of a career in films. The time was fast arriving when I would have to make a decision about my future. After four years, the army had become part of my life, and it was hard to imagine another kind out of uniform. However there were aspects of the peacetime army that I was finding less and less interesting. It had been an amazing stroke of fortune to be given the HLI film to make and it looked like some kind of omen. The wind of fate seemed to be blowing me in a definite direction.

Late in September I made up my mind. I decided on a huge gamble – use *Proud Heritage* as a launch pad for an attempt at a career in films. I told Roddy that I intended leaving the army, but would – if he approved – stay on as a civilian to see the film through. In this way I should look like a professional film director, rather than a soldier playing at one. He agreed, and I went to York to be formally discharged. I received a poorly cut "demob suit", and rail warrant to carry me home. When I said I was returning to Glasgow and Maryhill Barracks there were raised eyebrows. I went back to my comfortable room in the mess and resumed work on the film.

Work on *Proud Heritage* – the editing and sound recording – now needed to be done in London. I came home as a civilian, and as a "return to civilian life/get me started" gift, my father presented me with a generous £25. It was a significant sum then, worth something like a thousand pounds at today's prices. I was still due a few months' army pay as well to keep me going.

The Kodak people introduced me to a small company that specialised in adding sound to home movies made by wealthy amateurs. It boasted a grandiose name. United Motion Pictures – TA RA! Its studio was tiny, however, on the upper floors of a tall old building in Denmark Street – "Tin Pan Alley", the centre of the popular music publishing industry – off Charing Cross Road in London's West End. Music publisher and composer Noel Gay, the creator of the musical *Me And My Girl*, featuring the immortal song

Doing The Lambeth Walk – (Oi!) occupied the floors below. United Motion Pictures' principals were a Mister Sheppard and a Mister Stubbs. First names were not customary in those days.

I did not suspect that UMP was to play a crucial role in my subsequent professional – and personal – life. The managing director, Mister Sheppard, was a short, dapper, dark-haired man with a "film-star" moustache. He was very conservative and a little pompous, but we got on well. The film cutting room was in a gloomy basement devoid of daylight. It was only accessible via an ancient lift and when that broke down – which it did every trip or so – the occupants were imprisoned. The basement also housed the storerooms of the newly created British Film Institute, cared for by curator John Huntley. The young vault boy was David Kenten, who I was to encounter again many years later.

There were no Steenbeck editing machines or Moviolas for 16mm so UMP's bright young film editors worked with stripped-down film projectors. Cuts were marked up with "jelly pencils" and joined with "film cement". "Fade-outs" and "fade-ins" were made by slowly lowering the ends of the relevant scenes into test tubes filled with black dye – the longer the film was immersed the more opaque it became, and if all went well a smooth gradation was achieved. Joins in the optical sound tracks made a sharp *CLICK* when they passed through the projector, so they had to be "blooped". This was done by painting a triangle of black "blooping ink" across the join – the *CLICK* then became a more acceptable "BLOOP".

Proud Heritage's speaking scenes had been filmed without sound and now came the long and difficult business of "post-syncing", a technique that the UMP lads vaguely understood but had not before experienced. They learned along with me. The process involved making each short section of film into a loop that was then projected over and over again while the person providing the voice attempted to speak the words to match the lip movements. This was made the more difficult because I had sometimes neglected to take notes of the exact words that were said during filming. Roddy Leckie-Ewing recruited staff from his London club, the Caledonian, to provide Scottish voices. I was amazed how well the amateur and totally inexperienced "actors" managed it.

I had shot scenes of the HLI's Colonel-in-Chief, seventeen-year-old Princess Margaret, accepting the Freedom of Glasgow on behalf of the regiment, and we also needed to add sound to that. Quite obviously, only the real thing would do. General Telfer-Smollett worked his charm on the Palace authorities and the princess agreed to make a special recording for us. I believe we were the first film unit to be allowed inside Buckingham Palace. We spent a memorable day in the awesome surroundings. General Telfer "presented" me to the princess, and she fluttered her lashes and looked up at me with enormous blue eyes. She provided impromptu entertainment when I informed her that our recording machine had broken down, by imitating a broken gramophone record.

Somewhere or other I ran into Kim Kendall, the actress with "no talent" in Jerusalem, and I went to see a play that her sister Kay was in. We went backstage afterwards to meet Kay in a dressing room crowded with admirers. Among them was a strikingly handsome chap named Roger Moore. He had only recently left the army, having commanded a CSE unit similar to mine in Germany, and was trying to launch an acting career. He had a rich deep voice. I needed someone to narrate the commentary for *Proud Heritage* so I asked Roger to do it – for a pittance of a fee. He made a good job of it and we became friends.

After long hours of work in the film cutting rooms assembling the material and synchronising the sound, I had something like a coherent film, though running the better part of two hours. No film laboratory in England had the equipment to bring such a complicated 16-millimetre production to completion, so everything had to be sent to New York where professional 16mm production was more normal. The film would now be out of my hands for many weeks; I would have to wait for it to be returned before my career could be launched.

(As it happened, my prime (and sole) contact, Frank Launder, was not currently in production and was preparing with his partner Sidney Gilliat to quit the Rank Organisation.)

In the meantime the press kept up its interest. The London *Evening Standard* ran a full-page piece, suggesting that I must be hotly pursued by the film industry offering jobs. If only! I even received a paragraph in *The Hollywood Reporter*, written by the famous gossip columnist Louella Parsons, relating the experience with Princess Margaret.

Jack Gourlay came back into my life when he phoned with the news that he had been brought to London by Lord Beaverbrook to take over the prestigious show business column in the *Sunday Express*. At Lord Beaverbrook's command he was to be known by his middle name Logan. "Logan Gourlay" – a name to strike terror in many a tough showbiz heart for some years to come. I thought it sounded awful. Pompous and artificial. But naturally I did not say so.

One of "Logan Gourlay's" first projects was to devote his entire column, covering almost the whole of page three of the *Sunday Express*, to me. It carried the sub-heading "23-Year-Old Director Hailed As A Genius". By all the rules, this amazing puff should have transported me instantly to Hollywood and riches! – At the very least it might have been expected that *one* curious film mogul would be moved to enquire who this amazing creature was. There was nothing. Somehow the film industry's hot pursuit failed to catch up with me. The explanation, of course, was that the film *business* of the time – dominated, as it was, by self-opinionated accountants and semi-literate salesmen – was complacent and unimaginative. The people who ran things would have read Jack's column, and shrugged. In any case, "geniuses" are frightening. Too clever by half.

Just after Christmas, 1949, the first copy of the film arrived from America. We could hardly believe that our monumental project, conceived as a wild act of faith just under a year before, had been completed. After viewing it, however, we were forced to recognise that, at two hours, our film was far too long and indigestible for anyone to take at one sitting. As a training tool it was impractical in its present state. I went back to the cutting room and made a second, shorter version. There was no question of paying me of course – the regiment had long since run out of cash.

Unfortunately, changes had been happening in the army that removed the film's purpose. In the future an infantryman would not serve in a particular regiment throughout his career. Regimental pride was no longer relevant, or even desirable. What was *Proud Heritage* about if not pride in regiment? I was invited to the War Office, as the Ministry of Defence was called at the time, to sit with a party of generals while they viewed the film in a projection room in the basement (and was astounded when one of them asked the projectionist if he had any Disney cartoons). The generals decided that the army had no use for *Proud Heritage*.

The final cost of the film amounted to about £3,000 – about £85,000 at the time of writing. (It is interesting to compare this with the budget of an average one-hour documentary made today for television, at three-quarters of a million pounds – and that would not be a "costume epic" with large crowd scenes.) Although I never knew the full story, I am fairly sure that Leckie Ewing and perhaps one or two other dedicated enthusiasts dug into their own pockets.

Although our film did not fulfil its intended purpose it was well received, both within and outside the regiment. It had a public showing for a week or two at the Cosmo Cinema, an art house in Glasgow. Although it was creaky and often amateurish it did, I feel, have moments of greatness. Today it lies in rarely opened cans in the Imperial War Museum, entirely unknown to the army, much less the outside world. General Telfer-Smollett died soon after its completion and Lieutenant-Colonel (Retired) Roddy Leckie Ewing also died suddenly of a heart attack in 1956, at the early age of fifty-three.

The Highland Light Infantry itself expired a year or two later, swallowed up in an amalgamation with the Royal Scots Fusiliers. It has been further diluted in The Royal Regiment of Scotland.

There are probably few people today who recall the events surrounding the making of *Proud Heritage*. It was a remarkable achievement for totally inexperienced people, who made themselves producers, impresarios and film actors. Above all, the achievement was Roddy Leckie Ewing's, a modest, cultured man, who was dedicated to his beloved Highland Light Infantry, and who became, for the few years that remained to him, my closest friend.

I owe him a great debt.

For my part I now had to see whether the film's other personal purpose would be realised – whether it would catapult me into a glittering career in films. It was a very distinctive period. I was one of "the New Elizabethans" – the survivors of a war that had reduced the population and been a great leveller. We were going to put the "Great" back into Great Britain, and everything was possible...

6

ALASTAIR SIM had slept in the bath.

The film was *The Happiest Days Of Your Life*, and he was supposed to be the headmaster of a second-rate boarding school for boys. Because of an administrative error at the Ministry of Education, his school had been invaded and taken over by a girls' school – a girls' school headed by the formidable Margaret Rutherford. She had commandeered the headmaster's quarters, which is why he had been reduced to sleeping in the bath.

It was 1949. Riverside Studios by Hammersmith Bridge. The day was a memorable one for me. It was my first day in my new job in a film studio.

The shot called for the headmaster to wake up, climb painfully out of the bath, and walk over to a mirror to survey his bloodshot eyes. Frank Launder, the film's director, had set up a tracking-shot with the camera mounted on a vehicle called a dolly, running on rails and pushed by a brawny worker, called the Grip.

I peered over the backs of the technicians, craning to see what was going on, so Grip invited me to ride on the dolly with the camera-operator and focus-puller.

There were several "takes", until everyone was satisfied and Frank Launder gave the order 'Print it!' I did not see the result until filming had been completed, and viewing the "rough cut" of the film with Frank Launder one day I saw, to my amazement, the entire camera crew, including me, reflected in the bathroom mirror behind Alastair Sim's back as he crossed the room. No one else seemed to notice it, and when the lights came up I asked Frank if this was acceptable. He grinned and accused me of kidding. It took several attempts before I persuaded him to run the scene again. There was panic – amazingly, no one had noticed the mistake before. Oswald Haffenrichter, the film editor, saved the day when he found an alternative take on the cutting-room floor which had only a momentary glimpse of the unit.

So, whenever *The Happiest Days Of Your Life* appears on television – and it frequently does – watch out for it. If you are quick enough, and don't blink, you can see me in my first (and last) film role.

A few days after we received the first copy of *Proud Heritage* Frank Launder had told me that he and Sidney Gilliat wanted me to work for them. I asked Frank what he had in mind for me to do and he told me with a twinkle in his eye that the publicity I had received for *Proud Heritage* had convinced him that I must have talent – for publicity. A timely prick to my ego! But it was not the moment to feel offended. I had been offered a job. It must surely lead to more interesting things in the future. I had a massive problem, however. At that time trades union were powerful and the film industry was a "closed shop". Everyone working in it had to belong to the union, the Association of Cinematograph Technicians – ACT. But chronic unemployment had led to enrolment being suspended. Catch twenty-two: you could only join if you had a job, but you could not get a job unless you were in ACT. It was to be many years before I was able to resolve this problem and it made my path much more difficult. For the time being there were a few, unsatisfactory, ways around it (apart from bribing the union officials, which probably went on). In my case it was to call me "Personal Assistant", which was not a union "grade".

Launder and Gilliat had left the Rank Organisation after its arrogant and autocratic head (an accountant, of course) had decided that a cinema's primary purpose was the sale of ice cream. Pinewood was to make fewer films. The talented teams that worked there – Frank and Sidney, the Boulting brothers, Carol Reed, "The Archers" – Michael Powell and Emeric Pressburger – decamped en masse to a new organisation, London Films, headed by the legendary Alexander Korda. Korda had acquired Shepperton Studios and recruited a glittering line-up of creative talent largely from an injection of capital by the Labour government – encouraging a sound British film industry to take root was thought culturally important.

Launder and Gilliat were a brilliant and successful team. They were very different in character, and I never felt there was a close personal friendship. Frank had come from fairly humble beginnings, starting life as a clerk in the Official Receivers' office. He always laughed that he had begun his career in bankruptcy! Sydney was the son of a newspaper editor, and the more intellectual of the two. He was lugubrious and pessimistic but had a devastating wit. On one occasion we all went to lunch at the Screenwriters' Club, off Park Lane. The entrance was at the top of a flight of stairs, and when we reached the door the manager barred the way. He pointed behind him to a large gathering already at lunch.

'We have no room,' he explained, 'Mr Rank is entertaining a party of cinema owners.'

Without a moment's hesitation, Sydney said:

'Look – the face that lunched a thousand shits!'

On another occasion he said of a shifty actor, 'At least he has the honesty to look dishonest.'

The flat in Sloane Square that Paul, Thelma and Bernadette lived in had been requisitioned during the war by Chelsea Town Council and rented to Thelma for a modest amount. Thelma invited me to stay there too. She had a five-year-old daughter named Jennifer from a former marriage, and it had recently been discovered that the child was spastic, which was not then a widely known disability. It was pleasant living with Paul, Thelma, Bernadette, Jennifer – and the Irish maid, Katie. The summer was hot, and at night we had the windows thrown wide. There were few cars about in those days, and the square below was silent, except for the loud bell that summoned the taxi drivers stationed in front of Peter Jones.

The Happiest Days Of Your Life was based on a West End stage success. The plot's potential sexual undertones were incredible but it was a more innocent age. The location filming was in an exclusive girls' public school at Liss in Hampshire while the girls were on holiday. One or two eighteen-year-olds remained behind to appear in the film, dashing around with hockey sticks in their bottle-green gym knickers, much to the delight of the licentious film crew.

The stars were Margaret Rutherford and Alastair Sim. Joyce Grenfell was also in the cast. The *ingénue* part was played by Bernadette, who seemed to me to be growing more beautiful every day. There was a problem over her relationship with Frank, which for obvious reasons was kept very quiet. Frank had wanted to give Bernadette this leading role, but Sidney Gilliat thought Korda might assume that he was just having a bit of fun with a starlet, and disapprove – putting the production funds in jeopardy. A strange situation arose, involving me. When I turned up at the studio it was usually with Bernadette, and most evenings I took her home after work. Word got around that she and I shared a flat. It was therefore convenient not to contradict the inevitable assumption – if she was my girlfriend there was no reason for anyone to suspect Frank. (Such a subterfuge would be impossible in today's tabloid-led "celebrity" world!)

The antics of the trade unions in the studio made a powerful impression on me. The film's humour revolved around the need to conceal the presence of both boys and girls in the same school when the boys' governors and the girls' parents choose the same day for a visit. The playing field would be rigged with rugger goal posts for the governors to see, and then cleared for hockey for the girls' parents, then back again, and so on. All had to be done in rapid and bewildering succession. In the studio the field appeared as a painted backdrop seen through a window, and the distant rugby posts were represented by three lines in the form of an H. When Frank began a new scene the continuity girl pointed out that the posts should no longer be there from the scene that had just been completed. Frank gave the order to paint the H over and called a tea break.

When the unit reassembled no action had been taken, so the studio manager was sent for. With a red face he explained that he had sacked the scene painter that day. As a result, the union had decreed that the only person allowed to paint out the offending H was the Art Director – and he was away from the studio and uncontactable. There followed a high-level conference between union and management, which established that the only other person who might paint over the H without provoking a strike was London Films' Chief Production Designer – the eminent Vincent Korda, brother of Sir Alex. He was based at Korda's Shepperton studio in Surrey, thirty miles or so away. A Rolls Royce was despatched to fetch him and *The Happiest Days Of Your Life* suspended production until he arrived with his little brush.

It was incidents like this, humorous though they are in the re-telling, that helped hasten the demise of the British film industry.

In earlier days Launder and Gilliat had written the scripts for many of Alfred Hitchcock's successes and they shared his talent for suspense. While Frank was occupied with *The Happiest Days*, Sidney was at Islington Studios directing his own "Hitchcock" thriller called *State Secret*, with Hollywood star Douglas Fairbanks Junior, Glynis Johns and Jack Hawkins. The story was supposed to take place in a fictitious East European dictatorship called Vosnia, and I helped to devise a publicity stunt. We dressed two or three actors in "Vosnian army" uniforms and walked them round the West End. It excited a lot of curiosity and one passer-by even assured us that he had been to Vosnia.

The feeling of freedom was strange and exciting after years of military discipline. Paul and I were lads about the King's Road and during the summer heat, Bernadette and I lounged on the grass in Hyde Park and talked of the wonderful years that lay ahead, she a star and me a director of epic films. The only cloud on Bernadette's horizon was Frank Launder's marital status. His divorce was in process, but Bernadette was a devout Catholic, and a marriage to a divorced person – especially a non-Catholic – was frowned upon.

My rather unlikely friendship with Frank grew stronger all the time. He was renting a luxurious mansion in Mayfair that had been the home of the star Gertrude Lawrence. One evening he phoned and asked me to bring Bernadette to his house after work. I dutifully escorted Bernadette there, and we had a weird party – the three of us – polishing off half-a-dozen bottles of champagne, and rounding off the proceedings with Frank and I taking turns picking up a giggling Bernadette and throwing her to each other. Freud might have seen some hidden significance in it.

Our cosy little circle in Sloane Square came to an end when the council gave notice that the flat was to be reprivatised and sold off. Thelma was given notice to quit. I moved out to accommodation of my own in the Brompton Road, and the rest of the group broke up soon after, when Paul Connell made an honest woman of Thelma, and Frank's divorce came through so that he and Bernadette could be married.

An Irish actor named Charlie Fitzsimons, brother of the Hollywood star Maureen O'Hara, invited me to his "residential chamber", a few hundred yards from Harrods, opposite Brompton Oratory in Knightsbridge. The proprietor was a Mrs Fitzmaurice who was rumoured to be some sort of relative of the Marquess of Lansdowne, having been given the house as part of a divorce settlement. She let "chambers" to "young gentlemen" and others she judged suitable to share her roof. I passed the test and moved in. My room was comfortably furnished, with a telephone and small washbasin, and breakfast was brought each morning by a maid. For a small extra charge dinner was also available.

With *The Happiest Days Of Your Life* and *State Secret* nearing completion I spent most of my time in the Launder-Gilliat Productions office on the upper floor of Korda's palatial headquarters at 146 Piccadilly, Hyde Park Corner. It was one of a terrace of three large houses that had been the London homes of aristocrats. King George VI and his family had lived in the middle house, 145, when he was Duke of York. It was destroyed by a bomb during the war. Korda acquired the houses on either side and a connecting bridge was built over the bombsite, with a preview theatre installed in it.

Sir Alex loved titles and all that went with them. There was a butler in morning clothes, a uniformed commissionaire on the door. Recognising something military about me, the latter would snap out a smart salute and greet me with a crisp 'Good morning, sir!' It made me feel just a little less out of my depth. There was also a house manager in the shape of Captain Hussey, RN-retired, who had served on a battleship with King George during the Great War. Countless notables were seen crossing the elegant entrance hall to the wide sweeping staircase that led to palatial saloons above. One afternoon I was introduced to Baroness Moura Budberg, who was Korda's literary advisor. I was too young to know that she had been Maxim Gorky's secretary and H. G. Wells' mistress (and I doubt if Korda knew that she was probably a Soviet spy.

Korda's persona was felt throughout the building. One heard stories about him (perhaps "legends" might be more appropriate) and from that source I learned two of his important maxims to guide me through my future career. First, *Always use O P M – Other People's Money* and second, *Everyone I meet has two professions – their own and film producer.*

I came face to face with – I could not say "met" – the great man only once. It had been decided that the story of Sidney Gilliat's film would be serialised in a national newspaper. There were fears that rival papers would take offence and give the film bad reviews, so it was essential that the project was kept secret. I was alone in the office one lunchtime when Sir Alex's secretary phoned and said that Korda was waiting downstairs, and wanted to be briefed on the newspaper deal. I raced down and found the great man on the forecourt sitting in the back of his Rolls Royce. He wound down the window and listened as I told him what had been arranged. When I finished he just stared at me. Thinking he may not have understood, I rambled on, repeating myself. He was Hungarian, after all. Still no reaction. Covered with embarrassment, I repeated yet again the need for secrecy. Stony silence. Silence, now, also from me.

All I could think of, to bring the bizarre "conversation" to a close, was to say, 'Well, I'm going to lunch now.'

Again no reaction, so I backed away and began to make for the gate. I had just reached it when there was a frantic hooting on the Rolls Royce's horn. The chauffeur was waving energetically for me to come back. I did so in quick time. Korda looked at me for a long moment, then said in his heavy Hungarian accent, 'Mom's dee worrd, eh?'

It was just a short drive to Korda's regal headquarters from Buckingham Palace. The Palace did not have a cinema, and every week King George and Queen Elizabeth, dressed of course in evening clothes, motored up Constitution Hill to the site of their former home, where Korda received them to show them the pick of the current films.

On one wintry evening the King arrived wearing a splendid black Crombie overcoat. He asked where to leave it, and Captain Hussey suggested he drape it over the banister at the foot of the sweeping staircase. The King did so and took two or three steps upwards.

Then he turned back and retrieved the coat.

'Remembering your reputation on the "Collingwood", Hussey,' he said, 'I'd better keep it with me!'

With Frank and Sidney out of production I had little to do. I attempted to get newspapermen interested, roughed out ideas for film posters, and took phone calls from Frank's racehorse trainer in Ireland. Various well-known figures drifted in and out, including "Dickie" Attenborough.

Jack Gourlay and Squibs had bought a house in Strawberry Hill, Twickenham, and we revived our collaborative sessions, attempting to write the screenplay that would make us rich and famous. I also ran into my Lovat Scouts squadron commander, Peter Glass. He had returned to his acting career and was doing the rounds of the theatrical agents. Alas for Peter, it was a tough time for actors, with so much competition from returning servicemen. Peter was a good enough actor but without that essential "star quality". The car accident in Athens had also marred his good looks. He finally gave up and took a job as a tour guide for Thomas Cook's millionaire's cruises.

My job, also, did not last much longer. Korda had built his empire on the strength of the government subsidy. The fly in the ointment was that he was not the man to be in charge of such a precious – and finite – resource. He was a creative perfectionist first and foremost rather than careful manager. I doubt if his business plan was ever thought through. Too many productions were embarked on, Korda admitting afterwards that he did not even know what some of them were. The funds dwindled quicker than they could be replenished from the box office and inevitably the reckoning came. Korda ran out of money.

Frank and Sidney visited Sir Alex on a vain quest for funds for their next production.

"We are two straws clutching at a drowning man," Sidney said.

With the Rank organisation making even less films, the result was the famous 1950 "film crisis". I was told very sympathetically to seek my fortune elsewhere.

7

FORTUNATELY I had something to go on to. A retired RAF officer had called at London Films and enquired if anyone could advise him on making a 16-millimetre sales film about his company, Redifon's, new product, the "Flight Simulator". The world's first passenger jet aircraft, the de Havilland Comet, had just gone into service with British Overseas Airways Corporation and the Flight Simulator was a replica flight deck on which pilots could be trained without the dangers of actual flight.

The enquiry had been passed to me as the only person who had experience of 16-millimetre filming. When my job with Frank and Sidney ended I took the project to United Motion Pictures, and went with it.

It was my first professional job as a director so I was naturally apprehensive. Filming was straightforward, however. The simulator was an exact copy of the aircraft flight deck, complete with computer-controlled instruments and realistic sound effects. I shot a "GV" ("general view" in film language, which I was now learning) of an imitation flight, into which "emergencies" were introduced for the trainee pilot to respond to. I then made close-ups of the instruments and controls to be cut in at the editing stage.

The one piece of excitement was a trip in a real Comet – the original Mark I that was later condemned as nonairworthy after a number of disasters. I was amazed to think that I was eight miles above the ground, in a sky that was almost black. Commonplace nowadays, but a rare experience then.

The retired Group Captain was satisfied with my film and told us that a similar device, based on the Sabre fighter, was being constructed for the Royal Canadian Air Force. We could expect a commission to film it in due course.

That was at least a year or two away and I had to live in the meantime. I had not been able to solve the problem of the trade union ticket – without it the possibilities of obtaining employment were severely limited. I had spotted another chink in the armour, though. The small companies making "industrial" films, usually on 16mm film – films used for sales training, staff indoctrination, or simply for company prestige – mostly ignored the union. One of them was United Motion Pictures.

Mister Sheppard, the managing director, who I was permitted to call "Jack" out of the hearing of his staff, had a high opinion of me (his accountant had advised him that any person who could get into Buckingham Palace had to be impressive!). He had been called up in the army at the beginning of the war and taken prisoner at the time of the Dunkirk evacuation. After several years as a prisoner-of-war his health had given out, and he had been repatriated with other sick prisoners in exchange for Germans.

He had made a tidy sum out of the Flight Simulator film, so he welcomed it when I dreamt up an idea to make use of his small studio.

I was aware that aspiring actors and actresses spent considerable sums on having glamorous photographs taken, mostly to be reproduced in the casting directory,

SPOTLIGHT. I also knew that film producers shot "screen tests" of potential cast members, and they were sometimes "borrowed" by the actor concerned to show to other prospective employers. It seemed to me that an acted scene, filmed by us, must be more useful than a still picture. We would be able to film in colour, moreover, using 16-millimetre Kodachrome. If we could persuade actors to use their cash on making their own "screen tests" we might start a small business.

To try out the idea we made a pilot "test" of a young up-and-coming actress named Eileen Moore. I persuaded Roger Moore (no relation of Eileen's) to act with her.

Shooting sync sound was something entirely new to United Motion Pictures. The camera was a semi-professional "Cine-Kodak Special" with the shaft of an electric motor inserted through the side, in place of the clockwork winding-handle. To deaden the noise, the entire device was covered by a large homemade padded box called "the blimp". As the viewfinder was in the box it was out of reach. We solved the problem by removing the blimp to line-up shots. Adhesive tape was stuck round the top of the tripod, and we marked the positions when the camera panned to follow the actors. The blimp was then replaced, and the scene was photographed "blind". Amazingly, it worked.

In the end, however, the 16mm equipment was too limited, and the colour film and sound not up to it, and we were compelled to abandon the project. Eileen Moore went on to make a film or two before marrying (for a while) George Cole. Roger, of course, became a "mega-star", as James Bond.

Although that project had not worked out, I remained convinced that with a bit of tuning UMP's tiny premises and 16mm film could be put to use for some sort of speculative production.

An agent I knew introduced me to a friend who was looking for someone to team up with, to collaborate on any kind of film enterprise that offered promise. Charles Edmund duMaresq Clavell – or Jimmy Clavell, as he liked to call himself – was two or three years older than me. He had been a prisoner of the Japanese in Singapore's Changi Gaol, and the privations he had suffered then had left him with a chronic skin disorder. On his return home, he had also been in a motorcycle accident that left him with a rigid right leg. These afflictions proved no handicap when he met lovely actress and top model April Stride, the daughter of a retired naval commander. He swept her off her feet, married her, and they set up home with April's miniature poodle and Siamese cat in a tiny mews house near Harrods.

For me it was the start of an intense association that lasted for about a year and had consequences for a long time to come. Jimmy had been to the USA and told me that American television consisted almost entirely of thirty-minute films. The studio facilities in Hollywood were too expensive to use for this kind of product, he said – we could produce them more cheaply in England.

I took him to see Jack Sheppard and we got an enthusiastic reception – Jack would provide the facilities for making some pilots. I brought in Jack Gourlay to work with me on the scripts and we formed a company, which we called United Cine-Vision. We agreed to contribute our efforts on a "spec" basis for a share of the potential profits, and we went looking for like-minded performers who were prepared to participate on a similar basis. There was Jimmy's wife April, there was Paul, and there were one or two actors I had met while I was with Frank and Sidney.

I had kept in touch with Kim Kendall, the showgirl "with no talent" in Palestine. She was too busy to take part, but introduced me to her younger sister Kay, who was only too pleased to be invited. The two girls were the daughters of music-hall artistes. They and their mum lived in a flat in St Martin's Lane, a few doors down the road from the Marquis of Salisbury – the actors' pub. Mum was droll. 'They say we're descended from Captain Cook,' she told me. 'I don't know how he found New Zealand. I can't find Leicester Square on a dark night.' The girls' grandmother was the Victorian music-hall star, Marie Kendall. She was in her eighties, with a back like a ramrod. When the boyfriends arrived at the family to take the girls out, she looked them over with a stony stare.

Katy Kendall – or Kay, as she was billed – was suffering a downturn in her fortunes. She had been plucked from the chorus to play the lead in a dismal "Hollywood" musical made in England, called *London Town*. The film had flopped and it had blighted her career. She was a stunning beauty, with enormous hazel eyes, a skin so white that it seemed translucent, a perfectly chiselled nose (chiselled, I found out later, by a cosmetic surgeon) and an extraordinary mouth that could smile and look tragic at the same time. She was also an extravert who kept everyone in fits of laughter.

We decided to make two half-hour "pilots". *DIAL 999* would be a crime drama and would star Kay Kendall and *The Return Of Jekyll And Hyde*, with April in it, would mine the horror seam. We decided to shoot the latter in colour. 'Nuff said about them. They were pretty dreadful. Writing a script for a half-hour drama calls for great expertise and experience, and Jack and I had neither. I don't think there was much of Carol Reed in my directing. In an attempt to be "different" I was given to bizarre angles. Upwards from the floor, on a makeshift dolly, skittering to and fro. It only emphasised the shortcomings of UMP's facilities. The actors were kind enough to say they liked being directed by me, however.

I may as well complete my personal story of Kay Kendall here. She was "doomed to become a star", as they say. She became the brightest *film star* Britain ever produced, and she shot to Hollywood stardom. Rich and famous people cultivated her; she had a fling with one of the heirs to a supermarket chain. 'If I marry him –' she told me, '– I'll give birth to a seven-pound cheese.'

Alas, she was destined never to give birth to anything. We were sitting on the set one day during a break in filming and she began to cough.

'The old TB again, Katy?' I joked, with monumental bad taste.

'Oh, don't,' she protested, looking gorgeously tragic. 'I have a premonition that I won't make old bones.'

The premonition proved all too accurate. After marrying the star of *My Fair Lady*, Rex Harrison, she fell ill and died of leukaemia in 1959, at the tender age of thirty-two.

Jimmy Clavell was uncritical of our efforts and remained optimistic. He continually recited the mantra: 'We're potentially rich men.' Jimmy also had a piece of wisdom to impart. For me filmmaking was wonderful, and I said I was surprised that anyone got paid for doing it. He was serious. 'Never tell anyone the money is not important,' he said. 'It will frighten them. They'll think "Well, if he's not doing it for the money, it must be something else. Something we don't understand. We don't like things we don't understand."'

I did not take this advice seriously. Filmmaking was the only thing I could ever conceive of wanting to do. As Orson Welles put it, it was being allowed to play with the best toy train set there was. Of course I would do it for nothing if necessary (and sometimes did). It was many years before I realised that Jimmy was right and I was wrong.

I thought he and I hit it off rather well, and April was unfailingly sweet and generous. The three of us became almost inseparable during the few months while I edited the films. We spent Christmas together, and visited April's parents' country home at Chalfont St Giles.

While we were making our films, United Motion Pictures was going through a crisis. The company's founder and principal shareholder had retired to South Africa after appointing two of his oldest employees, book-keeper Sheppard and a former plumber and aspiring cameraman named Stubbs, to run things as joint boardroom directors. They couldn't stand each other. My productions brought things to a head. Stubbs was not up to photographing the sort of things we were doing, and covered his incompetence with rudeness and sarcasm. Sheppard seized an opportunity for forcing a showdown. Either he or Stubbs would have to leave, he declared.

Jimmy Clavell was drawn in as an apparently disinterested mediator. Sheppard sent him to the cutting room to ask me if I would consider joining UMP in Stubbs' place. I gave it some thought, but turned the offer down. I wanted to make my career in feature films. Declining a regular pay check in the pursuit of a dream was a brave decision, and I regretted it more than once in the years that followed. Stubbs was paid off and Sheppard continued to run the company on his own. It was a turning point in several people's lives, and many years later, towards the end of my career, it would return to haunt me.

It had been arranged that Jimmy would go to the USA to sell the films. Just before he sailed in the *Queen Elizabeth*, Jack Sheppard confided that he did not like Jimmy and wanted to sever connection with him – I should go to New York instead. It took me by complete surprise. I protested that Jimmy was being misjudged. I knew him, I said – I was confident he was a loyal friend and colleague who would do his best for all of us. I also pleaded, rightly, that I had no experience in selling.

As it turned out, I was forced to accept that it was I who was guilty of misjudgement. Jimmy went to the States for three or four weeks at our expense, and when he came back, having failed to sell the films, I found my phone calls were not returned. Our association ended literally in silence. Not long after, that I discovered that the bird – or birds – Jimmy and April – had flown. There was not even a "goodbye".

Jimmy had not sold our films, but had sold himself. The most galling irony was that the job he landed was with the only contact in the USA I had been able to provide, the company that had processed *Proud Heritage*.

It was forty years before I saw Jimmy again. In the interim he had become a multi-millionaire novelist with a semi-autobiographical "blood-and-thunder" about Changi Gaol called, rather appropriately in the context of our association, *King Rat*. He had also directed one or two films (without much distinction). He died, no longer "potentially", but seriously rich in his early seventies.

For me, 1950 came to an end with *Dial 999* and *Jekyll And Hyde* unsold, and the whole enterprise a professional catastrophe. I had to start all over again.

New year 1951 came. It was the centenary year of the 1851 Great Exhibition and the government decided that a similar festival was required, to cheer up a nation still suffering from rationing and drab austerity. A large area of the derelict South Bank of the Thames at Waterloo was taken over, and by summer an exciting array of exhibits was open to the public. There was a towering modernist installation called The Skylon, and a great hall of wonders called "The Dome Of Discovery". Among a maze of other buildings was the "Telekinema" (it survives today as the National Film Theatre), that showed a number of specially-made 3-D films, requiring the audience to wear horizontally- and vertically-polarised glasses.

A more disturbing portent for the film industry was the demonstration of large-screen television.

For me, the first two or three months of the year were anything but festive, with no prospects on the horizon. It began to look as if my dreams of a career in films might end in failure and disillusionment.

I continued working with Jack Gourlay, trying to come up with an idea we could develop into a screenplay to sell to a production company. As a child I had loved the Fenimore Cooper story *Deerslayer*, which I thought more atmospheric and sensitive than the same author's better-known *Last Of The Mohicans*. It told of an elderly pioneer living on a lake in 18th-century New York State with his daughters, one of whom is feeble-minded. They get caught up in wars between rival Indian tribes. I imagined the setting, and it occurred to me that it could be reproduced in Scotland, around one of the lochs near Aberfoyle. "Spaghetti Westerns" were being filmed in Italy – why not Scotland? ("Haggis Westerns"?) I wrote a screenplay, and Jack and I took it to the head of Hammer Films, James Carreras. He was enthusiastic but wanted the atmospheric stuff replaced with lots more blood and thunder. In the end he sold the project on our behalf to a small Hollywood studio and we shared the meagre proceeds. The film was eventually made in America on a low budget and I never went to see it.

Jack Gourlay and I continued developing ideas, working them up into short "treatments" – descriptions of the action with a line or two of dialogue. I had met a Russian who told me he worked for the official guide to the aristocracy, *Burke's Peerage*, which struck me as a bit odd, because we thought all Russians were communists. It inspired Jack and me to work on a comedy about an anarchist who gets a job on *Burke's Peerage* while plotting to blow up the House of Lords. We called it *Pardon My Pedigree*. Frank Launder thought it was a good idea and helped us to develop a workmanlike treatment.

Then I got a break. UMP was commissioned by a manufacturer of home power-tools to produce a training film for their salesmen, and Jack Sheppard asked me to produce it. My characteristic (and unjustified) self-confidence must have overcome any doubts in his mind from the United Cine-Vision fiasco.

It was to be a lavish little film, shot on 35-millimetre film, with sets, location shooting, a cast of actors and a generous budget that included a satisfyingly large fee for me. One hundred pounds a week (£2,000 in today's money), which at that time was riches.

We rented a small studio in Wardour Street, with a staff of experienced technicians. As producer-director I was their "employer", so there was no danger of shop stewards checking my non-existent union status. I contacted agents and had casting sessions, and was offered quite well-known actors. Among them was a former Korda star, Hector Ross, who had come down in the world.

For the first time I found myself directing a proper film unit and it was wonderful. I had been given "the train set" to play with! The actors and I worked out the moves. The camera-operator detached the viewfinder from the bulky sound-deadening "blimp" containing the Mitchell camera, and followed me round the set, peering through the finder and lining up shots. The focus-puller marked the selected camera positions on the floor with chalk, and the Grips laid steel tracks from one mark to the next. Then the hefty "Fearless Velocilator" dolly, carrying the camera, was manhandled on to the rails. Veteran Director of Photography George Stevens directed light on the scene while the sound-recordist manoeuvred his unwieldy trolley so that the microphone boom would not throw unwanted shadows.

We rehearsed the scene. Once, twice...

Then:

"Go for a take!"

The bell shrilled and the red light came on.

"Roll it!" my Assistant Director shouted.

"Slate one, take one," the Clapper Boy recited.

Clap went the board.

"Action," I said.

Then:

"Cut!"

Magic words.

I directed a smooth little half-hour film that pleased the tool manufacturer. It won First Prize in the Harrogate Industrial Film Festival the following year. It seemed I was "in business" once more. Saved by the bell.

With the Clavells gone, I struck up a friendship with Hector Ross. He had recently married June, the daughter of prominent playwright Vernon Sylvaine. She and Hector lived in a furnished apartment in Dolphin Square, Chelsea, and I began to spend a lot of time with them. I also got together with Roger Moore occasionally. He was having a hard time, living in a bed-sitter in Greenwich with his first wife, ice skater Doorn van Steyn.

The end of the year also saw a national sensation that involved some of my friends. On Christmas Day, Westminster Abbey was broken into, and the Coronation Stone – the Stone of Scone – was taken away. It is said that King George, when informed of its "theft", stammered, 'Any w-w-one who w-w-wants to s-sit on a b-bloody lump of Aberdeen granite, is welcome to it!'

Scots had been complaining for some time about a lack of concern for their country's problems by the (as they saw, English) government. The stone was believed, quite correctly, to belong to Scotland, and that is where it was taken to be hidden away. In the course of the robbery, the Stone was found to have been broken in two at some time in the past. It proved convenient in transporting the pieces to Scotland, and one piece rested overnight in the Covenanter's Inn, Aberfoyle, in the care of none other than my bosom friend Robin Steele. The Stone was eventually rejoined and "surrendered" to the authorities at Arbroath Abbey in April the following year, to be taken back to London.

Many years later, just before he died, Robin told me that the stone that had been returned to England was not the real one. One of the two bronze rivets used to repair it was hollow, he said. It contained a paper revealing the truth. I asked Robin where the real Stone was, and he said it was in a mason's yard outside Glasgow. Could it be true?

One of the pleasanter aspects of my life at this time were the regular invitations I received to stay for a few days with Roddy Leckie Ewing, who had retired from the army with the rank of colonel. His house, Arngomery, was a Georgian mansion near the village of Kippen in Stirlingshire. It was famous for the great yew tree, said to be eleven hundred years old, that grew beside its front door. According to tradition, the bows for Wallace's army had been cut from it. The house was set in a park, with a glen running through it. Roddy had read forestry at Cambridge before joining the army, and had established an arboretum, which contained, among other things, a Sequoia Giant Redwood. He had never married, and lived alone in the greater part of the house, looked after by his former batman "Sandy" Smart, and Smart's wife, who did the cooking.

Roddy suffered from chronic arthritis. Lumbago it was called in those days. He had moved his bedroom downstairs, so I was allotted the palatial upper rooms. They were freezing in winter, and it was also slightly creepy to be alone up there, because the house was reputably haunted. These interludes were a marvellous break for me, and I spent the time writing, ensconced in a large armchair in front of the fire in the elegant drawing room with its massive crystal chandelier and cabinets of precious porcelain. Roddy was out of doors most of the day, whatever the weather, indulging his favourite hobby, bricklaying. He built a group of pig houses himself. At four o'clock he would return to the house and Smart would appear with a tray of tea and Marmite sandwiches. We would face each other across the fire and talk "army".

In those days, television was regarded as a lower-class indulgence and Roddy did not own one. Smart had a set, however, and one evening he invited us to see a play. So after dinner we made our way through the winding upper passages to the Smarts' quarters, where we watched Terence Rattigan's *Deep Blue Sea* while Mrs Smart produced tea and fruit cake. Life was calm and uncomplicated in the 1950s.

But my life was about to be thrown into turmoil again.

8

NINETEEN FIFTY-ONE WAS not only the Festival of Britain year. It was the year that World War III nearly began. The Korean War had broken out twelve months earlier. It was going badly for the United Nations forces, and looked as if it might end in defeat. Things took an apocalyptic turn when the American commander of the UN force, General Douglas MacArthur, threatened to use the atom bomb. There was every likelihood that North Korea's ally China would retaliate, the USSR would join in, and a full-scale world conflict would be triggered off. While President Truman calculated his chances, Britain mobilised her reserves.

I took little interest in politics and world affairs. The war in Korea was just another of the recurring spots of bother that got the newspapers excited. So it was with some surprise that I opened my mail one July morning, and read a letter from the War Office, addressed to Lt F. E. P. Taylor, ordering me to join the 4th/5th Battalion The Black Watch at Spey Bay in Morayshire. In a little under three years I was back in uniform.

It did not seem at all strange to be in battledress again. I felt almost as though I had come home. The battalion was in tent lines on a former airfield, and the mess was in a large marquee. Life promised to be companionable and full of fun. On the first evening, the officers were assembled in a Romney-hut and addressed by a brigadier. He told us that there was a good chance we would be at war with Russia in the next few days, and we should expect to be in action before long. Needless to say, the news came as a shock.

I was given command of a platoon, and we got down to brushing up our weapon handling. The summer nights were warm, and we slept out in slit trenches. We practised river crossing in collapsible boats on the fast-flowing, but fortunately shallow, River Spey. My craft turned over in midstream and I ordered my men to abandon ship. We waded, chin deep, battling the strong current, and managed to manoeuvre our absurdly unwieldy vessel to the bank.

Thankfully, the threatened war did not materialise. President Truman sacked the bellicose MacArthur, the Chinese pulled back, and the reservists of the 51st Highland Division were told they could go home. Something unexpected happened to me, however. I received a message from Roddy Leckie Ewing asking me to come to Edinburgh. My "Services Cavalcade" boss, Colonel Malcolm of Poltalloch, was in trouble over a military tattoo he was producing at Edinburgh Castle, and was in need of assistance.

I had heard of the tattoo, which Malcolm had persuaded the generals to allow him to stage on the Esplanade in front of the Castle drawbridge for three weeks in August during the Edinburgh Festival. It was now in its second or third year.

As soon as I was released, I took the train south and joined Roddy, who told me the story. Edinburgh, like London, was celebrating the Festival of Britain. To kick off the festivities, Malcolm had sold another of his ideas to the

City Fathers. He invited the chieftains of all Scotland's clans to send a piper to Edinburgh, for a great march down Princes Street – "The March of a Thousand Pipers". The tattoo, however, was more than usually important in the Festival of Britain year. With the pipers' march to organise, Malcolm found himself unable to find time for both. Would I – he had enquired of Roddy – supervise the tattoo rehearsals?

No fee was mentioned, but I agreed to help. I was given accommodation in Edinburgh Castle, and reported to a lieutenant colonel named Maclean, who was in charge of administration. He was a small, wiry man, with a hooked nose and thinning hair and thin and bony legs below the gaudy Cameron Highlanders kilt. The Balmoral bonnet worn at a jaunty angle suggested that his personality was as odd as his appearance. Although he was in his late forties, it made him look a bit of a lad. However, the impressive row of medal ribbons on his battledress blouse indicated that he had had an exciting war.

I found myself on the square at Redford Barracks, but had no time to ponder on the strange irony that it had been on this very square, seven years before, that I had entered the army. There was a demanding schedule of rehearsals to be organised, for the many detachments arriving in Edinburgh to take part. They included the mounted band of the Household Cavalry from Windsor, and the band and drill squad of the Royal Marines from Deal, commanded by a Captain Blood. The colonel – Maclean – was never far away. He kept a sharp eye on things, but did not interfere with my efforts.

A day or two before the opening night, word got out of a fiasco in Princes Street. Malcolm had set off his "March of a Thousand [in actual fact a few hundred] Pipers" from the Waverley Station end of Princes Street. Unfortunately someone had forgotten to seal off the side streets. The crowds had poured in to see the sight, spilled on to the roadway, and caused a total jam. Just one especially determined piper succeeded in forcing his way through to the other end of the street, no doubt playing *Scotland The Brave*. The Edinburgh City Fathers were furious, we heard. Malcolm was responsible for the mess and he was very much out of favour.

Because he had not supervised the tattoo rehearsals, Malcolm was not prepared when the massive cast of performers moved on to the Castle esplanade for the dress rehearsal. He was also in the habit of giving the show's running commentary himself, so I more or less drifted into directing the performance. This was done from the wooden shed, rather like a bird-watchers' hide, beside the VIP box at the top of the stands facing the Castle. My name was not printed in the programme, though, and Malcolm took full credit.

In those early days, the tattoo was a very amateur affair. It seemed to me to have far less polish than the Glasgow show. Malcolm made up the commentary as he went along, delivering it in a breathy undertone, and the lighting, that played such an important part, was provided by salvaged naval searchlights that threw a dim, yellowish light. The seating scaffolding was inadequate for the large number of people who wanted to see the show, so a line of folding chairs was placed out on the edge of the performance area, along with the disabled spectators in wheelchairs. This gave hair-raising moments. The esplanade was paved with cobbles in those days, and the horses stumbled on them, nearly sending members of the audience flying.

After the performance it took several minutes for the crowd to disperse, and we control staff were confined in our "shed". On the opening night, a long cigar appeared at its open "window", followed by a face.

'Say – are you da prodoocer of da show?' the face asked, in a broad Brooklyn accent.

To save lengthy explanations I said I was.

'I'm a prodoocer too,' the intruder announced. 'My name is Michael Todd.' (It would be some months in the future before that name would be world famous.) 'I gotta tell you – dis show gave me GOOSE-PIMPLES!' he exclaimed. 'It gave my *goose-pimples* goose-pimples!'

Before I could reply, he waved to the distant seating. 'I got Mary Martin over there, with her husband. She's over to do *South Pacific*.'

At this moment Lieutenant-Colonel Maclean appeared.

'Bring your guests up to the officers' mess for a drink,' he told me.

Ten minutes later, we were part of a cheerful party in the Castle mess, with white-coated waiters circulating with trays of drinks and canapés. I acted as host to Todd, Mary Martin, and her husband Richard Halliday (they had a son who would grow up as Larry Hagman, the villainous JR of the TV soap opera, *Dallas*).

I took Todd's coat, revealing a gaudy tartan suit. He was soon flashing a photograph beneath the noses of bemused Guards officers. It was of his recently divorced wife, the veteran film star Joan Blondell.

'Dat's my "ex" and my "next"!' Todd boasted. 'I'm going to marry her again!'

I now learned the reason for his approach to me.

'Could I buy your show?' he asked.

It seemed hilarious, this brash Yank trying to "buy" the British Army. He explained. He was making a "road show" film using a revolutionary new wide-screen process called "Cinerama". It was being compiled from spectacular scenes – Niagara Falls – a ride on a roller coaster – and he had planned to include "The March of a Thousand Pipers". When that came to nothing, he set his sights on the tattoo.

I was astonished when Maclean took him seriously. He left us for a few minutes, then returned.

'I've talked to the general,' Maclean announced. 'You can have a daytime performance of the tattoo for five hundred pounds.'

I was bewildered. 'There won't be an audience,' I pointed out, rather reasonably.

Maclean nodded and went off again. After a few minutes he brought more amazing news.

'I've been on to the BBC,' he said. 'They will make an announcement before the morning news bulletins that anyone who wants to see the tattoo free should be on the esplanade at nine hundred hours!'

Next morning, I went out under the gate of the Castle to find a large crowd already filling the seats, and a long queue stretching down the Royal Mile almost to Princes Street.

The massive Cinerama camera, assembled from three cameras mounted side-by-side, was rolled out. It was operated by a man wearing the inevitable baseball cap.

Todd drew me aside and told me his director, the celebrated Fred Zinnemann, had been delayed in Europe. I was therefore asked to take over.

The cameraman was crouching behind his monster contraption, evidently expecting the show to blaze forth immediately. It didn't seem to occur to him that armies take a moment or two to get rolling.

Todd turned to me and announced that we should get some audience-reaction shots in the meantime.

'They haven't seen anything to react to yet,' I pointed out – rather reasonably I thought.

'I'll show you how...' said Todd, leading me out to the middle of the empty arena.

He cupped his hands to his mouth.

'You're the greatest bunch of movie actors I've ever seen!' he bawled at the crowd, 'and when I shout "action" I want you to shout and cheer and clap! OK?'

'Action!' he shouted, and the crowd went wild.

Utter idiots...

'Now you do it,' Todd said to me. So I did.

I don't remember much of the rest of the shoot, though it must have worked out satisfactorily. Strangely enough, I never saw *This Is Cinerama*, although it ran for several years in London. It is still regularly shown at the Bradford Museum of Photography. Todd "forgot" to put my name on the credits, of course, but I see from the British Film Institute database that I am listed.

I never set eyes on Michael Todd again. He became more and more famous, marrying – among others – Elizabeth Taylor, and producing the blockbuster *Around The World In Eighty Days*. He met an untimely death in a plane crash while at the height of his career.

At the end of the tattoo run I was taken aside by Lieutenant-Colonel Maclean. He confided that George Malcolm had been blamed for the "March of a Thousand

Pipers" fiasco. It was thought he should have concentrated his attention on the tattoo. It was financed by Edinburgh Corporation and generated much of the revenue to underwrite the Edinburgh Festival. As a result Malcolm was not to be invited to continue as the tattoo's producer. Maclean asked me if I would return the following year. The tattoo would become a more professional production. As a Scottish Command staff officer, he would be "Director" in command of troops. I would be producer, paid a handsome fee and promoted to captain (I could not help recalling Mike Todd asking me what my rank was, and gasping when I told him – 'Dey made me a Brigadier-General when I prodooced shows for de army dooring de war!'). I was just twenty-five-years-old, which might seem rather callow to be offered such a "command", but it should be remembered that during the recent war, major-generals commanding divisions were only in their mid-thirties, and many battalion commanders in their twenties. People were used to being given monumental responsibilities at an early age.

Behind it, however, I suspect the situation was less high-minded. Alasdair Maclean was due to retire from the army in a year or two. He had his eye on the tattoo producer job himself, which would keep him occupied and bring fame and extra fortune. I could be the catalyst to enable him to realise his ambition. I had made Malcolm dispensable, and could act as Maclean's teacher.

I returned to London, a civilian again for the time being, with the task of re-launching my film career. My fortunes had improved enough to contemplate renting my first flat. Hector Ross found one for me in a square off Lancaster Gate, Bayswater – as the memorable line from

Kind Hearts And Coronets said, "on the wrong side of the park". It did seem foreign after Knightsbridge and Chelsea. The flat was sparsely furnished, so I went out and ordered a sofa bed in case I had a guest to stay. My flat was on the ground floor, and when it was delivered I expected the sofa to be carried in. Instead, the van driver and his mate dumped the heavy, cumbersome item of furniture on the pavement outside my front door and drove away.

Fortunately, at that moment Roger Moore dropped by to invite me out for a beer, and I commandeered him to carry one end. I doubt if he moves much furniture these days. He is now *Sir* Roger Moore, with furniture in Monaco and Switzerland.

Frank and Sidney had gone into production on a comedy called *Beauty Queen* (Korda persuaded Frank to change the title to the awful *Lady Godiva Rides Again* – Frank always regretted it). Frank had seen Kay Kendall in my forgettable TV pilot and given her a small part, along with Bernadette. Diana Dors and Joan Collins also had minor roles. I was amazed that Frank bypassed them when giving the lead to an inexperienced unknown (who as far as I know, was never seen in a major part again). But casting was never Frank's strong point. I had an enjoyable day getting the feel of a film studio again when I visited the set at Shepperton to talk to Frank about the "anarchist" story. Afterwards, we foregathered in the bar and Katy squealed with joy when she saw me. She greeted me with hugs and kisses, until Bernadette claimed that it was her turn. Wonderful to be treated like that by two such beauties! I loved both of them.

Jack Gourlay and I formed a new company to try and put our ideas into production. We called it Senate Films. An elderly film industry veteran named David Henley, who was scratching a living trying to put productions together, was interested in our plans. He became a director of Senate Films and let us use an office in his suite in Clifford Street, off Old Bond Street.

We got some encouragement when John Woolf of Romulus Films bought an option to produce the anarchist film. We discussed the leading part with Peter Ustinov. He was appearing in a stage play in St Martin's Lane, and before his matinee we took him to lunch at an undistinguished restaurant, conveniently placed in Leicester Square. Ustinov had never been there before, but the manager greeted him like an old friend.

Peter did not look up at him. Instead, a strange sound came through his pursed lips. Beep-beep-beep-beeeeeeeep... beep-beep-beeeeeeeep... I realised that it was Morse code. I could read Morse, and spelled it out in my head... F... U... C... K... O... F... F...

The restaurant manager beamed delightedly.

Although Ustinov was enthusiastic about our story, he was too heavily committed with the stage show. We then thought of comedian Frankie Howard, who wanted to play the part, but his name proved not sufficient to get our project off the ground. For the time being, John Woolf's regular renewal payments for the option brought in a minuscule income.

9

IN THE spring of the following year I went north for a meeting at Edinburgh Castle, where I was formally appointed Producer and Stage Director of the Edinburgh Military Tattoo. I would have a number of majors and even a lieutenant colonel or two as assistants. Maclean had asked me to arrive with ideas for the tattoo's presentation and I described a number of innovations I would like to see. In particular I wanted the old naval searchlights to be replaced with something more effective, such as film-studio arc lights. I also proposed that the Castle floodlights should be used more imaginatively, along the lines of the new attraction called "Son et lumière" that was becoming very popular. I said I thought *ad lib* running commentary, garnished with waggish jests, such as Malcolm had delivered, was amateurish – there should be a commentary, scripted if necessary, and delivered by a professional. I proposed my old CO "Titus" Oatts, who had given a fine commentary at the Glasgow "Services Cavalcade" show, to deliver it.

Strangely enough, it was my father who contributed a really clever idea for the tattoo. Over a drink a week or two before, I had told him what I was doing. 'Why not put anti-aircraft searchlights in the Castle?' he had asked, 'and have them beam a massive V-sign in the sky during performances, so that Edinburgh and surrounding district would know that the Tattoo was on?' Parents are fated never to receive any gratitude from their offspring, and I confess that I presented the idea as my own. My father did at least have the satisfaction of seeing the tattoo on television.

All my ideas were received with enthusiasm, and I was congratulated on my efforts.

During the planning sessions that followed, I was invited to stay with Alasdair Maclean and his wife in their grand house in Murrayfield, the most select part of Edinburgh. Though a professional soldier, Alasdair was an instinctive showman, and we spent hours dreaming up ideas for our "new look" tattoo. It was a fascinating household to be taken into. Alasdair was a flamboyant eccentric. He had been born on Mull, and claimed to be either "the Maclean of Pennycross" or "the Maclean of Lochbuie" (wags called him – out of earshot – "the Maclean of Drambuie"). His wife, Mary, was the former wife of Lord Strathspey. She was a New Zealander, tall and thin with aquiline features. She had three children from her first marriage. All their names began with "J" – James, aged nine, who was "The Master of Grant" and heir to the Strathspey title, Janet and Jacqueline. All three were unfailingly polite and friendly. On Sunday afternoon, Alasdair and Mary would retire to their room for a siesta, and I was left to shoot arrows with the children in the garden. The only other member of the household was "Cookie", who ran the kitchen with unquestioned authority. Oh – and there was one other – Alasdair's brown-and-white Springer spaniel Duncan, who only understood Gaelic.

After three or four days I returned to London until August, when the tattoo was due to take place. In the meantime, I had a new Wolf Tools film to shoot. Again, we used the Wardour Street studio, and I had a good cast of very nice people, including Hugh David, who eventually became a BBC drama director, and Ann Bennett, who took me by surprise by revealing that she was Alasdair Maclean's cousin.

August came, and I travelled to Edinburgh and moved in to the North British Hotel. Again there was the massive operation of moving in, and sorting out, the tattoo performers, scheduling rehearsals on Redford Barracks parade ground, and seeing the innovative lighting and sound equipment installed. The list of performers ("the Order of Battle" as military orders liked to express it) included four regimental bands, the senior one conducted by Major Sam Rhodes of the Scots Guards. He was an old friend from the Glasgow "Services Cavalcade" show. There were also five pipe bands, including one from Canada. We had two other overseas contingents – the Band of the Netherlands Grenadiers from The Hague, and the spectacular mounted *Fanfare à Cheval de la Garde Républicaine* from Paris. The latter was commanded by a fat and garlic-breathed officer who had been bandmaster to the Sultan of Morocco. It was whispered that he had arrived in Edinburgh with multiple wives.

At the last minute, Alasdair Maclean informed me that there was to be yet another foreign contingent, the US Army Field Band, consisting of one officer, fifty NCOs and one Private First Class (who turned the pages of the conductor's music). They were to play in the moat while the audience was being seated. Noticing that they had violins, I enquired of their commanding officer what "field" they normally played in – I had in mind "battlefield" of course.

He scratched his head. 'The field of public relations,' he replied eventually.

My assistants, Majors Kelway-Bamber and Clark, were put out by this last minute change in the "Order of Battle". When Alasdair suggested including a further American outfit – the University of Iowa Girls' Pipe Band – which had turned up in Edinburgh and offered their services, they "mutinied". They asked me to accompany them when they made a formal protest to the commanding general, Sir Colin Barber. I advised them not to go ahead, pointing out that although my army status was unimportant to me, they had their careers to consider. In the end, Alasdair "got the message" and the girls did not perform.

The 1952 tattoo was a good deal more polished than the previous years. The film arc-lights brought out the gorgeous colours of the uniforms, "Titus" Oatts' commentary was dignified and commanding, and I ensured that the show ran steadily and smoothly, with the marshals positioned at the various points where performers made their entrances knowing exactly what they had to do and when. I gave the cues myself, via a complicated phone network operated by the Corps of Signals. It was nerve-stretching work for the two hours of performance.

A demonstration of precision drill by the RAF Regiment seemed to me a bit dry, and I searched for an idea to liven it up, preferably with something "aeronautical". The searchlights installed in response to my father's idea provided the answer. A Meteor jet fighter based at a nearby RAF station was allotted to us, and an air traffic controller installed amid the scaffolding below the seating stands – a woman officer who sensibly brought along a flask of "the water of life" to protect her from the icy drafts howling through the steel tubing. The aircraft circled over the Firth of Forth at Queensferry until I gave the cue, whereupon the lady ordered the pilot to home in over the Castle. The searchlight crews tracked the aircraft by radar *with their lights switched off* – and at the precise moment the RAF Band marched over the Castle drawbridge to the stirring strains of the RAF March, the searchlights were switched on – to reveal, as if by magic, the Meteor flying down the esplanade over the heads of its RAF comrades! It was marvellous theatre, and worked perfectly every night, except one occasion when an aircraft was not available. I just had the lights track the empty night sky! Such was the sleight of hand that most of the audience thought they had seen an aircraft...

Other officers did not always appreciate Alasdair Maclean's ways. His behaviour became more and more eccentric and flamboyant. Things came to a head when the youthful husband of the king's eldest daughter was present in the Royal Box. This called for the massed bands to play a "Royal Salute" – the National Anthem – at the end of the show. The audience got to its feet and we producers emerged from the control box at the top of the stands, the officers saluting. Alasdair was beside me.

Suddenly there was an astonishing sight. Alasdair – his right hand still raised in salute – clattering down the aisle between the raked seating, towards a very old man who was still sitting with his cap on. Alasdair snatched it from the startled man's head and thrust it into his hands.

Then he returned to his position at my side, still saluting, until the anthem finished. Alas, the drama had been witnessed – not only by scandalised fellow officers, but the *Daily Mirror*!

The next morning's headlines told the story in gruesome detail. The old man was *of course* an invalid, and likely to die from exposure caused by the fascist army officer. Throughout the morning, the affair rumbled around the Castle. My two assistants, majors in the Argyll and Sutherland Highlanders, asked me to accompany them when they made a formal complaint about Alasdair's behaviour to the Commander-in-Chief, General Barber. I advised them to cool down. I was not staying in the army, and had nothing to lose. They had.

There was a VIP lunch in the Castle mess that day. Alasdair was the last to arrive – in high spirits and basking in his press celebrity.

'Did you see the *Mirror*?' he asked the assembled diners.

The atmosphere was electric – at any moment, several military careers seemed about to come to a premature end. As the rotten novels say, 'His mind raced...'

A quip rose to my lips.

'You might at least have left his wig on, Alasdair,' I said.

There was laughter and the moment was saved.

The climax of the show was a recap of the idea that had brought the audience to its feet during the Glasgow show.

Once again, detachments in old uniforms – pre-1914 redcoats, Great War service dress and "tin hats", World War II battledress and desert khaki-drill – marched and counter-marched through each other's lines to nostalgic tunes – *We're The Soldiers Of The Queen, Me Lads* – *It's A Long Way To Tipperary* – *Roll Out The Barrel* – *Lilli Marlene.* The parade came to rest in the form of a cross. I had given each man a small hand-torch and, as the band struck up *Scotland The Brave* and the spotlights flooded the arena with blue light, the troops switched on their torches, producing an impression of Saint Andrew's Cross – the Saltire. There was tumultuous applause.

The tattoo ended in a blaze of glory and fireworks. The BBC broadcast it on Sunday night, and the following day I received a telegram from Bernadette saying all the gang had watched it.

After it was over, nothing was said of a further engagement the following year. I did not expect it. I knew Alasdair Maclean was retiring from the army – he became an honorary brigadier, and produced the tattoo for many years.

I was nevertheless disappointed to discover later that he had "written me out" of the record. It was a shabby action towards someone who "created" the format of the show that is still put on today, from a man who had no need of further celebrity. The tattoo authority still persists in "forgetting" to include my name in the role of honour of producers. Perhaps it hurts the pride of the brigadiers and generals, who followed me, to think that the job could once have been done by a twenty-six-year-old junior officer.

10

WHEN I returned to London this time, Frank Launder asked me to work for him again. It was only a brief engagement. He was going into production on a film called *Folly To Be Wise*, based on a play by James Bridie. Alastair Sim was besotted with Bridie, and had persuaded Frank to make it, with himself in the leading role. He was to be an army chaplain, and the main setting was an army barracks. Frank wanted me to be military advisor.

I enjoyed my few days at Shepperton, getting to know the female lead, Janet Brown, and the young male lead, Peter Martyn, who had been a Guards subaltern (tragically, he was to die of cancer not long after). The best moment was when Frank left me to direct a short sequence of National Servicemen being drilled.

My relationship with Alastair Sim was less cordial. I had met him before while working on *The Happiest Days of Your Life* but for some reason on this film he was unfriendly. Although an actor, he had achieved distinction in other fields, becoming Rector of Edinburgh University, with the award of a CBE. It gave him a lordly air on the set, and perhaps I was not sufficiently deferential. One morning he went for me in front of the film crew. A know-it-all had pointed out that one of the medal ribbons on his uniform was incorrect. It was the Africa Star, with three lines of colour – dark blue, signifying the navy – red, the army – and light blue, the RAF. As the senior service, the navy – dark blue – should be first, but the costume department had sewn on the ribbon upside-down, with the light blue first. I had not noticed it.

When Alastair had finished dressing me down in front of the embarrassed film crew I pointed out that, as the film was being photographed in black-and-white, the mistake was unlikely to be spotted (I might also have said that lots of people sewed their ribbons on the wrong way, and a chaplain was only too likely to).

But Alastair went berserk and accused me of being unprofessional. We did not speak to each other for the rest of my time on the picture.

Nineteen fifty-two had been a profitable year for me. After *Folly To Be Wise*, 1953 continued less promisingly. Money dwindled at an alarming pace and I now had a flat to maintain. When I had a film to make I was paid handsomely, but it was always a struggle to stay alive in the periods between. No one had any money in those days. The banks did not grant overdrafts, and there were no credit cards, so if you were out of cash, tough. That was when one's friends proved their worth. We were always borrowing from each other.

I was brimming with ideas. Jack and I developed another comedy, about piracy in the fashion industry. We called it *Pirates Of Paris*. Maurice Chevalier had been a major film star in the 1930s, but was largely forgotten in the years following the war. Now a veteran, Chevalier was appearing in cabaret in London. We took him to lunch to discuss the starring role in our project. This time, we chose a good restaurant, the plush *Mirabelle* in Mayfair. As soon as we were seated, the maitre d' rushed to our table with the visitors' book and a pen.

Chevalier flicked through the pages and came across the entry:

M est pour Mirabelle et M est pour Marlene

It could only have been written by the legendary Marlene Dietrich.

Chevalier took up the pen, and to the restaurant-owner's horror, scrubbed out "Marlene". He then wrote:

Non! M est pour Maurice

I think that might be called egotism…

Chevalier phoned me from Paris a week or two later, saying that at sixty-five he did not feel up to launching a new film career. So that ended that idea. A year or two later, he did allow himself to be lured back to films when the legendary director, Billy Wilder, offered him a film co-starring Audrey Hepburn and Gary Cooper. He went on to make many more films, eventually winning an Oscar for *Gigi*.

Another celebrity Jack Gourlay and I became involved with was the comedian Norman Wisdom. He had fairly suddenly become a very big star, and was drawing huge crowds as the unlikely leading attraction in an ice show at London's Empress Hall, Earl's Court. Norman had had a colourful life, beginning as an army bandsman, and now had ambitions to advance his career by becoming a serious actor. In this he had been inspired by the singer Frank Sinatra's recent dramatic performance in *From Here To Eternity*. Norman told Jack that he had been champion flyweight boxer of the British Army in India and a fan of the professional boxer Benny Lynch, "the greatest boxer Scotland ever produced". Lynch's story was a tragic one, of chronic alcoholism ending his brilliant career at the age of twenty-five and leading to his death at thirty-three of starvation. Norman wanted to make a film of the boxer's life with himself in the leading part. It sounded like an exciting project – Norman looked a bit like Lynch, and could also box, and the casting could not have been a happier one. Jack and I flew to Glasgow to see Lynch's widow and we received her blessing. Alas, the project foundered, in a way we did not expect. Wisdom's agent was only too happy to see his ten percent flooding in from Norman's work as a comedian and was in no mood to endanger it with a risky excursion into straight acting – especially in a tragic part. He forbad Norman from making the film. I have often wondered where Wisdom's life would have taken him had his agent been more visionary.

He made his film debut a few months later in his familiar "gump" guise, in a daft comedy that is still regularly shown on television when nothing else is available.

The broadcast of the Queen's Coronation in 1953 transformed television from a luxury enjoyed by a few into mass entertainment that ordinary people could afford. By the mid-fifties, a significant section of the population had television sets, though with tiny screens, and without colour. The cinema continued to be the major leisure activity. Most people were still in the habit of "going to the pictures" every week, though unlike the 1930s, were less loyal to a "local". You got three-and-a-half to four hours' entertainment for your money, with Disney cartoons, "travelogues" and ten- to fifteen-minute general interest "shorts" in addition to the two feature films, projected on a giant screen to emphasize the limitations of television. Some were shot in 3D or the newly invented "anamorphic" CinemaScope system. Early reports of these systems were not encouraging. It was said of CinemaScope, with its wide, wide screen, that Marilyn Monroe lying down was sensational but Gregory Peck standing up was a disaster. 3D did not last. It had been sold to Hollywood by a fast-talking salesman who explained that as the human eyes were four and a half inches apart, films could be photographed with two cameras placed in a similar way and the result shown in cinemas using two projectors with polarised lenses. "The guy's a genius," said Hollywood, and several features were shot that way. After thousands of complaints of splitting headaches from the audiences there was an inquest. A Hollywood mogul held a ruler before his eyes and said "Hey, fellers – my eyes are only two and a quarter inches apart!" "So are mine!" cried another. The first films – Warner's *House Of Wax* starring Vincent Prince among them – had been filmed for an audience of gorillas...

There were other misbegotten enticements to discourage desertion to television, too. The Empire, Leicester Square, offered a sixty-minute stage show, complete with music-hall stars and a chorus line of precision dancers. (The drawback was that the best seats for this – in the front – were the worst ones for viewing the film.)

Jack and I plodded on, trying to come up with the idea that would make our fortunes. We tried a story about debutantes, but it got nowhere. I can't think why we thought it a good idea – in 1950s austerity Britain, debutantes were far from anyone's minds. A better story, which we called *The Lady Is For Export*, was about innocent beginners in show business being lured abroad by shady nightclub owners. Working with Jack was becoming difficult, as he was riding high with his prestigious *Sunday Express* show-column and was increasingly reluctant to buckle down to writing sessions.

David Henley told me there was a demand for "second features" – the sixty-minute films that cinemas ran to make up their four-hour programmes. They could be made in three weeks for £15,000, a not inconsiderable sum, but realisable. I got out the typewriter, and decided to try a script on my own. Making use of my army experience I wrote a screenplay about the Military Police Special Investigation Branch. A daring young SIB officer, aided by his actress girlfriend, foils a plot by a renegade Guards officer and a crooked Hollywood film producer to steal the Crown Jewels from the Tower of London. While doing the research, I was surprised to receive unstinting co-operation from the Tower authorities, and actually had the Crown Jewels to myself on several occasions!

David Henley was enthusiastic about *Operation Crown Jewels*, and took it to an independent producer named Eric l'Epine Smith, who set about raising the money to put it into production, with me directing. An agent named Peter Eade signed me up and submitted the script to the British Board of Film Censors for their approval. I received by return a detailed critique that makes hilarious reading nowadays. Their principal concern was the suggestion that a commissioned officer in His Majesty's Foot Guards might be dishonest. But there were other worries:

P.36. The line "The other room's the <u>bedroom</u>. Don't let it give you ideas" should be omitted.

P.37. In view of its associations with the twenty-third Psalm, the phrase "the <u>valley of the shadow</u> of the Employment Bureau" would be better omitted.

P.51. Norma's line "Keep it nice and physical" should be omitted or changed.

P.53. The line "He's got more hands than an octopus" should be omitted.

P.56. The expression "a fate better than death" should be omitted.

P.62. Tim's suggestion, "Darling, what's to stop us?" might be interpreted as inviting Ann to have an immediate affair with him and would be better omitted.

P.91. The shots of Venable's corpse should not be too unpleasant.

P.95. A cosh should not be used, and the impact of the weapon should not be seen.

Perhaps surprisingly, some pages of script were left to make a film with! For a while, it really looked as though I was about to make a major breakthrough, but in the end the money was not forthcoming and the project withered on the vine.

Very little cash was coming in, and eventually my flat in Devonshire Street had to go. I moved back to cheaper accommodation in the house in Brompton Road that I had lived in two or three years before. It seemed a portent that I was not making any headway. Mrs Fitzmaurice had vanished from the scene and the premises were less luxurious than before. A Polish artist named Andrew Loret lived at the top of the building with his Australian wife, Joan. I became firm friends with them and spent much time in their cosy room. Joan was a good cook and I was entertained to boiled Polish sausage and dill pickles. Delicious. We were all short of money and chipped in what little money we had. There was a time when we lived on fruit cake for a few days, sent by Joan's grandparents in Australia.

I stayed in touch with the Lorets through the years. Andrew was a talented artist, and eventually began to be successful. He and Joan moved to Devon, then the Channel Islands, where Joan died of cancer. Andrew took up portrait painting, through which he met his second wife, with whom he went to live in Guernsey. By then, Andrew had discovered that he was heir to a Polish title and became Count d'Aquino.

One or two girlfriends drifted in and out of my life at this time. In the early fifties "Espresso Bars" were all the rage in fashionable London, and "Sloane Rangers" and "resting" actresses got jobs in them. It was not thought demeaning – quite racy, in fact, and very much the thing to do in pre- "Swinging Sixties" London. Such a place was Le Mistral in South Kensington.

I was on my way to the cinema one afternoon when I ran into an actor friend, Hugh David, who had been in one of my industrial tools films. He was standing outside Le Mistral, talking to a fellow actor, and we fell into conversation. As things do, the talk went on, and Hugh suggested we continue inside the restaurant. At first I declined, saying I would miss my film, but still we talked, and then it *was* too late for the cinema. We entered Le Mistral and sat on tall stools at the counter. The girl behind the counter who served us was extremely pretty, not to say beautiful. She was an actress *(of course)* and had recently been on tour with Hugh's friend.

We ordered coffee, and when the lady disappeared to make it, I admonished the other two not to tell her I was a film director. I was fearful that it would result in my being asked for help finding parts, and did not want to get into the complexities of explaining that film directors – me for instance – could be as powerless as actors. It came out of course, and predictably the lady asked if I could introduce her to any casting directors. The only one I could think of was David Henley (at least he'd been the creator of the Rank Charm School). I gave her his address and never expected to see her again.

A few days later I went into the office I used in David Henley's suite and ran into Hugh's actress friend just as she was emerging from her interview. It was midday, and curious to hear how she had got on, I suggested a drink.

'I'd rather have lunch,' Miss Mary Manson replied, with a flashing smile.

We repaired to The Intrepid Fox in Wardour Street, and she told me about herself. She had been at the Royal Academy of Dramatic Art, and had had two or three years' experience on the stage in provincial repertory and touring religious drama. Her home was at Oxford, where her father was librarian of Christ Church College, and her mother, who had trained at the Slade, was a painter of landscapes and flowers.

It was all very normal. I had met countless aspiring actresses with similar backgrounds. But there was something about this young lady. I heard myself asking her if she would like to have dinner one evening, and she said she would. I took her to an artists' club in Kensington, and there, between the courses, I realised with something of shock that I had found the girl I wanted to share my life with. What her thoughts were at that moment, she will have to reveal in her memoirs, if she writes them. Suffice it to say, that we began to go out together.

I took her to Scotland (by overnight coach) and introduced her to the Covenanters and Robin Steele, and we went to Arngomery for dinner with Roddy Leckie Ewing. He was quietly approving but I sensed a change in his manner. He was very much a man's man and had never married. Not many months after this, our last meeting, I heard with a shock that he had died. He had had a heart attack while out shooting. I could hardly believe my ears. Roddy was only about fifty. I felt shaky. Roddy had been an *especial* friend. I could not believe I would never see him again or stay with him at Arngomery.

11

OWNERSHIP OF television sets had continued to grow and people were increasingly deserting their local cinemas for the small screen at home. There was a further threat when Parliament voted in 1954 for the introduction of a commercial TV service. The film industry met the challenge with the production of blockbuster films that ran up to four hours and could only be shown in cinemas. A result was the demise of the second feature – there was simply no room for it. Instead there was a new demand for thirty-minute "shorts" to fill out the programmes. David Henley told me that a small firm of distributors in Wardour Street was looking for product, and he introduced me to two unprepossessing individuals who were only too keen for me to make something – at my own expense – for them to sell. I discussed the idea with Jack Sheppard, and once more he agreed to provide the production facilities "on spec".

My new girlfriend Mary had told me about the Royal Academy of Dramatic Art, and I thought it might make an interesting documentary film. I approached RADA and received approval from its principal, Sir Kenneth Barnes. With Mary re-living her tender years as a student, we spent several weeks filming the drama classes. They contained several students who in later years became famous. I then "opened" the subject out by showing something of what happened to students after they graduated. We filmed Mary being interviewed by agents, posing for publicity "stills" and having a screen test. We shot the latter in an elegant Mayfair flat belonging to one of Jack Gourlay's journalist friends.

I delivered the film to the distributors, and they sat through it with undisguised puzzlement and dismay. The inner workings of RADA bored them and they were probably waiting for Mary to take off her clothes. I had wanted to call the film *First Act Beginners*, which I thought was a quite clever play on a theatrical term, but the wooden heads didn't understand it. In the end we called it *Prelude To Stardom*, which was pretty banal. They took it to the market, however, and seemed stunned when it was booked into the prestigious Odeon cinema at Marble Arch – they'd probably never had a film in the West End before.

Our little offering supported a worthy-but-dull British feature called *A Pattern Of Islands*, a stiff-upper-lip saga of colonial rule in the Pacific. The cinema manager delighted me by saying more than once that the audiences preferred my film. Surprise, surprise – although the film went out nationally, no money arrived for either United Motion Pictures or me. It was all swallowed up by expenses, the distributors explained. And that's how it remained. We never saw a penny. The sole consolation – for me – was that the film was selected for permanent preservation in the British Film Institute National Film Archive.

The journalist in whose flat we filmed the screen test, Frederic Mullally, also managed publicity for a number of celebrities, including Audrey Hepburn, Frank Sinatra and Vera Lynn. He had recently discovered a builder's labourer from Hull named David Whitfield. Whitfield had a fine tenor voice, and Mullally had masterminded the recording of a song called *Cara Mia*, with a backing by the famous Mantovani's Strings, which had become a smash hit.

One of the biggest Hollywood stars of the period was tenor Mario Lanza. Unfortunately he was passionately fond of pasta; he had become grossly overweight, and his employers, Metro-Goldwyn-Mayer, were fearful that he would go to an early grave through cardiac failure, cheating them of the riches he was bringing in. MGM decided that the way to discourage him was to threaten him with rival singers who could replace him. They sent all over the world for screen tests of potential alternatives, and Freddy Mullally's protégé David Whitfield was one of those chosen. I was asked to direct the test, and we shot it in Freddy's flat on the same day as the test sequence for my RADA film, with Mary acting opposite Whitfield.

The filming had to take place on a Sunday, as Whitfield was appearing in a show somewhere in the north of England. We rented 35mm equipment from a film studio, and I hired a cameraman I had never worked with before. I was slightly put off when I saw he had a perpetually runny nose, which he sniffed back just as the mucus reached his upper lip.

As I busied myself lighting Freddy's flat and working out the moves my two "stars" were to perform, I became conscious that all was not right in the technical department. I eventually confronted the cameraman and asked what was wrong.

'There's no viewfinder in the camera box,' he told me.

The rented camera was an ancient contraption called a "Debrie Super Parvo", which its owners had assured me, had been used to photograph many famous films, so I got on the telephone and spoke to the person who had supplied it.

'The Super Parvo does not need a viewfinder,' he said. 'The eyepiece is focussed on the back of film itself, and you see a perfect image *through* the film, without parallax error.' Well, that sounded all right.

The cameraman then opened the can of film MGM had sent us. It was a mysterious new type called "Eastmancolor", and when we examined it we discovered that it had an opaque black "anti-halo" backing. You could not see through the film. It looked as though we were in trouble.

My intrepid cameraman however gave a mighty sniff, which took care of the hygiene for a while, and reassured me.

'All right guvnor,' he said, 'leave it to me. I've had worse problems before.'

He proceeded to wrap the camera in the sound-deadening quilt that had come with it, then pinched a rudimentary "foresight" and "backsight" in the material. Using these, he succeeded in following the action without losing the artistes once!

We shot a nice little test, with David Whitfield and Mary exchanging a few lines of dialogue, and Whitfield miming *Cara Mia* to playback. I personally delivered the can of film to MGM's British head, Ben Goetz, at the large studio they then occupied at Borehamwood. He was a genial host, and treated me to a slap-up lunch in the "commissary", followed by a tour of the studio.

'What do notice about this studio?' Goetz asked.

I could have replied that nothing seemed to be going on, but instead said something bland about it being in a nice place.

'It's a *tidy* studio,' Goetz said, 'and a tidy studio makes good films!'

I don't know what MGM did with the test, which was probably one of hundreds from all over the world. No one replaced Mario Lanza, and he did die of over-eating not long afterwards. His sound tracks were used in *The Student Prince*, and an English actor named Edmund Purdom mimed to them. More about Purdom later. It was ironic that David Whitfield should also die of a heart attack while still young.

The next eighteen months were a testing time for me. Romulus Films dropped the "anarchist" project, for which Jack Gourlay and I had been receiving regular option payments. A lifeline was cut off.

Despite having made a film or two, I had no real idea where I was going, or how I was going to get there. There were long periods of inactivity when I was hard pressed to keep my head above water. But there seemed always to be a prospect of a future production, usually from UMP, to make it worth hanging on if I could only hold out. Mary was away much of the time in "Rep", first at Bath, then Chesterfield, and finally Ventnor on the Isle of Wight.

I even contemplated – reluctantly – a move into television, which in those days meant, of course, the BBC. I sent off a letter and was invited to attend an "Appointments Board". It was awful. The title "board" was well chosen. Its members seemed bored, as well as themselves being boring and patronising. Most of them seemed to be civil servants. I found myself persuading them that I was not the BBC type.

Things brightened up on the films front when the second flight-simulator film for Redifon came back on the scene – it had been promised for so long that I had almost given up hope. This was the one about the Sabre jet, the USA's front-line fighter that had been in active service in the Korean War.

A replica of the cockpit had been constructed in Redifon's factory in south London, and a team arrived from the Royal Canadian Air Force, which was to take the Sabre into service, to help us make the film.

In order to photograph the pilot at the controls we set up the camera on a rostrum, ten or twelve feet above the simulator. On the second day of filming, I felt distinctly strange. My head was swimming. I clambered down the ladder to *terra firma,* and all went black – I hit the floor with a resounding smack. I came to, to find myself in the factory sickbay. Somehow I climbed to my feet, and staggered back to finish the film sitting in a camp chair. Then I went home and took to my bed, thinking how fortunate it had been that I had managed to climb down from the rostrum before fainting. The consequences of a fall from that height would have been serious.

Mary was in town at the time, doing the casting rounds.

She gasped when she saw my appearance.

'You know what's wrong with you?' she asked. 'You've got mumps!'

I felt my cheeks, and was astonished to discover that they were about twice normal size. Mary took charge and called the doctor, who prescribed medicine – and a dire warning: 'The danger with a man of your years is that it can affect your marriage equipment,' he said. 'If you're not careful for the next week or two, you could end up sterile.'

So I stayed in bed, while darling Mary administered to my needs.

After about a week, the phone beside my bed rang.

'Get out of that bed!' drawled a Canadian voice. 'Get up here to North Luffenham. We've got a Sabre flying, and it's the only chance you'll have of filming it.'

With plenty of misgivings, I dressed myself, collected a cine-camera and drove to Rutland. There, the Canadian Air Force crew dressed me in a "g-suit" and "bone-dome" flying helmet, and installed me in the rear ejection seat of a T33 Shooting Star jet. We took off alongside a Sabre and climbed like a rocket into the blue, high above the clouds for me to take shots. The rear cockpit was so small and the Perspex canopy so close to my head, the straps restraining me so tight, that I had difficulty getting the viewfinder to my eye. When we did a tight "peel off", the gravity – the "g" – became so great that the camera became many times its normal weight, and dropped into my lap.

When we landed, I realised that I felt better than I had for some times! The mumps had gone. Subsequent events proved that the doctor's grim warning had not come true.

I finished the film, and again weeks passed without sign of a breakthrough in my career. One meagre commission kept me from starvation. Jack Sheppard got an order for "a personal film" from the circus owner Billy Smart. I picked up a camera and some film, took the train to Scotland and joined the circus on tour at Arbroath. It was a fascinating fortnight, watching a way of life that is now vanished. I liked visiting the animals between shows, especially the elephants and Palomino horses, but was disturbed by what looked to me cruelty in the way they were trained. I have no idea what Billy Smart did with the film.

When I got back to London, Frederic Mullally telephoned me and told me he had been appointed editor of the ailing magazine *Picture Post*. It had been prestigious in its time but now suffered from a catastrophically falling circulation, partly due to television. One of Mullally's solutions was to introduce an "up-market" cartoon strip. It would be exciting, with cliff-hanger endings each week, but "documentary" enough to live up to *Picture Post*'s traditions. Would I like to write the script? Of course I jumped at the chance.

I had been reading Ernest Hemingway's *Death In The Afternoon*, and was fascinated by the techniques and artistry of bullfighting, so I decided to make it the background for a story about a lady detective. A cartoonist was recruited, and we produced a full-page strip called *The Adventures Of Ricki* (Freddie came up with the name for our heroine – I hated it). It started in January 1955, and ran for two series before coming to an end when *Picture Post* finally ceased publication.

The modest weekly fee kept me reasonably solvent, but now there were no prospects on the horizon. UMP had always had something in the pipeline, but suddenly there was nothing. It looked as if I was facing the end of the line. It was eight years since I had embarked on a career in films, and I was still as far as ever from making a steady livelihood. It was at this moment – it would be, wouldn't it? – that an elderly screenwriter friend told me he had been at a union meeting the evening before when I had been elected into membership. I phoned the union and was told this was true – all that was necessary was for me to send the large entrance fee. I just did not have the cash. Another "Catch 22"!

All I could do for the moment was get *any* sort of job to bring in the rent. A friend in the shipping industry happened to mention that a firm he knew of was in difficulties. Its business was shipping Russian timber to Britain from the Baltic ports. This was only possible in the summer, when the Baltic was sufficiently free of ice; as soon as the thaw came there was a mad rush to cram in as much business as possible, and temporary help was needed to cope with the load. I went along and offered my services. An odd little adventure was about to begin.

The firm was called The Russian Wood Agency. It was housed in Aldwych and was jointly owned by a British timber importer and the Soviet government. It was a very odd concern. The Cold War was at its height, with Russia the centre of "the Evil Empire", and communications with it were almost non-existent. The agency had a direct telephone line to Moscow, however.

My job was helping to draw up the massive documents which detailed the placing of timber aboard the ships. All recipients had to accept a percentage of their order carried on deck, where it was exposed to the weather, and the loading pattern of the different ships was a highly skilled task, calling for a thorough knowledge of ships and their trim. The clerks worked alongside me at a breakneck pace, and I found it unexpectedly interesting.

There were two bosses, a mild, elderly Englishman and an unsmiling Russian. There were few Soviet citizens in London at the time and the Russian staff lived together in a commune somewhere in North London. They were forbidden to fraternise with the capitalist British – presumably in case they were corrupted by Western values. It was whispered that among them was a secret KGB "minder", and it was very obvious that the Russian staff were scared of being caught out in some indiscretion which would result in being shipped home.

There was much talk in the papers just then about mysterious disappearances of members of the Iron Curtain community who were suspected of being "unreliable". A Polish ship, the *Josef Batory*, made regular visits to the Pool of London and it was believed that miscreants were spirited out of the country aboard her to be taken home for execution or imprisonment.

The Russian managers were paranoid about their British colleagues, especially newcomers, and when it got around that I was a writer with some journalistic background, the Russian director manufactured a reason for me to visit his office where he could examine me. As he questioned me, I noticed a scorch hole in the shoulder of his unfashionable wide-trousered Soviet suit, presumably caused by a cigarette.

A few days later, I received another summons to take some documents to the Russian boss's office. The *Batory* was in London at the time. When I entered the office I was surprised to see, not the familiar grim-faced manager, but a stranger. He showed little interest in me and I did not linger. But as I turned to the door something made me glance back. A thrill passed through me. *The shoulder of the newcomer's jacket had a cigarette burn on the shoulder. He was wearing the former director's suit!* We did not see the missing man again and his departure was not discussed.

I left too soon after, as I shall explain.

12

THELMA CONNELL had become supervising editor on a filmed series being made for American television called *The Adventures Of Robin Hood*. She knew that I was despondent about my future, and invited me to supper for a heart-to-heart talk.

"Would you take a non-directing job?" she asked.

"I'd take any kind of job," I answered.

The company Thelma was working for had begun work on another series called *The Buccaneers*. An eighteenth-century sailing-frigate had been constructed in Falmouth, and the preceding months had been spent filming action sequences, to be used when the production came into the studio. Thelma said that the director had gone on to other things, and would not be available to sort out the thousands of feet of material he had shot. An enormous task lay ahead, preparing it for use by the film editors, and advising the episode directors how the scenes could be used. Thelma thought my directing experience might qualify me for the job.

The following day I went down to Walton-on-Thames studio in Surrey, where the company, Sapphire Films, was based, to meet the producers. Thelma's recommendation was all that was needed, and the American managing executive said the job was mine if I could sort out my position with the union. I hurried back to town and went to ACT's head office in Soho Square.

A scruffy character identified himself as "the organiser".

'Buy me a beer round the corner and we'll discuss it,' he said.

A few minutes later, leaning against the bar, he pronounced – without so much as a blush, 'Course you c'n 'ave a card. I'm the one 'oo decides. Pay up when you can.'

I accepted my pristine new membership card, and notified the Wood Agency that I would be leaving at the end of the week. The occasion provided another – pleasant – surprise. When I went to collect my final pay-packet the British director said, 'I'd hoped you might want to make a career in shipping, but I know where your heart lies, and –' he reached in his desk and brought out an additional twenty pound notes, '– here,' he said, 'you always need this. Good luck.'

It was a wonderful gesture. Twenty pounds meant something in those days. (About a year later I ran into one of the staff in the street. He was working for a different company and I asked him about the Russian Wood Agency. 'Finished,' he told me. 'One Saturday morning we were all working when the door burst open and a group of armed plainclothes men entered. We were made to get up and face the wall. The next thing we knew was that we were out of work. They said the direct line to Moscow had been used for transmitting intelligence.')

At long last I was a recognised member of the film industry. *The Buccaneers* was in the early stages of production at Twickenham Studios not far from London.

For the first time I noticed how "blue collar" most of the studio's permanent staff appeared to be. Not a university education in sight. The make-up chief had begun as a casual crowd artist – he had been pulled from the crowd to slap greasepaint on his colleagues. An assistant cameraman had the job because his father was the studio carpenter, and a sound recordist had been a laboratory deliveryman. The assistant directors gave the impression of having shady backgrounds. One told me he was a "tally man" – whatever that was – in his spare hours...

The irony was that despite being quite ostentatiously wealthy, all the *employers* – British or American – were communists! The boss was a former journalist named Hannah Weinstein. It was rumoured that she, and most of the other Americans, had conveniently absented themselves from Hollywood while the McCarthy witch-hunt was in full cry. The British executive producer, a legendary figure named Sidney Cole, was a lifetime member of the Communist Party. He had had a distinguished career at Ealing Studios as one of Michael Balcon's "bright boys".

Like Jimmy Clavell and me, five years before (though in our case prematurely), Hannah Weinstein had seen the opportunities for filming series for American television away from expensive Hollywood. She set up in England, and prepared to produce *King Arthur And The Round Table*. Sets were built and the cast assembled. Then just as shooting was about to begin, the sponsors arrived from America with bad news. American viewers did not like *kings*! They liked their characters to be *republican*.

Hannah was shattered.

'If you had something like Robin Hood...' one of the sponsors remarked helpfully.

'OK,' the desperate Hannah said, 'we'll make Robin Hood!' – the *King Arthur* sets were not so different from Robin Hood, after all... cassles... furests... all that stuff... even the scripts could be doctored. For "Sir Lancelot" read "Robin". Hannah's substitute series went into production at Walton Studios, with superannuated Hollywood idol, Richard Greene, in the title role. Maid Marian was none other than Bernadette.

As a child, Hannah Weinstein had dreamed of one day being a great lady living in a "cassle". Now she bought one – well, perhaps not a castle, but a large, rambling Victorian Gothic monstrosity called Foxwarren Park. It stands in several acres of meadow beside the Portsmouth road in Surrey and is said to have been the artist Ernest Shepard's inspiration for "Toad Hall" in his illustrations for *The Wind In The Willows*. No comment.

Another kind of "cassle", made of plasterboard, was erected in the grounds for exterior scenes. Wisley Common, not far away, was nominated "Sherwood Forest".

I don't know how much "stately home" life Hannah managed at Foxwarren, because she was on a rollercoaster. *The Adventures Of Robin Hood* was an instant hit. Thirteen episodes became twenty-six. The money flooded in. The sponsors demanded more product. Hannah expanded into the small studio at Twickenham and got *The Buccaneers* going, with Robert Shaw as "Captain Dan Tempest". He was a troubled, complicated man, who went on to do much better things, before dying of a heart attack at an early age.

I was given a cutting-room at Twickenham, with a "Moviola" editing machine, and turned my attention to the enormous pile of cans containing the film shot at Falmouth.

Devising ways of integrating the scenes into the studio-based sequences came naturally to me and I went on the sets to advise the directors – Leslie Arliss, Bernard Knowles – industry veterans who had made noteworthy films in the thirties and forties. My contribution was more valuable than my employers had expected, and after a week or two I was asked to look at setting up a similar project for *Robin Hood*. The Robin Hood "second unit" had shot a large number of scenes out of doors over the preceding eighteen months, and I saw that much of the footage could be re-used, saving expensive shooting time. An assistant film librarian was recruited to keep *The Buccaneers* operation going at Twickenham, and I moved to Walton where *Robin Hood* was being filmed.

It was nice to be among old friends. Bernadette was there, and Thelma was also about of course. Bernadette and I had lunch every day in her dressing room, but all too soon she decided that she had been with the production long enough. She "retired" from being Maid Marian, and the part was taken over by Patricia Driscoll.

Walton was a nice, compact little studio. In fact it didn't *look* like a studio at all, just a row of semi-detached suburban houses lining one side of a leafy *cul de sac*. The middle house had been the home of Cecil Hepworth, a pioneer film-maker, who in 1905 made what was reputed to be Britain's first cinema film in his back garden – *Rescued By Rover*, starring his pet dog. He actually developed the dangerous nitrate film himself. As his fortunes increased, he acquired the neighbouring houses to use as a laboratory, and built studios in his large back garden with lighting powered by an electric generator driven by a massive diesel engine taken out of a Great War

U-Boat installed in a house across the road. By the time I arrived at Walton, there were three large sound stages, together with construction workshops, offices and studio restaurants.

Again I was able to use my experience and imagination, and old material was given a new lease of life. My talent for coming up with fresh ideas got me invited into the small circle that surrounded Hannah Weinstein. It included Thelma, who had been promoted to Associated Producer, Sid Cole, the casting director Basil Appleby, and dynamic production manager Harold Buck. We met weekly to discuss future plans.

Like most Londoners I did not have a car. To save the expense of travel I left Brompton Road for what proved to be the last time and found digs in Walton. Having little to do in the evenings, I repaired after work to *The Bear*, opposite the studio, where I shared the bar with Sid Cole. He did not seem to have a home to go to, though I knew he had a house in Ealing and a wife, Jean. He was a prodigious boozer, which somehow did not affect his small, wiry physique. He was an interesting companion, and although he was nearly twenty years older than me, we became bosom friends. It was indeed strange to think that he had been the film editor on *Midshipman Easy* when I was a nine-year-old (and even stranger to think that I should be working with him on a production starring Richard Greene, who I had met when I was seventeen at Drury Lane). Life is full of coincidences.

Sid and I spent long hours arguing politics, with him engaged in soul-searching over the recent Soviet invasion, with great brutality, of Hungary.

'I've been a communist all my life,' he said. 'How can I now say that everything I believed in was wrong?'

Mary was sharing a house in London with four other girls. She had joined the English Stage Company at The Royal Court Theatre, and was making real progress in her career, playing a lead in *How Shall We Save Father?* with Robert Stephens, and understudying the leading part in John Osborne's *Look Back In Anger*. She "went on" in the latter role when the leading actress was taken ill, and gave a memorable performance opposite Richard Pasco and Alan Bates. As a result she was considered for the ingénue lead in *The Entertainer*, starring Laurence Olivier, until it was decided that the part must go to an established "name". She decided to stay with the play, as understudy to Dorothy Tutin, with whom she had been at RADA.

After *The Entertainer*'s first night there was a party on the stage at the Royal Court. Several barrels of beer were set up at the back of the stage and things got lively. After an hour or so, Vivienne Leigh arrived from the theatre where she was appearing. Relations with Olivier were at breaking point by this time, but he was in high spirits after his roaring success in the play. He went into the orchestra pit and banged away at the piano, which made Vivienne decide to sing. They were soon shouting insults at each other across the footlights.

At that moment, someone realised that the Royal Court staff had not emptied the theatre, and several members of the "Gallery First Nighters" were in the Dress Circle, watching the proceedings. They got their money's worth that night!

When *The Buccaneers* ended production, Hannah embarked on new projects. She decided to make *The*

Adventures of Sir Lancelot, using the old King Arthur scripts and playing-down the offending "regal" character. It was the first television show in England to be shot in colour. Mary had the leading part in one of the episodes, playing a medieval woman's libber. She also had the lead in an episode of *Robin Hood*, called *Bride For An Outlaw*.

Next came a series set in Renaissance Italy. The setting was medieval Florence, and the stories featured villainous rulers like the Medicis and Borgias, politicians like Machiavelli, and "a fighter on behalf of the poor" in the person of "Marco The Magnificent". To play this part, Hannah brought over from Hollywood a minor English star named Edmund Purdom. As with *Robin Hood*, the scripts were written under pseudonyms by top Hollywood screenwriters who had been exiled from the USA, and the "championing the underdog" theme chimed with their sentiments.

The US sponsors turned down the title *Marco The Magnificent* and Hannah's "inner cabinet" was summoned to come up with an alternative. After half-an-hour of feeble and increasingly desperate suggestions, Thelma – inspired by the advertisement for Polo Mints – got a laugh by suggesting *Marco Polo, The Man With The Hole*. I was the one who came up with *Sword Of Freedom*. It got as big a belly laugh from the Brits as Thelma's suggestion. Hannah silenced everyone with an imperious 'No, guys – this is *interesting*!' I had stumbled on the Americans' sacred word. Freeeeedom! And it was my title that the series went out with.

Harold Buck, the production manager, gave me my break. The editors required some additional sound effects and he sent me out with a recording team to get them.

Everyone seemed to like the way I handled the unit. Then the studio bought a new kind of camera mount that could move in any direction, and I was assigned a unit over the weekend to direct tests with it.

The real break came as a complete surprise.

The episodes were made on a "conveyor belt" system, and a method had evolved in which the main unit and its director concentrated on the principal acted scenes in the studio, while a "second unit", with another director, filmed the outdoor sequences – which were also, of course, the action scenes.

Harold Buck told me that the second-unit director was to be given a chance to direct in the studio. He then broke the good news – I was to be his replacement.

I had got the train-set back!

The news got even better. 'It's a point of principle that the director is the highest-paid member of the unit,' Harold said. 'The cameraman gets thirty-five pounds a week, so would – say – thirty-eight be OK?'

I said it would be very OK. It was a massive increase over the seventeen I had been getting, and was riches at a time when the national average wage was seven pounds. (At the time of writing the equivalent would be around £1,000 a week.)

And you could rent a really nice flat for four or five pounds a week, which was very much to the point, because Mary had found one, overlooking Shepherd's Bush Green. There was no reason for not getting married. It was a small ceremony, on a Saturday, at Caxton Hall, Westminster. Paul Connell was Best Man. Mary's parents were unable to be there, so out of fairness, my father was not there either. Mary was "given away" by her much loved godfather, Sir

Keith Falkner, who was Director of the Royal College Of Music. The *Evening Standard* took some nice pictures on the steps outside, and the "Wedding Breakfast" was at Rule's Restaurant behind the Strand, before Mary had to dash away to do a matinee at the theatre. I collected her that night at eleven.

That was how our marriage began. No honeymoon as such. We saw each other for a few hours each night. I was up with the lark to get down to the studio, and Mary had evening performances at the Royal Court. We managed a "flat-warming" party, however, to which most of her fellow cast members came, including the author of *Look Back In Anger* John Osborne, and Bob Stephens (later Sir Robert, the great Shakespearean actor).

The second unit that I took over was headed by a cameraman named Ian Craig, a figure of enormous dignity who rarely smiled, and appeared to disapprove of everything, especially me. On my first day, when the unit assembled outside the production office to travel to "Sherwood Forest" on Wisley Common, I was mystified to spy several props men carrying young trees on their shoulders.

'The trees are never where I want them,' Ian Craig pronounced, 'so I take my own.'

Of course! What an idiot God is, I thought.

I was canny enough to know that I had to make my number with the unit. To them, I was the wide boy who had got the job by drinking with the boss. They set me up. My first shot was of "Robin" – Richard Greene – setting out on a horse. I intended to be careful with Richard, as I had heard he had an uncertain temper. After carefully setting up the shot, using a "stand in" for Greene, I was ready to go for a take. Richard climbed on to his mount, none too athletically, I thought. As soon as he was set, I called 'Action!' The horse shot off like a cannon ball from a gun, with Richard Greene hanging on for dear life. The unit howled with laughter.

'Don't you know that you never say "action" with Richard's horse?' one of them scoffed. 'It knows the word, and always bolts.'

Richard trotted back, staring down at me with hatred in his eyes. Fortunately, by the time we had filmed a few more set-ups, the unit grudgingly admitted that I knew what I was doing.

We were to film a number of action shots, for an episode called *The Inventor*, in which an eccentric (medieval) professor – played by "Steptoe's son", Harry H. Corbett – invents a catapult capable of destroying the Sheriff of Nottingham's castle. A full-size catapult had been constructed and taken out to the location. Time for some interesting (read "weird") angles, I thought. I had the assistant cameraman, Nobby Smith, shin up a tree with a hand-held camera, then got the catapult to shoot its large plaster missiles past his left ear. The "rushes" next day caused a sensation. Novelty and ingenuity had not been expected from the second unit in the past. Hannah's voice was heard in the darkness of the preview theatre loudly congratulating me. I thought the hushed assembly must have roundly hated me. I had failed to fail!

But a day or two later, Ian Craig told me that it was the first time anyone had used the unit with any imagination.

It was hard work. Filming began at eight-thirty a.m. usually some distance from the studio. At midday, I would come in to the studio for a production meeting over beer and sandwiches, to plan the next episode. In the afternoon, I would grab an electrician with a couple of lights and set up in a corner of a sound-stage to shoot "inserts" – close-ups of hands signing death-warrants, et cetera. "The Sheriff of Nottingham's" hands in many of the episodes are actually mine.

Things hotted up when the American sponsors, Johnson's Baby Powder and Schlitz Brewing Company of Milwaukee (a rather unlikely pairing!) demanded more product, quicker. The British end of Sapphire's operation was overseen by Lew Grade. He suggested that the half-hour episodes, that once had been produced in five days, then four, should now to be filmed in two and a half.

The only way to achieve this was to break down the scripts more radically and shoot at least a third of each story out of doors, using the second unit. Of course I accepted this eagerly. I was too naïve to insist on a screen "credit", however. I was working at something I loved and was being paid handsomely for it, and that seemed enough. Thus, my name does not appear on any of these series.

13

WINTER WAS far advanced and shooting was usually impossible after three o'clock in the afternoon. We went out to Wisley each morning, with a sheaf of scripts for various episodes, and filmed, filmed, filmed. I bought a thick, loden duffel coat and fur-lined flying boots, but it did not keep out the cold. The weather was awful, Wisley was a swamp, and only the egg-and-bacon sandwiches brought out to us by the location caterers kept us going.

I often had Richard Greene to direct, though I never mentioned that we had met before, at Drury Lane Theatre. He was a cold, stand-offish character, and it was hard to get to know him. He was the complete professional screen actor, however, with a thoroughgoing understanding of film technology. He knew the depth of focus of the lenses, so that he could stop just slightly short of his marks, so that the actress playing opposite him would be forced to turn away from the camera to face him, switching the attention to him. This was so widely known that Bernadette decided to show him up.

She called across the set to the hairdresser.

'Is my hair all right at the back?' she asked.

'It's fine, Bernadette,' the hairdresser replied.

'Oh good,' said Bernadette. 'Rather a lot of it is being seen in this shot.'

Richard caught on immediately.

'Oh, I'm sorry,' he blushed, shuffling forward an inch or two.

The rest of the cast was a joy to work with, "Friar Tuck" – portly Alex Gauge, "the Sheriff of Nottingham" – gentlemanly Alan Wheatley, and "Little John" – a former Glasgow stevedore named Archie Duncan. Most of the time I had "the rep" – as we called them – to direct, a resident company of actors and actresses who were expected to play any part the situation required. Among them was a marvellous actor named Paul Eddington. We all loved directing Paul. He was always word perfect, and always gave exactly the same performance, however many times the other artistes in the scene fluffed their lines and made us go for another take.

The use of a stock company of artistes had its dangers. It sometimes led to dire "accidents". Shot in the way they were, by a multiplicity of directors, many of the episodes did not cut together too happily. Much of my work involved "picking up" additional scenes to smooth out inconsistencies. Often this was done some time after the original footage had been shot.

I did not have a "continuity girl", and relied on briefings from the cutting-rooms. One day I was asked to do a close-up of "Peasant", lying on the ground, being kicked by "Man-at-Arms". I grabbed a couple of members of the resident acting team and told them to put on costume and join my unit out on "the lot". Only the legs of "Man-at-Arms" would be seen, so I told that actor not to bother with the top-half of the costume – just wear the "chain-mail" leggings and boots.

I filmed a good kicking and delivered the result to the cutting-room, where it was joined into the main scene.

Panic! It was only too obvious that the man being kicked (my shot) was also the man kicking him (the studio scene)! It provided a good laugh that time, but when the next fiasco happened, Hannah was cross.

In this episode, Robin Hood is imprisoned in a Castle tower. He drops a note from the barred window, which is picked up by "Blind Ned" below – who is actually one of Robin's "Merry Men". Blind Ned (who of course isn't blind) ties Robin's note to an arrow and shoots it from the town wall into the forest. "Woodcutter" retrieves it and shoots it onwards. It flies into a tree in the outlaw camp where one of the "Merry Men" pulls it from the tree and takes it to "Little John", who is to mount the rescue.

The trouble was that all the shots for this sequence were photographed on different days, across two or three weeks. When they were joined together, it was discovered that "Blind Ned", the "Woodcutter", and the "Merry Man" in Robin's camp were *all* the same actor! It all had to be re-shot.

It wasn't all chaos, of course. Most of the time we were in control. We had to be, shooting at that rate. One episode I especially liked was *The Fire*. I directed well over half the scenes out of doors, with a full unit including sound and lights. Paul Eddington played the Sheriff's evil lieutenant. We got permission to set a section of the wood on fire, and although the local fire brigade was on site to control things, the blaze very nearly got out of control. Nobby Smith, operating the hand-held Arriflex, had the eyebrow that was not behind the camera burnt off.

The Fire had unfortunate consequences for me, too. It was produced in the last days of December, and on the morning of Christmas Eve I had an appeal from the editor for a close-up of Richard Greene. "Robin" was supposed to be in the burning forest and hit by a falling tree, but the studio sequence had not made that clear. What was needed was a shot of Richard glancing up at the tree (out of shot), as it was about to fall on him.

The light was too poor for us to film outside, so I found a corner of a sound stage on which another episode was being filmed. As I framed a head-and-shoulders of Richard against a bit of "forest" background, I realised that something else was needed to make the scene convincing. A suggestion of fire. Obviously I could not have a smoke machine, as it would drift across on to the other set. I had a bright idea. I smoked at the time, so I put a line of cigarettes in my mouth and blew smoke into Richard's face from behind the camera. All very clever – but Richard, blast him, could not get it right.

We went for take after take. By the time I called 'Print it,' wrapped up, and joined the rest of the studio staff in a farewell Christmas party, my throat was sore. That evening, Mary and I went to a theatre party in the palatial apartment of a wealthy member of the Royal Court Theatre cast named James Villiers. Among the guests was the actress Brenda de Banzie. She greeted us as we arrived, coughing and wheezing and claiming that she had "*pneumonia*, darling!"

The following morning, Christmas Day, I woke up feeling like death. I was in a muck sweat and shivering violently. 'Only flu,' I told Mary – but it was obvious that I was too ill to get up.

On Boxing Day, I was whisked across London to the Catholic hospital at Dollis Hill, where a pretty young nun stuck a needle in my posterior and injected me with penicillin. I was there for the next fortnight, very ill with double pneumonia. I was probably the only non-Catholic in the hospital. They put me in a private room and at night I could hear the nuns passing through the neighbouring ward, wishing the patients "Good night – God Bless". My door would then open, and I would hear just "Good Night". God did not bless Protestants!

They were lovely, though, these little nuns, who were training to go out to Africa. They brought me safely back from the brink.

The illness broke my run of luck at the studio. Someone else had had to carry on filming my scenes, and I was no longer the new "boy wonder". Everyone was very kind and solicitous when I returned, however, and even Richard Greene asked how I was.

I worked hard to get back in the swim, but events conspired against me. I don't know why, but the American writers started sending scripts that required far more complicated staging than we had either the time or facilities to provide. There was a lot of moaning, and morale was on the decline. Hannah had a new man in her life, a disbarred US lawyer, we heard, and he was spending her fortune like it was going out of fashion. Her two brothers, Seymour and Albert, who had given loyal service to the company, resigned and returned to the States. Hannah became autocratic and difficult to work for, and was no longer the leader of an enthusiastic collaborative team.

Robin Hood came to an end after seventy-eight episodes, and I found myself giving all my time to *Sword*

Of Freedom. Its star, Edmund Purdom, was an amusing buffoon who spent all night on the town, and reported each morning not having learnt his lines. He had developed a clever ploy for covering it. When he "fluffed" or forgot a line, he would stop and say something like, "Shouldn't the camera have moved then, Forbes?" or "Sorry – I caught sight of the mike boom". He would then do some quick mugging-up while we reset the shot. The marvellously professional team that supported him – Martin Benson, Adrienne Corri, Bill Owen, Joan Plowright – were exasperated by his unprofessional conduct.

We were shooting at a frantic rate by this time; most of the time on the studio's "back lot". I would often finish shooting a scene, and then have to rush to the open window of the writer's room to snatch a page of script for the next scene, fresh from the typewriter. We even carried on when it was raining, if the cameraman decided it was not quite heavy enough to notice.

One drizzly morning I began to shoot a little love scene between Edmund Purdom and Adrienne Corri. We had hired a freelance cameraman, who had come straight from working on *The Bridge On The River Kwai*. He didn't think much of our shenanigans, or the way Purdom and Adrienne were fooling about. A large umbrella protected the camera, but the actors were out in the rain. I went for a take, and as usual, Purdom fluffed his lines and stopped.

I waited for the excuse.

'Won't the rain be seen, Forbes?' he asked (rather reasonably, for once).

From behind the camera, the cameraman answered.

'Don't worry, Edmund. The audience will all be in tears by this time...'

Sword Of Freedom rang few bells when it went out on TV, and it began to look as though Hannah's luck was running out. The series came to an end and further production was halted for a much needed recess. Along with all the other staff, I was sent home. Mary was currently without a part at the Court so we went on a delayed "honeymoon". We went by coach to Oban, and then by Macbrayne's ferry boat to the Outer Hebrides where we stayed with a crofting family on South Uist. It was idyllic.

When Hannah's final series, *The Four Just Men*, starring Jack Hawkins, went into production, it did not have action sequences requiring a second-unit, so I did not return to Walton Studios.

None of the later series produced by Hannah enjoyed the success of *Robin Hood*. She over-committed herself financially and became entangled in complex arrangements to buy the studio. Eventually she returned to America, leaving massive debts, including a great deal of salary owing to the film technicians and actors. She eventually began a new career in Hollywood, before dying of a heart attack.

The break with Sapphire after a year of well-paid employment came at a sensitive moment in my career. I had succeeded at last in being recognised as some sort of film director, but because of my carelessness in not insisting on screen credits I was without a vital advantage when "going on the market". Roger Moore was at Beaconsfield Studios starring in a *Robin Hood* clone series called *Ivanhoe*. I went down to see him, but they were reaching the end of production and had all the directors they needed. Mary and I had £35 in the bank, and I needed to find another job, fast.

Jack Gourlay and I still met to dream up ideas for screenplays, but the occasions became increasingly rare and it was obvious that our lives were moving in different directions. He was mixing in high circles and in any case, unlike me he had a growing family that he needed to spend time with. Our friendship simply faded away, and I have not seen or heard of him for many years.

There was one sort of job I had no doubt I could get – directing "industrial" films. UMP was a bit *too* "amateur" to descend to, so I turned to the top company in the field, Film Producers Guild. They owned a studio at Merton Park, near Wimbledon, and an office block in St Martin's Lane. They had made many information films for the government and army training films during the war. One of the partners, Oswald Skilbeck, gave me an enthusiastic welcome and a job as a staff director. It meant a cut in the luxurious salary I had been enjoying, but it was a secure job – essential for a married man.

Having tasted the thrill of working in a large studio with first-line technicians, set designers and actors, I was not enamoured at finding myself directing non-theatrical information films again. The films were indeed unexciting. I began with a studio-based acted production designed to promote sales of disposable babies' nappies! It was filmed partly on location, in a maternity hospital in Birmingham. I was allowed to give Mary the leading part – she was the only woman to leave the hospital in the same condition as when she went in! Another project (which fortunately never got made) was about packet cake-mixes.

The Guild was a conservative company that guarded production budgets very carefully. I had a struggle persuading them to let me use a dolly and tracks in the studio, but when I demonstrated that it speeded up production as well as making the film look more slick and professional, I won their surprised approval.

At last I was assigned to write and direct something worthwhile. Two important films for the Home Office, about Civil Defence control in a nuclear war, were to be made on an unusually generous budget, with a large cast of actors. I went down to Merton Park Studios and supervised the building of complicated sets, which would allow me to "fly through walls".

My occasional agent, Peter Eade, told me that a newly arrived American producer was calling for scripts for a new television series to be called *A1 At Lloyds*. The stories would be thrillers about insurance frauds. I went to the briefing and knocked out a treatment about a medical scam – a murderous nurse takes revenge on someone who has wronged her by switching the right type of blood to the wrong type during a transfusion, killing the victim by anaphylactic shock. It triggers off an insurance claim, and the investigator unmasks the killer, after nearly being murdered himself. I may have been guilty of raiding Frank and Sidney's *Green For Danger* for the idea. Anyway, the script editor liked it and handed me a cheque for £250. Riches. I wrote no more stories for the series however, and in any case it never went into production.

Although the Civil Defence films allowed me to flatter myself that I was at the helm of a major production I yearned to get back to entertainment films. But film studios were experiencing another recession; cinemas were closing and being converted to bingo halls wherever one looked. The reason, of course, was television. The industry seemed stuck in a time warp, dazed by the breathtakingly high-speed growth of its rival, and at a total loss how to respond to it.

The British film industry had always been Byzantine in its complexity. Everyone concerned in it, from cinema owner to film producer, appeared prosperous, but below the surface it was riddled with patronage, corruption and crookery. Exactly how the finance worked was an arcane mystery, and deliberately so. Unlike the film producers, the "distributors" – companies that transported the reels around the country – were in direct contact with cinema owners, the "exhibitors". They were in the happy position of being able to demand payment immediately, regardless of whether a film they delivered was successful or not, and built up enormous caches of capital. Film producers had to wait for their rewards to trickle in and (then, as now) had an abiding problem of remaining solvent between pictures. They had to go cap in hand for finance to the distributors, who eventually exercised almost total control over what films were made. Headed, as they often were, by accountants, their concerns were less with aesthetics than making quick profits. They set up "arrangements" with the cinema owners, who combined into powerful chains, but in all cases the distributors took the largest share of the spoils. They covered their operations with a smokescreen, the smaller ones often refusing to open their books to their producer "partners". Unscrupulous ones even made undercover deals with venal exhibitors, ensuring that a film's creators received little or nothing in return for their efforts. Frequently the producer was told that no money had come in for his film. I learned that Frank Launder once had a blazing row with his distributor after spotting long queues outside a cinema for one of his films, after having been told that no one was going to see it.

The distributors were not creative, but hard-headed businessmen, so they were instinctively conservative when choosing what films to finance. The staple fare was stiff-upper-lip war films (mainly about officers, of course) and *Carry On* – type comedies, made in one or other of the factories – Pinewood, Borehamwood, Shepperton. Nearly all were directed by the same cosy group of people who began their careers in the 1930s. Some were genuinely brilliant, but many were just "safe pairs of hands". Others were *spielers* – trading on the snobbery of their "mittle-European" names – who got by on the backs of skilful technicians. And there were thoroughgoing charlatans, like the notorious Gabriel Pascal, who managed to charm Bernard Shaw and nearly bankrupted the Rank Organisation with *Caesar And Cleopatra*. At least one was plain mad. He was given to walking round the set asking people if they could prove they were sane. He would then produce his discharge certificate from a mental institution to show he was the only one with the proof.

This group took care to guard their interests, making it hard for newcomers to get a foot in the door – a door that anyway the unions kept firmly shut. One could not predict that we were about to enter "the swinging sixties", when everything would change – when new creative forces, many university educated, would elbow their way into the film industry with intelligent projects that would never have been produced before.

For the time being, the chances of crashing in and getting a feature film to direct seemed somewhat smaller than winning the Irish Sweepstake.

Part Two

The Idiot Lantern

14

AT A quarter past four on the afternoon of October 27th 1959, all across East Anglia a new age began.

In the centre of Norfolk's ancient county town, the red-stone Victorian Agricultural Hall stood foursquare and characterless, as it had for the preceding seventy-seven years. Within, however, the atmosphere was charged with excitement. Two hundred people waited – tensed – for a moment of historical importance. A moment that would usher in this new age.

High in the building, staff at control desks watched the sweep-hand of a large clock. Thrilling music played – Holst's *The Planets* – *Mars* – tumpety-tum-tum tumtumtum – tumpety-tum-tum tumtumtum…

As four o'clock approached, a red light glowed over the door. A voice boomed out:

'Ten minutes to the beginning of Anglia Television!'

Throughout East Anglia, from King's Lynn in the north to Chelmsford in the south, Cambridge in the west to Lowestoft in the east, thousands upon thousands of people sat before their television sets.

Again the voice:

'Five minutes to the beginning of Anglia Television!'

The music reached a crescendo.

Then – at last – a picture appeared on the screen. A towering television mast with waves emanating from it.

'Tuesday the twenty-seventh of October, nineteen fifty-nine! Anglia Television is on the air!' the voice announced triumphantly.

Inside the Agricultural Hall, champagne was opened and the staff of Britain's newest television company congratulated one another on getting the service on the air on time. It had been due to begin broadcasting two days later, on October 29th, but the date had been brought forward because Ulster TV in Belfast had chosen the same day to go on the air.

For me, it was an especially poignant moment. I had written those opening words and directed the first pictures that appeared on Anglia Television's screen.

"Commercial Television", financed by advertising, brought about an enormous change in the cultural life of the country. Prior to its introduction, the only television had been provided by the BBC, its hours of broadcasting limited so as not to distract the working class from its tasks, and operated under strict Presbyterian guidelines by its authoritarian Director-General, Lord Reith.

In 1953 Parliament voted by a narrow margin to end the BBC's monopoly. It was terrified, nevertheless, that broadcasting might fall into the hands of "unsuitable" people, so it created the "establishment's" favourite kind of regulatory body – an *Authority,* made up of members of "the great and the good" who would graciously award licences to broadcast ("licences to print money", Roy Thompson, the newspaper-owner head of the Scottish ITV company, later put it).

When the first three or four licences were granted in 1954, the Authority's dignitaries refused to allow the leading entertainment tycoon, Lew Grade, to participate, presumably because they thought him vulgar. They were forced to reverse their decision when it was explained to them that Grade and his brothers controlled most of the country's pool of light-entertainment talent.

Parliament decided that the new service should be "regional" in character. The first commercial stations broadcast nationally, however, and were based in London, Birmingham and Manchester. There were strange anomalies. A classic announcement was heard each week:

"From the North! – Granada presents – *Chelsea At Nine!*"

The programme was produced in London's Fulham Road, but was beamed from studios in Lancashire (the reference to Spain would have really baffled a foreign visitor).

By 1958, the ITV audience approximated twenty-eight million. By then, a clutch of truly regional stations had been commissioned and a pattern of *local* programming, of marginal interest outside the borders of the particular area, began to emerge.

East Anglia was among the last parts of the country to get commercial television. The east of England franchise was known to be a curiously tricky one. The designated region embraced Norfolk, Suffolk, Essex, and parts of Cambridgeshire, Hertfordshire and Lincolnshire, making it one of the largest. But it contained the smallest population of any broadcaster, at around two million.

Norfolk in those days was almost as remote as Outer Mongolia. It was estimated that for every ten people there in the summer only one was there in the winter. The region was also somewhat primitive. A researcher discovered that there were more television sets than bathtubs! (The figures were actually 371,000 TVs to 358,400 baths.)

As far as potential advertising revenue was concerned, Norfolk seemed an especially tough nut to crack. The locals had a daunting boast. 'We "du different".' 25,600 of them were fish-owners and 139,200 owned birds, as *The Daily Telegraph* rather curiously discovered. Would they desert their bird cages and fish tanks to watch *Opportunity Knocks*? It was said of Norfolk folk that they were so bloody-minded they would deliberately *not* buy something they saw advertised. The general view was that commercial television would last about three or four weeks, at best.

Several groups, nevertheless, applied for the licence to provide programmes for this uninviting area. All of them called at the monumental Marble Hall of the Norwich Union Insurance Company, with an invitation to participate. In nearly every case, that august concern was frightened off by wild promises of large dividends, which suggested correspondingly large risks. Only the consortium headed by one of Norfolk's most respectable landowners, Marquess Townshend of Raynham, quoted a steady four percent. It won the coveted support, and went on to win the television contract.

The inspiration for the bid had come from John Woolf, the head of Romulus Films, and producer of blockbusters like *The African Queen* and *Oliver!* He had teamed up with Laurence Scott, the proprietor of *The Guardian* and son of that newspaper's legendary founder, C.P. Scott. They had gone in search of true East Anglian blue blood to give the company respectability, and it materialised in the person of

George, the 7th Marquess Townshend of Raynham, whose ancestors included "Turnip Townshend", the inventor of crop-rotation, and a general who lost the Heights of Abraham after Wolfe had been killed capturing them. His current lordship had been stage struck in his young days.

The company's aristocratic credentials were further augmented by the recruitment of one of the Duke of Edinburgh's best friends, Aubrey Buxton. He was an Essex grandee who had previously worked in public relations.

One senses that the award of the franchise rather bowled its recipients off their feet. At any rate, the four original partners found themselves without an office and almost entirely without any knowledge of how to create a television service. By 1959 – the year the service was to open – the board of directors had grown to include a representative of Cambridge University, archaeologist Glyn Daniel (who was also a television personality. He had taken a prominent part in several of the BBC's early programmes, most notably as chairman of the panel game *Animal, Vegetable, Mineral.*). Sir Robert Bignold (whose ancestor had helped create the Norwich Union) represented the worlds of finance and brewing, Alderman Will Copeman was a proprietor of the local newspaper, *The Eastern Daily Press*, Donald Albery was a London theatre owner, and Sir Peter Greenwell a Suffolk farmer. *No one* professionally involved with television was invited to join. A characteristic pattern had been established. As in every decent English game, there were to be "gentlemen and players" – proprietorial amateurs and employee professionals with clearly defined places in the hierarchy. One irreverent engineer put it more brutally – *"Aristocrats and peasants"*.

There was much discussion among the new board members concerning the station symbol. Some wanted a statue of Boadicea, others the three crowns of the ancient East Anglian kingdoms. The issue was settled when one of their wives chanced to pass Asprey's window in Old Bond Street and saw a massive silver model of a mounted knight in armour. It was going cheap, so the company bought it. Suitably modified with the addition of a silver pennant bearing the word "Anglia", and accompanied – for what reason, no one now remembers – by a passage from Handel's *Water Music*, it became the company logo.

Had I been around, I could have advised that the relevant few bars of Handel could be culled from a gramophone record. Instead, the Philharmonia Orchestra was assembled on Elstree film studios' massive sound stage to make a special recording. On the principle that nothing but the best would do, Sir Malcolm Sargent was invited to conduct. Pleading other engagements, he nominated his assistant, John Hollingsworth. Aubrey Buxton appointed himself to supervise the recording and the filming of the silver knight revolving on its base.

Lord Townshend chose that day to invite his neighbour at Holkham Hall, the Earl of Leicester, to lunch.

'Where's Buxton?' demanded "Tommy" Leicester.

'He's shooting at Elstree,' answered George Townshend, demonstrating his newly acquired knowledge of television vernacular.

The earl's eyebrows shot up.

'Oh?' he said. 'Who has the shoot at Elstree?'

(I visited Lord Leicester, at his palatial home, a year or two later. He told me he could not see television because his wife would not let him put up an aerial.)

To address the mind-numbing prospect of creating a company to service their imponderable area, the new franchise owners turned for advice to the London broadcaster Associated Rediffusion, and with its help the nucleus of a staff was appointed. (There was an unkind suspicion that Rediffusion used the opportunity to off-load some of its less reliable executives.) The first appointment, engineer Tom Marshall, was a laudable one, but other senior recruitments were more questionable. Stephen McCormack, the head of programming, had been a "floor manager" in the BBC, a fairly lowly position. His easy-going, alcoholic enthusiasm had powered his rise through Rediffusion's ranks. The Head of News had come from a minor provincial paper. The production manager had all too recently been a salesman at Harrods. Most of the programme producers and directors had been in the theatre, like the senior lighting and sound technicians. Other department heads had had only a year or two's experience in television. *No one* senior, apart from me, was from the film industry. Given how much film and television technologies have in common, it seemed bizarre. This reluctance of television to have anything to do with the film industry seemed to go back to television's earliest times – the BBC's first electronic cameras were equipped with primitive viewfinders that turned the image upside down. The poor suffering cameramen had to remember to tilt up when they wanted to go down and vice versa. A trip to any film studio by one of the BBC's haughty engineering masters would have led to a proper viewfinder.

I celebrated my thirty-third birthday by travelling with my new wife, Mary, to see Anglia's embryo studio under construction in Norwich. We took the train from Liverpool

Street and, as we approached Manningtree, we caught sight of the great, empty, East Anglian landscape, the wide estuary of the River Orwell at Mistley. Ancient rotting boats were marooned on the mud, and seabirds wheeled in a soaring sky. It promised an improvement on our flat in Shepherds Bush.

Norwich seemed a pleasant city. Anglia's production manager met us off the train and drove us down Prince of Wales Road to the studio, which was being converted from a redbrick Victorian monstrosity nestling below a mound topped by the imposing Norman Castle. The former Agricultural Hall had been thrown up in just seven months in 1882. Presumably someone thought it was needed in the centre of one of Britain's most productive farming areas. There were cattle shows and corn sales, but no one was quite sure how the place could or should be used. Optimistic entrepreneurs put on occasional pantomimes, fairs, banquets, balls and circuses (the tightrope-walker Blondin trod carefully across the vast space) and there were even early demonstrations of the new-fangled cinema. But most of the time, the building was silent as the morgue. It was therefore something of an inspiration on the part of whoever saw it as a potential television studio.

The adventurous conversion threw up massive difficulties. Huge concrete piles had to be sunk through the flooring to support the heavy broadcasting equipment. (A dark rumour got around that a number of skeletons, almost certainly medieval and probably executed Lollard heretics, were unearthed in the process. Such a discovery would have resulted in an inquest, entailing lengthy delays in the construction schedule, so the bones were quietly taken out and disposed of.)

Mary and I arrived to see everything covered in brick dust. Enormous pieces of polythene-wrapped equipment were being manhandled into position by a white-coated army – supervising them was a balding, heavily built chain-smoker, with a moon face and reflecting glasses.

'This is Tom Marshall, the Chief Engineer,' the production manager introduced us.

I made a fatal error. I greeted him in a friendly rather than deferential manner. Coming from the film industry, I thought of "engineers" as relatively unimportant personages compared with the likes of me, concerned with the primary purpose of the operation, making programmes. I did not know that in television, engineers are god, and Chief Engineers are *super* god. They had created the beast after all, and no one should forget it. They could transmit a beautiful test signal, and toads like me just spoilt it with programmes.

Marshall put on an appearance of civility, but his manner (as I learned to be wary of later) was designed to trap.

He feigned respect.

'I apologise that we did not have time to wait for you to be appointed before ordering the film equipment,' he said. 'I hope you will be happy with what we have purchased. I had to make a decision about the kind of cameras we went for, so we decided on combined-sound models. They are not the highest quality engineering, unfortunately.'

I had heard poor opinions of the American combined-sound cameras and agreed with him. But Marshall's preamble fooled me into assuming that I had a say in matters concerning my future department's equipment.

'We can always replace them with Arriflex cameras and separate sound recorders later,' I said.

The Chief Engineer went very red.

'You won't get any additional cameras,' he barked. 'I can assure you of that!'

He turned on his heel and stalked away. Charming.

The production manager grinned.

'You'll get use to old Tom,' he said.

Had I been able to foresee much of what would happen in the next year or two with "old Tom" and others, I might then have decided to change my mind about making the jump from film into television. Which would have been a pity, taking the longer view. But I was optimistic, and after a tour of the complex – the last word in "high-tech" being created within the shell of the nineteenth-century "bygone" (a word that would become the title of one of Anglia's most enduring programmes) – Mary and I returned to London, to prepare for the enormous transformation about to sweep over our lives.

15

IT WAS quite an opening night. Anglia immediately established its unique credentials by transmitting a drama on the national network. It was a play called *The Violent Years*, and the leading players were two stars John Woolf had managed to lure from Hollywood, Laurence Harvey and Hildegarde Neff.

I thought back on the previous hectic days.

Three weeks before, the BBC had stolen a march on its new rival by opening a tiny television studio in Norwich, broadcasting local news. Hitherto it had been content to provide a sound-only radio service to the region. (The "Beeb" has always been contemptuous and patronising towards commercial television. One of its executives told me recently that it had passed into the record that "owing to teething troubles in Anglia's film department" Anglia had been forced to borrow a BBC film editor to cut its first news items. I was happy to tell him that no such thing had happened.)

Nothing had been easy about installing a television service for East Anglia. Curiously, although East Anglia is notoriously flat it was difficult to get a television signal everywhere. The VHF mast, erected as close as possible to the centre of the region at Mendlesham in Suffolk, was the highest in Europe, at 400 metres. It had a reception footprint of 10,000 square kilometres (but never managed to reach Raynham Hall, Lord Townshend's home!). Television sets needed to be modified to receive the new service, and it was essential to convince people that it would be worth the effort and expense.

A large Wessex helicopter, carrying the sign "ANGLIA – YOUR OWN ITV OCT 29TH" on its sides, landed on town sports fields and village greens. Three beauties, called "The Anglia Helibelles", tumbled out, accompanied by the board member responsible for publicity, Aubrey Buxton. An Outside Broadcast vehicle also turned up and performers gave a show, perched on top.

It was at one of these jamborees, at Haverhill in Suffolk, that I met Aubrey Buxton for the first time. We became firm friends, a friendship that endured to the end of his very long life. Aubrey was a great enthusiast for his new career. He had a distinguished war record, serving in the Far East, where his courage earned him a Military Cross. His name is a prominent one in Norfolk and Essex. Glyn Daniel, who was a "collector" of practical jokes, told me that a former Buxton was a notorious practical joker in the 1920s. With one or two wealthy friends, he had booked every seat in a theatre for an invited audience. They had placed bald men in certain seats in the stalls, so that when viewed from the dress circle, their heads spelled B U M. I never asked Aubrey about it, but can't help feeling that he would have enormously enjoyed such a joke.

August was nearing its end, and there was little time to lose if we were to get on the air on time. A film department needed to be recruited, and I spent the evenings in London interviewing prospective staff. My cameraman at Walton-on-Thames studios had been the unfailingly reliable Ian

Craig. I phoned and offered him the job of chief film cameraman. To my surprise and delight he told me he had always wanted to move to the country.

I had heard the rumours that Walton Studios were about to close, and made a return visit to see how my old colleagues were faring. I found an atmosphere of gloom. The studio was bankrupt, and had been bought by a property developer who intended to demolish it to make way for a supermarket. Britain's oldest filmmaking facility was about to come to an ignominious end. There was therefore no difficulty in recruiting staff for my new department. I hired Sound man Charlie Earl, and was fortunate in landing a first-class camera technician in Peter Fuller, who could also be assistant cameraman. Peter also did me a great favour by putting me in touch with his friend, Harry Aldous, a film editor with a distinguished career at Ealing Studios. He had been badly wounded during the war, which left him with damaged fingers and facial disfigurement. I took Harry on to supervise Anglia's editing needs.

On Friday the 28th August, I made my farewells at Merton Park, and took the train to Norwich to spend the weekend setting up the film department – the cutting room, film-processing room, offices and stores. On Sunday evening, I returned to London, and Mary, and set about buying our first car. The £250 I had earned from *A1 At Lloyds* bought us a three-year-old Riley Pathfinder, a sleek monster in British Racing Green, leather seats, twin carbs, a curious gear-lever on the right-hand side – and a faulty braking system that required "pumping" some distance before the car came to a stop. We loved it.

Monday the thirty-first was our second Wedding Anniversary. It was also my first official day as an Anglia employee. Mary found us a flat in Norwich, in a new tower block that was already crowded with television "immigrants". Stephen McCormack labelled it "The Sin Bins" (whatever "sins" went on there, it was not long before Mary delighted me by announcing that we had an addition to the family on the way).

Michael Seligman had a flat upstairs, and took to joining us for breakfast. He had severed his connection with his advertising agency, and formalised his position with Anglia, becoming Company Secretary. It was not a totally happy choice of job for someone without legal or accounting qualifications. He was invaluable to the company in those early days, though, bringing a wealth of production, budgeting and technical experience. He maintained some of his outside business interests, which stood him in good stead in the future. As far as Mary and I were concerned, he was a delightful companion, and we began a close friendship that has endured to this day.

There was now about eight weeks to go before Anglia commenced transmission, and an enormous amount still had to be done, completing the installation, "working up" and stockpiling material. I took pains to ensure that my part of the operation was as professional as possible. In this (ironically) I was aided by my old enemy, the union, now renamed the Association of Cinematograph and *Television* Technicians. It maintained its iron grip on recruiting and crewing standards, which prevented Steve, and some of the board members, offering film director or cameraman jobs to people they met on the train.

By the end of September, the studio was almost ready for action. There could not have been a more dramatic contrast between the dreary exterior of the nineteenth-century building and what was going on inside. At the top of the timeworn steps, the visitor passed through plate-glass doors into a cavernous entrance hall, with large glass windows at the back through which technicians could be seen crouching over flickering screens. Behind the hall was a building *inside* a building. A wide passage encircled an inner wall of brick, behind which was the heart of the complex – a television studio insulated from the noisy outside world.

Myriad new staff members wandered through the confusion of passageways and empty areas. Among them strolled a cheery, rotund figure who gave all the appearances of owning the place. He introduced himself to me as Dick Joice. He was a north Norfolk farmer ("the jolly farmer" of my fairy tale) – and he would be presenting the weekly farming programme. There was a constant reminder of the importance of agriculture to the fledgling company. On my first Saturday, I was amazed to glance out of a window at the back of the studio, and see a herd of cattle approaching down Norwich's Ber Street to the accompanying whoops and yells of stockmen. They were driven into pens beside our car park. The cattle-market had been held here, in the shadow of Norwich Castle, for the past five hundred years. Our architects had thoughtfully placed the air-conditioning intakes on that side of the building, and the delightful aromas provided one of the pleasures of working in a country station.

Rather unexpectedly, Lord Townshend was everywhere to be seen about the studio. It was clear that he intended to be a "hands on" manager. The Marquess was a mixture of almost royal hauteur and simple chumminess (the latter probably a legacy of wartime army comradeship). I got to know our tall, debonair chairman quite well. We would run into each other in the car park or the entrance hall, and a simple greeting would develop into a lengthy gossip. Sometimes I would be summoned to his office – much smaller than those of the other senior executives – and we would talk for an hour or so about all sorts of things – often about our lives in the army. On one occasion, at a large reception for archaeologist guests, he detached himself from the gathering and spent the entire time with me. His eyes lit up as he described his pleasure when, as a Guards officer in the Far East, he supervised the execution of Japanese war criminals.

I heard the story of George Townshend's strange history from a feature-writer on the local newspaper. George's birth, upbringing and youth was anything but conventional. His eccentric father, the 6th Marquess, was virtually penniless, and went to America in search of a wealthy bride. He narrowly escaped marriage to a woman who turned out to be a barmaid before being introduced to a lawyer who offered his daughter, Gwladys, in exchange for settling Townshend's debts. After the marriage the lawyer tried, unsuccessfully, to have the Marquess declared mad.

His daughter, however, proved anything but a liability to the dynasty. She was extremely strong-minded, and when her husband died she fought off several complex legal challenges to ensure that her five-year-old son George would succeed to the title and estate.

As a youngster, the boy seemed accident-prone – a near death from blood poisoning compelling him to leave Harrow, two driving accidents in his early teens – and the tradition continued during the war when he was commissioned in the Guards. He was with a group of soldiers when they were machine-gunned by mistake by the RAF, killing twenty-five officers and men. Townshend was left with severe injuries.

During the 1930s, much of Britain's agriculture was in decline and the Raynham estate became virtually bankrupt. In Townhend's absence on war service the farms were managed by the Joice family, of which Anglia's Dick was an energetic member. Under their shrewd stewardship, and aided by government subsidies, the debts were repaid and the estate was handed back to the returning warrior in a healthy state.

Two or three weeks after I joined, Lord Townshend called a conference to decide what sort of programme should be put together for Opening Day. Everyone sat round the table looking blank. By this time I had got the message. Coming, as I did, from the film industry I was a second-class citizen among the "tele" people. I deferred to them to put forward their ideas. When none were forthcoming, I ventured to put in a word. I suggested that we might begin with a helicopter-ride over the region, identifying the places we passed over, and finally soaring into the studio in Norwich, where Lord Townshend would be waiting to welcome the new viewers. Townshend thought it was a super idea and promptly ordered me to be the producer. It put not a few noses out of joint.

Almost simultaneously, Steve informed me that he had made a commitment with Rediffusion for Anglia to produce a fifty-minute documentary about the local RAF station at Coltishall. The presenter would be Hughie Green, and I was to direct it. He now added that it was due to be broadcast on the network during our first week on the air. We were less than a month away from that date, so it rather took my breath away – the more so when I learned that the programme was already "billed" in *The TV Times*! In my former incarnation I would have expected to spend at least two or three months on such a production – the laboratory work alone might take several weeks. But this was not film. This was television. And others knew television better than me, didn't they?

Making the opening programme was exciting and enjoyable. The helicopter ride over my new home was an eye opener, in more ways than one. I was amazed by how large Norfolk was. Despite the aircraft's speed, it took hours to pass over the acres of scrubby Breckland in the west, the miles of lonely coastland on the east and the seemingly limitless expanse of weirdly ridged mud around the Wash.

After an hour or two's filming, we landed in a field to go behind a hedge for a pee. When we returned to the aircraft, we found two farm workers staring at it.

'Mornin',' one of them said, very nearly touching his forelock, 'Oi see yew got 'elicopter.'

'Yes,' I replied.

'Oi say ter m' mate 'ere – 'at's an 'elicopter.'

'Yes,' I confirmed.

I climbed in beside the cameraman, and the pilot switched on.

'Mornin',' said the farm worker.

'Morning,' I replied, and we soared into the air. Obviously it was the most natural thing in the world – dropping out of the sky to take a pee behind a hedge.

Not long after we ran low of fuel, and set down behind the pumps of a rural petrol station for a refill...

Rehearsing on the barrack square for the "Services Cavalcade" pageant in the Kelvin Hall, Glasgow.

My toy cine-camera.

The Covenanters' Inn, Aberfoyle

Roddy Leckie-Ewing.

Briefing Paul Connell as Lord Macleod.

Aboard the paddle-steamer "Jeanie Deans" to film the wreck of the troopship "Birkenhead" – Robin Steele in foreground.

Screenshots from *"Proud Heritage"*.

Previous page: Scenes from *Proud Heritage* – Paul Connell as Lord Macleod raising the regiment, 1778; Roddy Leckie-Ewing as Captain Baird threatening to shoot the entire regiment for disobeying orders, 1778; cavalry charge for the Battle of Assaye, 1803; French cavalry charging at a British "square" at Waterloo, 1815.

My first day on a film set. Roddy Leckie-Ewing on my right, visiting. Frank Launder far left, talking to the star of *The Happiest Days*, Alastair Sim.

Bernadette on The Happiest Days of Your Life set.

Below. Paul (leftt); Thelma (right).

The Boyhood of James Bond… The Roger Moore "screen test".
Kay Kendall in *Dial 999* with Cyril Coke.

Committee

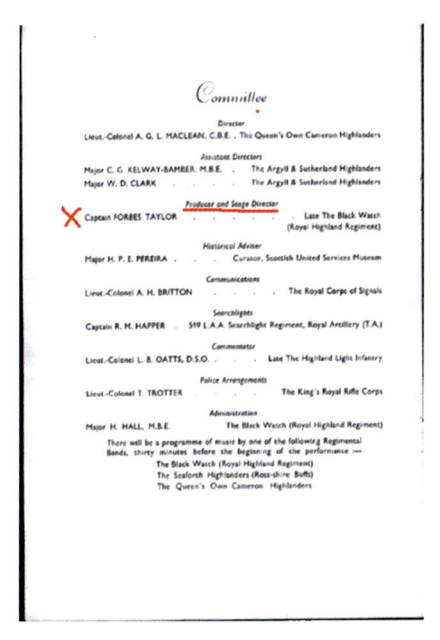

Director
Lieut.-Colonel A. G. L. MACLEAN, C.B.E. . The Queen's Own Cameron Highlanders

Assistant Directors
Major C. G. KELWAY-BAMBER, M.B.E. . The Argyll & Sutherland Highlanders
Major W. D. CLARK . . . . . The Argyll & Sutherland Highlanders

Producer and Stage Director
✗ Captain FORBES TAYLOR . . . . Late The Black Watch (Royal Highland Regiment)

Historical Adviser
Major H. P. E. PEREIRA . . . Curator, Scottish United Services Museum

Communications
Lieut.-Colonel A. H. BRITTON . . . . The Royal Corps of Signals

Searchlights
Captain R. M. HAPPER . 519 L.A.A. Searchlight Regiment, Royal Artillery (T.A.)

Commentator
Lieut.-Colonel L. B. OATTS, D.S.O. . . . Late The Highland Light Infantry

Police Arrangements
Lieut.-Colonel T. TROTTER . . . . The King's Royal Rifle Corps

Administration
Major H. HALL, M.B.E. The Black Watch (Royal Highland Regiment)

There will be a programme of music by one of the following Regimental Bands, thirty minutes before the beginning of the performance :—
The Black Watch (Royal Highland Regiment)
The Seaforth Highlanders (Ross-shire Buffs)
The Queen's Own Cameron Highlanders

My "Tattoo", 1952. The present authorities have "forgotten" me.

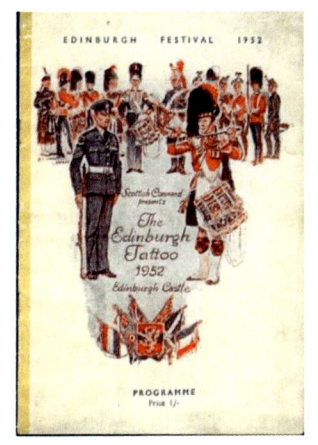

Mary age 23.

Mary with Richard Gere in "*The Adventures of Robin Hood*".

Norman Hackforth, Stephen McCormack and Tom Marshall.

Michael Seligman and Mary on the beach at Cromer.

Our new home – White Horse Farm.

I begin work with Brian Hope-Taylor. Filming at Stonehenge for "*Who Were the British?*"

Studying the script in a Stone Age bed at Scara Brae in the Orkneys.

Brian Hope-Taylor – 'This is Wembley, the White City, and the Madison Square Garden of Ancient Rome.'

The Dome of the Rock in Jerusalem.

Rome – in front of St Peter's for a travelling shot.

A helicopter is a useful camera platform. Ian Craig with Arriflex before the days of stabilisers.

Below. Directing *Shooting Stars.* On set of "Billy Bud" with Peter Ustinov.

Lost in the desert. With Brian Hope-Taylor, setting out hopefully for Palmyra.

The Lost Centuries – shooting at El Azraq when the Israelis crossed the Jordan.

At Qasr Al Amra in the Jordan desert.

The impromptu war correspondent.

Divided Berlin – filming the infamous wall.

The East German police attempt to spoil our film with mirrors.

Danish Boy Scouts provide a magnificent "Viking" long ship.

The "Lost Centuries" preview at the National FilmTheatre. Archaeologists Professor Glyn Daniel and Sir Mortimer Wheeler with Brian and me.

My last association with Brian, on his dig at the Devil's Dyke, near Cambridge.

Africa... National Geographic Society photographer Bob Campbell looks out across the wilderness east of Lake Rudolph, northern Kenya.

The Leakey expedition camp at Koobi Fora, Lake Rudolph, Kenya.

With Richard Leakey examining a fossil find.

Alan Root with the pet baby hippopotamus that he kept in house.

Cats come before filming!

Not our usual mode of travel – the replica of George Stephenson's "Locomotion" which we financed. First run at Beamish Open Air Museum, Durham.

My first Anglia filming in 1959 had been with Dick Joice…

I ended it eighteen years later with Dick. *"Digging For Yesterday"*…

Salalah, southern Oman, on the shore of the Indian Ocean – the TV studio on the beach.

My office. My trainee Director-General of Broadcasting, Ghamen Salem, seated back to the window. The others in for a gossip.

On my way home from Oman I stopped off to stay with Frank and
Bernadette in their home at Cap d'Ail, close to Monaco.

Frank – in characteristic pose – with Mary.

16

MY STRONGEST impression on switching from film to television was how amateur it all seemed. I tried to think what it reminded me of. Then it came to me. The whole operation was for all the world like Lady Bountiful and the vicar marshalling the villagers to get up a show. Even the news was like a parish magazine.

There seemed to be a complete lack of discipline. People wandered in and out of the studio while we were on the air – in a film studio it was a sackable offence to enter when "the red" was on outside the door. I was amazed by the way things were managed. Everything was informal, decisions were made on the hoof, and muddles and crises were the order of the day. Senior people carried on as if they were independent gentlemen of leisure, spending the company's money without giving it a thought, on boozes, slap-up lunches and joy rides. Many had worked for the large London company, Associated Rediffusion – where, so it seemed, the profits were so enormous that nobody bothered about such things.

Watching over the chaos was Stephen McCormack, a delightful muddler, whose principal – perhaps sole – quality was his eye for an interesting picture. Everyone who worked for him, including me, adored him. We had hit it off from the first moment, and he took to calling me into his office first thing every morning and consulting me on nearly everything that was going on. I was flattered, until I realised that he extended a similar invitation to nearly everyone who walked past his open door. I suppose Steve bemused me. He was the first television supremo I had encountered, and I ignored the gossip – among those who knew him better – that the company already viewed him as unreliable, and that he was unlikely to stay the course. I did not see the danger when I allowed myself to be drawn into his projects.

As I was putting the opening programme together, Michael Seligman muttered in my ear that Lord Townshend had a very high regard for me. I believe now that at that moment, the top job at Anglia Television was potentially mine for the taking, had I recognised the weakness of the other department heads and been sufficiently ambitious. It was increasingly obvious that Stephen McCormack's days were numbered and his job would be up for grabs in the not-too-distant future. But I lacked the necessary ruthlessness – and experience – in a crucial area, the "executive rat race". I had not been in a formally structured company before, and had still to learn the importance of "empire-building" and "one-upmanship". A fatal flaw in my character also hampered me. I was *creative*. I had not yet finished playing with "the train set" and wanted direct participation in programme production.

What I wanted, of course, was to "have my cake and eat it" – enjoy the power that went with management, but also work as a filmmaker. So I failed to exploit my initial success, and in the months that followed all kinds of mischief went on while I was away from the centre of things making films.

Things began to go wrong, in fact, almost immediately after the opening programme. I failed to recognise the trap that was lying in wait for me. *Battle Formation*, Steve's wild scheme for a major documentary about the historic RAF station at Coltishall on the Norfolk Broads, to be run up in a few days.

Perhaps it was my army training that made me ignore the warning bells. You didn't ask questions, but "bloody well got on with it". At first, forgetting all past experience, I really thought we had a chance. It was fascinating working with Hughie Green, the selfsame star I had sat in Walpole Park as a small boy and cheered on (though I didn't tell him). He was mad about flying, and had been in the Canadian air force during the war, which is why Steve chose him to front the programme. He was a mixture of vain exhibitionism, feigned brainlessness, and shrewd opportunism. It was impossible to really know what made him tick, but we got on like a house on fire.

We filmed operational activities, including a spectacular formation "scramble" by Javelin and Hunter fighters, and interviews with the pilots and ground crew. After a week or so I had enough material to make a programme. We would have to start editing as fast as possible if we were going to make the transmission date. At this point, however, Steve arrived at the RAF station rather merry from a good lunch, and informed me that he had invited half a dozen Battle Of Britain aces to come to the base to swap yarns about their war escapades; I must hold things in abeyance for several days while this was arranged. I began to feel an unpleasant sensation in the pit of my stomach.

Eventually the aces were gathered in the officers' mess to be filmed – legless pilot Douglas Bader, Air Marshal "Johnny" Johnson, Bob Stanford-Tuck, "Crow" Crowley-Milling, and Coltishall's station commander, Group Captain "Birdie" Bird-Wilson. They asked me what I wanted them to talk about. I said I had no idea – this was Steve's department. He was busy in the bar, of course. They began to chat, however, about aerial dogfights in Spitfires and Hurricanes, the Battle of Britain, the "Big Wing" controversy, and we churned out mile after mile of film. It *was* very interesting.

I took several hours of film back to Anglia House, and Harry Aldous and I got down to editing it. It was then Wednesday. The programme was due in London the following Tuesday evening for transmission by Rediffusion, and what time was available had to include the laboratory work, so it was really just a case of throwing the shots together. There was no time for real editing. Harry and I worked right through the night on Saturday to get it completely assembled, and I drove us down to London in the small hours of Sunday morning. As we passed through the empty Norfolk countryside I fell asleep at the wheel, and we had to pull off the road for a catnap. I opened my eyes, in the dawn light half an hour later, to find we were parked in a corporation rubbish tip. It was prophetic.

Battle Formation went out on schedule, but it wasn't up to network documentary standard. The narrative was confused and meandering, and Hughie Green's presence detracted from the *gravitas*. I must take part of the blame. I had not yet grasped the essentials of tailoring the shots to suit the limitations of television. The end of the process was a picture on the tiny, fuzzy screen of the average home TV set and wide-angle scenes didn't work. I was not helped by a poorly engineered camera, with a zoom lens that was hardly better than shooting through a milk bottle, and grainy negative processed by fairly amateur equipment. Anything other than big close-ups was a waste of time in those days.

The only bit Harry Aldous and I were proud of was the opening sequence, the operational "scramble" – but as Harry said, it was the only part we had edited properly.

The following morning Lord Townshend sent for me. He was less friendly than he had been.

'You should not have allowed it to go on,' he said.

I politely pointed out that Stephen McCormack made that sort of decision.

The Chairman shook his head. 'You should not have let it go on.'

I played my last card.

'It was billed in *The TV Times.*'

'You should have stopped Steve,' said Lord Townshend, bringing the interview to a close.

My problems were beginning.

Nineteen sixty began with a portent. A New Year's Eve staff party, held in the studio. Some ill-advised members of the staff got up a cabaret, with thinly disguised "send-ups" of board members and senior managers. They drew forced smiles from the victims. We had been in existence for only four months, and it was far too soon for people to know each other well enough to "take the mickey".

The most lethal gaffe came from the musical director, Norman Hackforth. He had been Noel Coward's accompanist, and in songs at the piano he gave his version of *The Master*'s song, *Let's Do It – Let's Fall in Love.*

Newly written ribald verses were aimed at old pals like Stephen McCormack.

But then he ventured into more dangerous territory, ending with the unforgettable verse:

> *The silver knight does it*
> *With that ruddy great lance,*
> *And even Lord Townshend does it*
> *When he gets the chance...*

There were roars of knowing laughter, and all eyes turned on the chairman, seated at the back beside the marchioness.

How could "Hacky" know the Townshends were beginning an acrimonious divorce, and they were there together to keep up appearances?

The company's New Year activities commenced with the dismissal of Norman Hackforth. During the next few weeks, several other members of the initial establishment failed to come up to expectations and were invited to say goodbye. The most exciting departure was the Head of News, who was observed by a board member directing the News while dead drunk.

As well as the problem of scenic shots establishing a sense of "place", filming for television was different in many ways from the kind of thing I had done before. The idiom was also quite different from the cinema, where no one ever looked directly at the camera. It was the day of the "talking head" (though still much in evidence in these days of colour and fifty-inch screens). The presenter stood in front of the camera holding a microphone, and told us what was happening behind him. I say *him* because there were very few women doing it in the '50s and '60s, and none at all in the News programmes.

It was apparent to me that the television directors had little, if any, training, especially in film. They were lost when put in charge of a film unit. For the time being, at least, I had no choice but to direct film myself alongside running the film department. In those first weeks I got around much of our large region – Orford Ness in deepest Suffolk, Blickling Hall near Aylsham in mid-Norfolk, Brightlingsea on the Essex coast – where we filmed the oyster harvest, Yarmouth, Felixstowe, Hunstanton, Cambridge, Leiston, Sizewell – where a nuclear power station was about to be built. And I visited Walberswick for the first time, little suspecting that it would play a major part in my life, far in the future.

Film had to be processed in a machine that the engineers had chosen to install on the top floor of Anglia House. To run it, I poached a cheery cockney named Norman Wood from a London film laboratory. He coped manfully with a poorly designed piece of apparatus, which was made even less reliable by being plumbed into the building's main sewage system. At moments of heavy usage elsewhere, the dreaded happened.

One afternoon I discovered Norman at the rural task of "mucking out". 'I've processed some crap in my time, but this is the first time it's come back out of the machine!' he said.

The schedule's voracious appetite for more and more material led to changes in my staffing arrangements. Steve McCormack told me one morning that a celebrated comic had arrived at his door, claiming to have been born in

Norwich. A half-hour film, showing the star searching for his home, must be made right away.

I had seen Richard Hearne, as his alter ego "Mister Pastry", and thought him monumentally unfunny, so it was not entirely altruism when I gave Harry Aldous his first directing assignment. Harry did sterling work, and the result almost made me laugh. From that moment Harry was on the strength as a film director.

To take Harry's place as film editor, I engaged David Kenten, and got a surprise when he reminded me that he had been the British Film Institute's vault boy in United Motion Pictures' basement at 24 Denmark Street. David was not to remain an editor for long, and I soon had to promote him, too, to director. Peter Fuller had also proved his sterling worth, and it delighted me to give an old friend from Walton Studios days a leg up to become a film cameraman alongside Ian Craig. It was a good time to make a career in television.

One of television's staple offerings (as it still is) was old cinema films. They had been made to whatever length the story dictated, but television had rigid "time-slots" to work to. We also ran films slightly faster – at twenty-five frames per second – than in the cinema, where it was twenty-four frames per second (I wonder how many people notice that, as a result, their favourite film stars sound a bit squeaky on television?). The film department's task was to prepare the films to fit the transmission schedule. "Big" films that lasted an hour and three quarters had somehow to be pared down till they ran for only sixty minutes. There also had to be regular interruptions for the commercials to be spliced in. We became quite adept at this – only occasionally ending up with something that made no sense.

Nevertheless, various myths went the rounds. When we ran the Powell and Pressburger war film, *One Of Our Aircraft Is Missing*, someone remarked that by the time we finished with it a whole squadron had disappeared.

Some local viewers assumed that all these films were made by us. When we showed *The Drum*, the Korda epic about the Northwest Frontier of India, someone phoned in and asked, "What par' o' Norfolk was that made in, then?" (On the other hand, some viewers were sceptical that anything of what they saw really came from Norfolk – a belief that appeared to receive confirmation when one of our new announcers wished everyone, "Good night from everyone here in our studio in Cardiff".) I was Duty Executive that evening and had to take the flack.

Film, from outside or shot by us, made up only a small part of the station's output. The flagship offering was *The Midday Show*, hosted by a very young Susan Hampshire. It went out each lunchtime, and was a mishmash of musical items and "general interest" bits and pieces in which local worthies were invited to take part. Sometimes their contributions were alarming.

Steve McCormack slammed down the phone one day, grabbed me by the arm, and raced me to the Viewing Room with an ashen face.

'Christ!' he gasped, pointing at what was happening in front of the cameras in the studio below. A party of ladies from a local Women's Institute was demonstrating old Norfolk folk dances.

'We *think* this is a fertility dance,' their chairlady was saying, 'the "Broom Dance"…' The WI ladies were mounted astride broom handles and hopping round the studio with the priapic poles jutting skywards from between their legs.

Steve hammered on the glass window of the adjoining control room and shouted to the programme director, 'Get them off!'

The band struck up a pop tune...

Following *The Violent Years*, George More O'Ferrall's drama department, based in London, produced many more excellent one-off dramas for the national network over the next ten years. Most featured important stars, Alec Guiness, Richard Todd, Anna Neagle, Dame Sybil Thorndyke, Margaret Rutherford and Louis Jourdan – some from Hollywood, like John Ireland and Dawn Addams. We also had our own "bathing beauty" and "quiz" shows. Weather was a vital topic in a largely agricultural area. Our "weather man", Michael Hunt, had been a wartime RAF meteorologist and looked every inch the part, with his large "Flying Officer Kite" moustache. One could easily imagine him standing in front of an assembly of young pilots: 'There's ten-tenth cloud over Hamburg at present, but a break in the cloud around 23:59 hours should give you time to make your bomb runs, while giving you cover from flack on your way home...' Michael was stocky and running to fat, but he received more fan mail and proposals of marriage than any other presenter! He produced his local forecasts from mysterious equipment he kept in the upper reaches of Anglia House (I suspect that much of the data was begged from former comrades at the local RAF station).

Mary was pregnant and the race was on to find a home fit for a child to be brought up in. We had no capital to speak of, but assumed we could get a mortgage, and my old army bank, Lloyds Cox & Kings, had pledged a loan for any balance required. House buying was entirely new to us and we had no idea what kind of home we should like. Newly built little boxes did not appeal to us, or the thought of living in a provincial town. A little thatched cottage deep in the country caught our eye, but it had already been sold. It seemed the sort of thing we should like.

We found our ideal because of an accident. While we were filming the opening programme, I had shot a scene of the film unit piling into a minibus and speeding to a news assignment. The van had a sliding door that was left open and Ian Craig, sitting in front, was holding on to the windscreen pillar to steady himself when the driver suddenly threw on the brakes. The impetus made door slide forward, crushing Ian's fingers.

One result was that he was unable to drive to his home in London at the weekend. To cheer him up, Mary and I took him for an outing in the country on Sunday afternoon. Returning to Norwich, on almost deserted country roads, we passed a large thatched farmhouse that appeared to be unoccupied. I stopped and called at a neighbouring cottage and enquired of the aged occupant if he knew anything about it.

'Would that be the White 'orse?' he parried, with the caginess we had come to expect of Norfolk people. Eventually he owned up. The house – *if there was one* – belonged to the squire 'up at the 'all' – Morton Hall. A telephone box nearby had a directory inside it (happy days), and I put in a call to Morton Hall. Its occupant, John Berney, answered and told me he did indeed own the house, which was formerly the White Horse inn. He had moved a geriatric lady tenant out to an old people's home the previous day. He was unlikely to want to sell, he said. I left my Anglia phone number in case he changed his mind.

The next morning he called me and said I should contact his agent if I wanted the house. We were eventually offered it for £2,250 – not cheap at the time for something with no electricity, water drawn from a well, and a "thunder box" in a garden privy. A local builder told us we would need another £2,000 to make it habitable. Perhaps understandably, the building societies did not fall over themselves to offer a mortgage. A friendly estate agent suggested that we look for a "solicitor's mortgage". I had never heard of such a thing, but when we called at the Dickensian office of one of Norwich's most eminent law firms, a partner opened a tin box in his strong room and produced all but a thousand of the required £4,250, to be loaned at a rate of four percent. Cox & Kings came up with a loan of the rest.

The house sat on the edge of an open field, so John Berney met us on site on Saturday morning to mark out our boundaries. I thought we had bought a house with a small front and back garden, but he led out across the field towards a large oak tree. I thought he was never going to stop. After marking out the boundaries, we found we had bought nearly an acre of garden, plus an adjoining two storey thatched building (known, mysteriously, as "the reading room"), two cart-sheds, and a flint-walled pound with another shed. We had become Norfolk landowners.

17

IT WAS spring and the weather was balmy. Harry Aldous and his wife, Ann, came out to Morton to see what we had bought, and we sat under a hedgerow bordering the garden, eating wild strawberries and pondering the twist of fate that had transported us from vibrant London and the glitzy film industry to rural torpor and Toy Town Telly.

John Berney invited us to dinner at Morton Hall – 'Don't bother to dress on this occasion...' Our hostess was Berney's wife, Jill, who was also a consultant-anaesthetist in the Norwich hospital. Their house was a gracious Regency building that been in the family since 1815. The other dinner guests were a local stockbroker and his wife. We were moving in "county" circles.

We found a genial, fatherly local builder and embarked on the task of creating our first real home, learning for the first time the pitfalls of restoring an ancient historic building. But at least there were few planning laws or building regulations at the time. The work took much longer than we had expected and went well over budget. But there were bonuses, such as the discovery behind the Victorian grate of a magnificent arched eighteenth-century brick fireplace, large enough for an inglenook.

I drove out from Norwich one lunchtime to check on progress. The builder's foreman drew me aside with a worried expression – was I aware that the house was haunted? He had heard it in the village post office. To confirm the rumour, one of his men would not work there without his dog beside him. He had seen "a man in a top hat" emerge from the wall of the cellar and disappear through the wall opposite. Mary insisted on having the cellar filled in.

We had spent considerably more than expected, but our splendid builder agreed to accept payment for the overspend by instalments. Work was just about completed when Mary went into the local maternity home. I asked if I could be present at the birth. The matron looked horrified. 'This is woman's private hour,' she said. I resisted the temptation to observe that it wasn't so private nine months before. Mary returned with our first son, Timothy, to a very austere White Horse Farm. Life had really begun in the heart of Norfolk's countryside.

We were forced to revise our opinion of the builder's talk of ghosts on our first night in residence, when we were awakened in the small hours by a violent banging on the back door, followed by a woman's voice below, calling 'Is anybody there?' There was no one below or within half a mile of the house. We got used to strange, unexplained happenings over the next twenty years, but as we told ourselves, a lot of people had lived there over the centuries, with every sort of drama, and they had probably left something of themselves on the old building.

For me, at least, life at White Horse Farm was idyllic. Mary had to get used to total immersion in a new, unfamiliar way of life, besides coping with a baby who was weakly to begin with. For the time being, she was compelled to put her acting career to one side. The neighbours were welcoming and generous, and we made friendships that were to endure for years to come. Reggie and Stella Tricker lived in the farmhouse across the road. They farmed the surrounding land as tenants of John Berney. Their son Tom was married to Maureen, and they had small children. Down the road was another young farmer named Michael Jones, and he and his wife Dorothy also had a young family. A mile or two away, Darryl and Silvia Oram grew fields of daffodil bulbs. They too had young children. So Mary found people with interests and problems in common.

We made other lasting friendships in the neighbouring area. The Frys lived not far away at Booton, in a former rectory. Alan was a "boffin" who did mysterious scientific and mechanical things in his barn, and Marianne was a jolly mother of three children who were roughly the same age as ours. We did not dream that the eldest, Stephen, would one day become a world celebrity. The Halletts lived in another old rectory at Lyng. Nick was a former soldier, in the Norfolk Regiment, and we had much in common. He was also the Independent Broadcasting Authority's regional officer, so I shared professional interests with him as well. Oddly enough, I did not make many close personal friends with Anglia people, though I had a good rapport with everyone, and especially liked being with my film colleagues.

Not long after the dinner at Morton Hall we decided to respond with a housewarming party. Unfamiliar with the Norfolk class situation, we invited the Berneys from the hall, together with the Tricker family. Tom Tricker, indeed, was only a lowly tractor driver. There were initial moments when everyone looked at everyone else, wondering what on earth they were there for, but before long they were gossiping like old friends. We learned later that everyone round us was related in some way; one had only to look round the local cemetery to see the same names recurring again and again. Before the introduction of the railways allowing ordinary people to travel there must have been an enormous amount of inbreeding throughout the land.

I was reminded of this when I attended a reception at Anglia House for local dignitaries. The Chief Constable assured me that I would not need to lock my doors at night. 'Norfolk has only two types of crime,' he said, 'not renewing car tax discs, and fathers getting at their daughters. In that, Norfolk Assizes are second only to Bodmin in Cornwall...'

Norfolk people proudly boast that "we du different", and we certainly did think our neighbours lived up to that principle. We took on an aged gardener named Prime. He told us that he only left the village every two years, when he went into Norwich to buy a pair of boots.

'Have you never been out of Norfolk?' I asked him.

'Oh ar,' he replied, 'Oi were with Lawrence of Arabia...'

With that he got on with his digging.

Norfolk in those days was virtually feudal. Everyone kept to one's place – but knew everyone else's business. Even Lord Townshend played that game. One day he said to me, 'I see you've made a lawn in front of your house.' He passed White Horse Farm every day in his Bentley, en route to and from Raynham Hall.

Unaware that his employers' confidence in him was draining away, Stephen McCormack fixed up another major documentary, this time about the local army battalion, the 1st East Anglians – "The Vikings" – which was on active service in Germany.

Germany had been divided into four regions after the war, under the control of the four "powers" – Britain, France, the USA and Soviet Russia. The atmosphere between the Soviets and the Western allies was poisonous, and the Cold War had reached a new low. Germany's pre-war capital, Berlin, was itself divided into four "Control Zones", policed by the same nations' forces. It happened to be in the Russian area of Germany, so the British, American and French forces in the city found themselves deep inside territory controlled by the "enemy", and a hundred miles from the nearest point of the western sphere of influence, from where any reinforcements could be expected. I called my film about the British garrison *Encircled Force.*

I flew to Berlin's Templehof aerodrome, in the centre of the city, to begin production. I had my usual unit with me, headed, of course, by Ian Craig. We stayed with the army, and it was nice to feel "at home" in an officers' mess again. The general, moreover, was a "Royal Scot" and had been a friend of Roddy Leckie Ewing's.

It was the first of several fascinating visits to the "enemy city" of my childhood. One evening, after a day's filming, an Anglian officer suggested that we all go out "on the town". As we were parking our cars in one of Berlin's gloomy backwaters, we were hailed by a large man standing in the doorway of his shop. It appeared to be a "curio" shop, with a shrunken head decorating the window.

The shopkeeper announced that he was an American, and had been one of Al Capone's gang in the nineteen-thirties. We accepted his invitation to join him inside, and he took us through to the back room where he lost no time opening bottles. His tiny wife then put in an appearance, but was quickly despatched to prepare spaghetti. We spent a hilarious evening listening to our host's tall stories, and when we eventually made our departure, he made me promise to bring some English tea the next time I was in Berlin.

The following morning, the Anglian officer and I were summoned to British headquarters in the former Olympic Stadium. It seemed we were in deep trouble. The chief intelligence officer, a gentleman with the unlikely name of "Crash" Abbott, interrogated us about our host of the previous evening, who was suspected of being a double agent, working for both the Western Powers and the Russians. The Anglian officer was warned to stay away from him. As I was a civilian, the order did not extend to me, so when I returned to Berlin a few weeks later, this time accompanied by Mary, I called at the curio shop to deliver the promised tea. Our host's wife put her head round the door and accepted the gift but did not invite us in. I asked my army friends what had happened, and was told that the mysterious shopkeeper had disappeared.

The regiment was scheduled for a training exercise on Luneburg Heath in West Germany. This meant moving out of Berlin into Soviet-controlled East Germany, then down the "corridor" – the autobahn connecting Berlin with the so-called "Free World". Mary and I travelled in the rear of an army staff car. When we arrived at the Russian checkpoint I asked if I could film it. A charming young Russian soldier smilingly agreed – as long as I pointed the camera in the opposite direction. He gave Mary a gallant salute.

I wanted to end the film with a dramatic scene that would vividly convey the vulnerability of the tiny British contingent, marooned deep in potentially hostile territory. In the event of a real war breaking out, they would face the first onslaught, and have little chance of extricating themselves without heavy losses.

The dividing line between the British and Russian sectors was at the Brandenburg Gate, and I decided to film the regimental band parading in front of it and marching down the Tiergarten playing the regimental march, *Rule Britannia*. I wanted to film it from a helicopter, "tracking" back before them, and a massive American troop-carrying helicopter was provided for us, piloted by a young army "lootenant". He landed it beside the Reichstag building and Ian Craig and I climbed in with the camera, to sit in the doorway with our legs dangling over the side.

In order to get the shot, our pilot would need to turn the aircraft side on to the road, and hover like that as he backed away before the band. We took off, and the "lootenant" manoeuvred the unwieldy craft round until it straddled the roadway, hovering about ten feet above the ground. To my dismay, I saw that we almost filled the space between the streetlights. The tail-rotor whirled a foot or so away from a very solid object that could have brought instant death to all concerned. The "lootenant" knew how to fly the monster, however. I had arranged with the bandmaster that the shot would begin when I waved a handkerchief. The band then marched off towards us, and we pulled back, gaining height, to widen the scene until the symbol of British presence was a tiny dot surrounded by the panorama of divided – largely hostile – Berlin. It made a spectacular and stirring end to the film.

Encircled Force was transmitted on Friday, June 16th, and was well received. It was the first time since I had joined Anglia that I had a real chance to show what I could do, and the programme restored my reputation after the *Battle Formation* fiasco. The Royal Anglian Regiment was also well pleased, and when the battalion was posted back to England, not long afterwards, the officers gave me a superb – alcoholic – dinner in the mess. They had a tradition of inviting guests to take a turn at conducting the band, and I was touched and honoured when it struck up *Hieland Laddy*, the regimental march of The Black Watch.

ITV transmitted sixty hours of programming per week, of which eight or nine were produced by the regional stations, primarily for local viewers. It was black and white, of course – colour was still some years in the future. Most of the film output was five- to ten-minute general interest "filmlets", for inclusion in the daily and nightly "magazine programmes". Nearly everything included an "into camera", a brief scene in which the reporter on the spot spoke directly to the viewer. The early presenters were usually former journalists who by and large recited what they would have written in newspapers in their earlier days. Often they came over badly, either through unattractive appearance or dull delivery, and the BBC and ITV turned more and more to fresh-faced youngsters who could be trained in the developing art of television. Newly graduated university students, schoolteachers, even actors. We put out word at Oxford and Cambridge, offering undergraduates a test attachment during the "long vacation".

I don't really know who chose our candidates. I was too busy out on the road filming. A succession of aspiring TV stars were sent to me, and I did what I could to teach them how to present themselves, and their material. (Looking at today's presenters, I wonder who it is tells them they have to do everything walking, starting their piece half a mile away and talking with their hands held out, palms upward, in that daft "imploring" gesture. And they *still* don't know that the modern microphone is sensitive enough not to need being thrust up the interviewee's nose.)

The first trainee problem child I recall with clarity did not come from the universities. He appeared in a pork-pie hat, affecting a jaunty manner that reminded me of the music hall comedian, Max Miller. A "cheeky chappie". It was immediately obvious that he was a vulgarian in the classic Fleet Street mould. We went out to film an archaeological excavation on the North Norfolk coast, being conducted by the eminent and very touchy director of Norwich Castle Museum.

Before I knew what was happening, our lad had leapt into an open grave and grabbed up a skull.

'I'll say something like this –' he told me, holding up the skull '– "alas poor Yorick, I knew him well – well, actually I didn't know him, and this is a prehistoric skull, and we are at an archae – "'

'– Hold it!' I broke in, seeing the museum director's horrified expression. 'If I were you I'd get out of the excavation. And don't you think that kind of thing is a bit silly?'

Later, when Lord Townshend saw the result, he declared that our "cheeky-chappie" was not in the Anglia image.

Another aspiring presenter also attracted Lord Townshend's disapproval. I was told that he was waiting for me at Norwich railway station. I should try him out conducting "vox pops" – the television term for off-the-cuff interviews with passers-by.

I found a thin young man with a curious haircut and a nasal voice who introduced himself as David Frost. He was no matinee idol, but at least had plenty of cheek in front of the camera, as he waylaid people coming off the trains. Over the next week or two, I took young Frost out and about on several filming forays. He knew the area well, as his father was a Methodist minister in a small Suffolk town. His main talent seemed to me to be abounding enthusiasm and energy, but these qualities were not sufficient to win the chairman's approval. He disliked Frost's appearance and lower-class accent.

'In my opinion this man has no future in television,' Lord Townshend pronounced, in a memo that, I believe, still rests in the company's files. (He could never have imagined that the lad would eventually become *Sir* David, confidant of prime ministers, presidents and film stars, and son-in-law of a duke.)

Another young man on the university scheme was more in the accepted mould. In any case, David Dimbleby's father, Richard, was a legendary BBC figure, and Anglia was flattered to have his son for training. I enjoyed working with him. He was at Christ Church, Oxford, and knew Mary's father. We made one or two little films, and he was clearly a natural. However, David had other and bigger fish to fry. After he graduated, he naturally joined the BBC.

One of the most delightful presenters to work with was gentle, cultured Bob Wellings. He had been a schoolteacher, and had an instinctive talent for communication. We made a little gem together, a half-hour film about Sir Christopher Wren's library at Trinity College, Cambridge. The highlight was an elegiac piece on the character of students, written by me and spoken by Bob beside a bust of Byron. The college Fellows were enraptured by the film, and the Senior Bursar wrote me a charming letter, saying that "both Wren and Byron would have approved wholeheartedly if they could have switched on at three p.m. on 1st January." Praise indeed!

Bob accompanied the unit when we took a party of elderly Great War veterans to visit the trenches of Flanders. It was an emotional experience. During a break in filming at the vast Tyne Cot war cemetery, Bob and I unwisely peeped into the visitors' book in the Gate House. 'Christ!' gasped Bob beside me, tears streaming down his face. An entry read – *Australia. A son sees his father for the first time.* On the way home across Belgium, Bob and I got well and truly drunk.

The other recollection I have of Bob, before he left Anglia for a long and successful career at the BBC, is when the film unit spent the night in a "haunted house". It was a derelict moated Elizabethan manor house, reputedly haunted by a woman at a spinning wheel.

After an eventless night, Bob interviewed a psychic "expert", standing either side of a gaping window with the dawn breaking beyond.

'The house is not haunted,' pronounced the expert.

We transmitted the programme two evenings later.

The moment it ended, Anglia's switchboard began ringing. Nine callers, from various parts of the region, reported that they had seen a ghost – a hooded monk – between Bob and the expert. I took the film into our preview-theatre and ran it. No sign of a monk... It was a strange enough incident to warrant re-running the clip during the following evening's local news. We did not say what the viewers claimed to have seen, but as soon as it was shown, the switchboard was jammed. Hundreds of people phoned in. All had seen a hooded monk.

18

AUBREY BUXTON was a keen and knowledgeable countryman, and had ambitions that Anglia should produce wildlife programmes. The only natural-history programmes were on the BBC. They were presented by Peter Scott, the son of the Antarctic explorer, and were rather dull reels of silent film, with *ad lib* off-screen commentary delivered with copious "ers" and "ums" and uncomfortable silences. Aubrey Buxton thought he could do better.

He took me out to the Norfolk Broads with a film unit, and we put together a half-hour programme about the shooting lodge on Hickling Broad once used by King George V. The programme was called *Countryman*. It proved very popular with our largely rural viewers and began a series that went out regularly during the early part of 1962.

Aubrey was confident that it could attract a wider audience, and he persuaded the network companies to give it a try. The reaction was sufficiently encouraging for Anglia to form a specialist unit, based in the company's London premises, to produce an ambitious series of programmes that would deal with the vanishing natural world. Aubrey christened it *Survival*. He invited me to take charge, but it seemed obvious that I would have to relocate to London, and the prospect of giving up our delightful new life in the country was not attractive. Mary and I were just getting ourselves established in White Horse Farm, and we wanted Timothy to grow up in pleasant rural surroundings. So I asked to be excused, though I directed one or two of the early episodes.

While I lived my exciting, varied life, Mary was increasingly isolated in the thatched farmhouse with our baby son. She had to make do with our Scottie, Mac, and a succession of Labradors for company. There were also three geese, Tip, Tap and Top, for a while – this venture came to an end when the dominant male challenged me for mastery of the household and we had to find them a new home with someone who promised not to eat them. Our unusual and attractive home brought visits from Mary's parents, my father and aunt, Thelma and Paul and other friends. There were classic "white Christmases", with the house full to bursting.

The following two years were busy. I had the film department to run – ordering film stock, seeing the News was edited in time, checking expense sheets, interviewing and recruiting additional staff. There were now 325 employees in Norwich and London, and my department had become much bigger. Tom Marshall's prediction that the days of film were numbered, and that I had better not count on a long career with Anglia, seemed fanciful.

Nevertheless, revolutionary developments were taking place in video engineering. It had at last become possible to *record* pictures to a reasonable standard, on enormous rolls of four-inch magnetic tape. Our engineers went further and built an Outside Broadcast facility, consisting of a single video camera connected by cable to a recording machine installed in a motorcoach (known in the television industry as a "scanner"). Because it could only shoot one view at a time, the unit was called Cyclops, after the mythical one-eyed monster. There was no known electronic process for joining scenes up, or editing them, but one of Anglia's brightest technicians devised a crude solution. He discovered that by sprinkling iron filings on to the tape, the "wave-form" of the shot was revealed – and more importantly the exact place where it ended. Using a razor blade, he carefully cut the tape at that point and stuck it to the beginning of the following scene with cellotape. If he was out by as much as a millimetre there would be "frame roll" (when the bottom of the picture would roll up to the top – as often happened in television's infant days). However, he became very expert and the result more often than not was very acceptable. He was probably the industry's first "video editor", and ought to have become a millionaire!

I took an immediate interest in Cyclops, because it seemed to me that it was more like filming than conventional television production, when a number of cameras were used simultaneously. Moreover there was an obvious advantage over film, in being able to see one's rushes more or less immediately.

Steve approved of my idea to devise a soap opera using the new medium. As a change from television's fixation with the "Met", it would feature a rural police force. At the end of 1961, with the enthusiastic cooperation of Essex County Police, based at Chelmsford, I made a pilot called *County Force*. We used film for the action sequences, but recorded the exterior acted scenes with the electronic equipment. I cast my old friend Hector Ross in the lead, together with a veteran film star who lived in Suffolk, Jean

Kent. They were both fine actors, with years of experience in film. Hector, however, was showing signs of physical degeneration. (Perhaps it was the cancer that was to kill him, not many years later. His devoted wife June died a week after him. I never knew why. Perhaps it was a genuine case of "a broken heart". I lost two cherished friends.)

Although we were able to broadcast the pilot programme, *County Force* never made it to the screen as a series. The actors' trade union, Equity, chose that moment to call a strike throughout ITV, and by the time we were able to resume production, the BBC had beaten us to it, with a similar series about a provincial police force called *Z Cars*.

Although Harry Aldous and David Kenten were kept very busy, I still directed much of the film myself. Among the programmes I directed was a weekly series called *Shooting Stars,* which was presented by the *Daily Mirror* film correspondent, Donald Zec. Donald was a small, rather wizened man, with a sardonic sense of humour who had become a great favourite of the countless stars he had interviewed. This gave him outstanding access to those currently making the headlines. Each week we interviewed stars – often at work on their films – Steve McQueen, William Holden, Peter Finch and Peter Ustinov.

I also directed a full-length film featuring the comic Norman Wisdom, at his home in Hampshire. I had a problem with this, because although it was meant to be a portrait of the star's personal life, Norman tried to make it relentlessly funny, and I found that his sense of humour was not mine. When we arrived in his village, we found him waiting in the middle of the road, dressed in his "gump" suit. He then raced off ahead of our car, frantically waving for us to follow. Ho ho! However, although I did not find him funny, enough people did not share my opinion. We shed a metaphorical tear together, though, over what might have been, had he done the Benny Lynch film.

I also experienced a bit of *déjà vu* when I visited Peter Ustinov on the set of *Billy Budd*, which he was directing. We both wondered if our "anarchist" comedy would have been any good. I found myself surprised when I watched Ustinov at work. He seemed to me to have no idea how to direct a film. I ached to take over. My instinct seemed somewhat borne out when the film turned out a flop.

We were very excited when we were offered an interview with the superstar Sophia Loren. She was coming to London, with her husband, producer Carlo Ponti, to make a film at Pinewood, and the studio's publicity chief promised to make her available, exclusively to us, immediately on her arrival at Heathrow. The airport PR people did not have a suitable venue, so I persuaded the most expensive of the restaurants to let us use one of its private dining rooms.

We arrived from Norwich in good time, with a larger than usual crew to handle the lighting and 35mm camera equipment. From the window I saw Miss Loren's 727 landing, and we prepared for her to appear in the next few minutes. Instead we were kept waiting. Then we received word that the star had been offered to the BBC for a live insert in the 6 p.m. news. I looked up a TV set hanging from the ceiling, and saw the gorgeous Sophia Loren being greeted by a female newscaster. To my horror, I heard the bitchy reporter say, 'Miss Loren, you look tired. Don't you feel well?'

The interview that followed was awkward and embarrassing, and I was not surprised when we received a message that Miss Loren had left for her hotel. Carlo Ponti was gracious enough to come and apologise. He even offered to let us film his wife "in the bath" the next day. That never materialised, and we were left with an expensive shambles.

It is perhaps surprising that Stephen McCormack lasted as long as he did. His unwillingness to plan anything, and penchant for creating chaos, even where there was none before, became more than the company could tolerate. In the three years since we went on the air, the company had become more professional, and the proprietors – Lord Townshend especially – had learned a thing or two. So poor Steve was given his marching orders. No doubt a generous parting gift was included. I was amazed when he told me that he had no idea what to do next. I took him to meet my former employers at the Film Producers Guild, but nothing came of it. He subsequently drifted from one job to another, each less important than the one before, and was last heard of as a doorman at Madame Tussaud's waxworks. He died a year or two later, when it was revealed that he was a good deal older than any of us had suspected.

The next person to leave the company was Michael Seligman, who had brought me to Anglia. His was an amicable departure. Michael had outside business interests and wanted to set up his own film studio and production company. Mary and I were sorry to see him go, as he had become a staunch ally – and godfather to our son Timothy.

No Programme Controller was appointed to take Stephen McCormack's place. Instead, a new post was created, that carried less power than Steve had enjoyed. On the other hand, it went to a man with a formidable reputation. Arthur Clifford had been one of the founders of Independent Television News.

Clifford was a very large man with a huge reservoir of energy. It frequently boiled over, and his office had to be provided with a regular supply of telephones, to replace the ones he hurled at the door or through the window. The principal cause of his ire was the wretched "Programme Planning Committee", which made all decisions about what programmes should be produced. The weekly meetings were held in London, because its leading figure was John Woolf. As far as I know, Woolf never came to Norwich in all the time he was a director of the company. Apart from him, the committee consisted exclusively of Anglia's gentlemen proprietors. (*Everyone I meet has two professions – their own and film producer* – Alexander Korda...)

Despite this, under Arthur Clifford's influence (which was to be all too short-lived) Anglia became more professional, and a number of programme strands were begun that would define the company's reputation in the future. In particular – as one would expect – the News changed from a parish magazine to a first class local service.

Anglia became a far more important broadcaster when a new transmitter mast was erected at Belmont in Lincolnshire in 1965. For the first time, north Norfolk was able to get a good ITV service. Anglia's signal also penetrated into Nottinghamshire, and – most significantly – South and East Yorkshire, including the city of Hull. There was immediate controversy. What was a crucial gain for Norfolk's King's Lynn was greeted with dismay in the north. We responded by establishing a News bureau in Hull, and began taking an interest in affairs on either side of the River Humber.

It became apparent that the journalists were in the ascendant. I thought this a not entirely welcome trend. It seemed to me that they saw things in newspaper terms – words came first and pictures were an add-on. Only there to brighten things up. In contrast, I thought of television as, first and foremost, a *pictorial* medium, and I was amazed at how little journalists and news editors valued pictures. A film unit would arrive back in the early afternoon with ten minutes or so of excellent footage. By the time it emerged from the processing machine and arrived in the cutting room, the news staff would be in a frenzy over the approaching deadline. They would view only a minute or two of the reel and select a couple of shots from the beginning before rushing back to their typewriters. The rest went into the waste bin. The cameramen learned to shoot what they thought was the most important scene first, on the front of the roll.

As far as my own fortunes were concerned, I was about to direct the series that set the course for most of my subsequent television career.

The Ancient Britons was a pet project of Anglia's archaeologist board member, Glyn Daniel. He proposed an ambitious series about the earliest inhabitants of these islands. Important prehistoric monuments all over the country would be filmed, many for the first time, and the presenter would be a distinguished Cambridge archaeologist named Doctor Brian Hope Taylor.

By an odd chance, the chairman of London's network company, Associated Rediffusion, at the time was Paul

Adorian (he had been head of Redifon when I made the flight simulator film). Adorian was a keen amateur archaeologist, and he agreed to transmit the series nationally. However, Rediffusion would have overall editorial control via one of its senior producers.

I was appointed director of the project, but not before a substantial amount of work on the script had been done by Dr Hope Taylor and the Rediffusion man, a current affairs specialist with an unconcealed scepticism of academics in general, and archaeologists in particular. Hope Taylor detested him.

Fortunately, Brian Hope Taylor and I formed an instant liking for each other, and so began a close collaboration that was to continue for many projects in the future.

Our immediate problem was what to do about Rediffusion's current affairs specialist, who we suspected had been assigned to the project to give him something to do. It was clear to me that an important series could not succeed with two of its principal people at each other's throats. The solution was to free Rediffusion's man to concentrate on other projects that interested him, by allowing him to take the credit as *The Ancient Britons'* producer while Brian and I actually made the programmes.

The scripts and the general thrust of the series emerged as we were actually shooting. Hope Taylor and I worked long into the night in the hotels where we were on location, throwing ideas at each other and generally enjoying an exciting creative experience.

It seemed to me that the script, as first devised, lacked any strong line. I did not think it enough just to say, "This is what the Ancient Britons were like – weren't they interesting?" There were too many similar worthy, but flabby and complacent programmes drivelling out from the small regional companies. Brian and I saw that we could construct a more interesting and meaningful theme. The series should be a study in depth of an ancient people – the Britons – seen through the eyes of another ancient people – the Romans. In this way we would bring both peoples vividly back to life. We would also demonstrate that our remote ancestors were not quaint sub-humans (if not cave-dwellers, as many people evidently thought) but were essentially similar to ourselves.

In recognition of how little most people knew about the Ancient Britons, we gave our series a more intriguing title *Who Were The British?*

We may have been the first television producers to use modern visual metaphors to describe ancient events. To emphasise the strong, ever-present sub-theme, that the study of the past helps us understand the present, I placed Brian Hope Taylor in a sort of Roman "Battle Of Britain ops-room", with a plotting table on which he moved symbols about, like the WAAF girls in wartime newsreels, as he described the Romans marching across Britain subjugating tribe after tribe.

Computer animation had not yet been invented. The kind of reconstructions we see today, complete with artificial people walking around digitally generated ancient cities, were not only impossible, but unimaginable. *We* conjured up ancient scenes and sounds by suggestion, with a heavy dose of imagination required of the viewers. Who can say that it was less effective than modern techniques? It might even be said that today's over-explicit reconstructions detract from the romance of the remote past.

19

THE FIRST programme in our series had a brief introduction by Glyn Daniel. He had to smuggle us into his room overlooking "the backs" in St John's College for me to film him, because Cambridge University disapproved of frivolous activities like television.

Anglia's board threw itself behind the series without reservation, and came up with the necessary extra finance to send us to Rome – a brave decision from a company whose only responsibility was to depict the lives and activities of local people. Rediffusion's engineers did not approve of 16mm film, so we had to hire 35mm equipment. The large, heavy, "blimped" Arriflex camera required an extra member of the unit, but we still set out on our adventure with only six members, including Hope Taylor and myself – a director of photography (Ian Craig), camera operator, sound recordist, electrician, and PA – my regular, cheery Annie Balmforth.

I chipped in the extra cash to take Mary and Timothy to Rome, too, and in mid March we set out for Italy – by train, because Brian Hope Taylor hated air travel.

Filming began in the Coliseum. We had no trouble getting permission, and the authorities closed the site off from the public for a few hours while we worked – unthinkable in these days, when television crews from all over the world line up for access to such places. I set up a spectacular shot looking down into the arena from the top of the seating terraces, and Brian perched on a rail in the foreground and talked:

'This is the Wembley, the White City, the Madison Square Garden of ancient Rome...'

I thrill to the memory. We had a television star on our hands!

The creative buzz grew daily. We had the Imperial Forum to ourselves, for Brian to call up the shades of the people who walked and talked there two thousand years before. We went to Ostia Antiqua and "animated" the mosaics of galleys and elephants while Brian told us about the emperor Claudius, "drooling at the mouth" as he prepared his invasion of Britain.

Mary, Timothy and I stayed with the unit in the Albergo Nazionale, opposite the parliament building in the Piazza Colonna. Although it did not serve meals, the staff fussed over little Tim, bringing him enormous scrumptious apples. We ate equally delicious meals round the corner in a cosy *trattoria* called Piccola Roma. I wonder if it is still there. All that, with after-filming aperitifs ("Negronis" – gin, Campari, vermouth, slice of orange and soda) beside the Trevi fountain in the cool of the evening, made it a heavenly, never to be forgotten, location.

The following month's filming was spent in Britain. We went to Stonehenge, Avebury, Hadrian's Wall and the great hillfort known as Maiden Castle in Dorset, all of which I had never seen before. The most memorable locations were in the Orkney Islands, where we were the first people to film the Neolithic village of Skara Brae and the chambered tomb called Maes Howe.

It is a lot easier to get to the Orkneys these days than it was then. I had planned a tightly scheduled tour of the northern places we needed to film, beginning at Hadrian's Wall, then onwards to Edinburgh for some shots in the National Museum, after which we intended to fly to Stromness in the Orkneys. From there we would fly to Copenhagen to film the mummified body of a man who had died during the Iron Age, 2,400 years ago. I had booked a series of scheduled flights, but a bout of violent gales made mayhem of my arrangements. Orkney was reported to be especially wild and no airline was prepared to risk a flight there. A film unit is an expensive thing to be keeping idle, and in answer to my appeal the helpful airline clerk suggested chartering an aircraft. A desk along the hall was labelled "Strathallan Air Services", and a burly, bearded man sporting four gold rings on his sleeve was in attendance. The RAF wings on his chest, rather than the usual airline ones, invited confidence. He announced his name as Captain Peter Tunstall.

Yes, he said, he would be prepared to take us to Orkney. We must fly first to his headquarters in Perthshire, where he could get an up to date report of weather conditions further north. We walked out across a parking area jammed with redundant planes, until we came to a smart little blue and white Piper Aztec twin-engined aircraft. Something about the registration number on its tale, G-ARYG, rang a bell – as well it might, for I had flown in that plane several times before. Tunstall confirmed that it had formerly belonged to the Norwich Union Insurance company, and then the short-lived Norfolk airlines. It occurred to me that the craft must be rather long in the tooth, but it looked OK.

We packed our film equipment in the hold and climbed in, me in the right-hand co-pilot's seat alongside Tunstall. The winds did not seem too violent during the first ten minute hop, and our plane landed without incident in a clearing in the Strathallan forest. Tunstall – "call me Pete", he insisted – led me into a shed that served as his headquarters and made a few phone calls. Then we went outside and he scooped up a handful of light soil, which he tossed in the air. The result obviously satisfied him, because he said, 'OK – we go.'

The surrounding trees shielded the grass "runway" from the high winds but this also had a less welcome effect. There was nothing to help the heavily-laden aircraft lift off and gain height, and I shut my eyes as the treetops raced towards us. Somehow we cleared them, though when we eventually arrived at our destination we noticed foliage in our undercarriage.

It was only a short flight, but wildly bumpy, and the wings were all over the place in a vicious crosswind as we made our approach and touched down at Stromness. The airport's fire engines raced down the runway alongside us.

As we climbed out into the teeth of the gale I saw that all the other airplanes on the airfield were tethered by their wingtips with guy ropes. We rode to the terminal building in the fire engines.

The Stromness Hotel was amazed to see us – and I was amazed to see the manager, who I had met before when he had visited our mutual friend Robin Steele at The Covenanters' Inn. He clearly thought a celebration was called for, and at dinner that night he produced a "special menu". I still have it – it offers Melon Seed Cocktail or Tripe Soup followed by a choice of Boiled Cod Heads,

Scragged Chicken Neck à la King, Liver and Kidney Hash, or Cold Rabbit with Myxomatosis Sauce and Fresh Garden Refuse Salad, served with Rissole Potatoes, Dressed Docken Leaves and Garden Pea Shells. To follow was Bread Pudding and Sour Milk, Leftover Trifle or Sillock Savouries, washed down with Coffee Dregs. My PA, cheery and trusting Annie Balmforth, actually ordered from it.

Pete Tunstall retaliated the following night. He had picked up the skull of an otter during the day, and placed it in his soup, before loudly complaining to the waitress.

'I've had some things in my soup during my time, but this is too much.'

The pretty little Orcadian waitress was not put out.

'Och – it wasnay there when I sairved it, sir,' she replied, whisking it away.

After dinner we all travelled into the far-flung interior of the island to a barn dance. It was an astonishing sight. As we approached the wooden building we could see it positively shaking from whatever was going on within. It was taking place in the upstairs of the building which was approached by a ladder in the centre of the floor, at the foot of which was the sergeant of police, being carried away mumbling incoherently by a bevy of jolly helpers. We climbed through a trapdoor into the large room. The noise was deafening. A cacophony of clumping feet, hysterical shouts, fiddle and accordion music.

It took only a couple of drinks to enter into the spirit of the thing. Pete Tunstall thought it the moment to tell me he had escaped several times from POW camps and ended up in Colditz. I learned in later years that he was a famous wartime celebrity.

I felt ghastly next morning. We were to film the interior of the massive burial mound called Maes Howe. The centre chamber was approached by a long passage too low to stand upright in. I could not face bending over and ordered Ian Craig to film it on his own...

The gales had died down when we flew onwards to Denmark to film the mummified man in the Silkeborg museum, near Aarhus. I was surprised when the curator handed me a head – it was all that remained of the famous "Tollund Man". I held the blackened, leathery object as Ian flooded it with light. We took several shots when I noted to my alarm that the dead gentleman was perspiring.

'We're melting Tollund Man!' I cried.

The jolly curator smiled.

'Your lights have melted the wax in his skin,' he said. 'I'll give him a wash with hot water and he'll be quite all right.'

Before we returned to England, Pete flew us up a fjord. He turned the Aztec around, however, before going very far.

'You have to be very careful in these mountains that you do not run out of space to turn round,' he explained. 'You might not have enough height to fly yourself out over the tops.'

I was to remember those words a year or so later in another aircraft.

On the way home we ran into trouble. The Aztec's radio packed up, and Tunstall could not make contact with our destination – Newcastle – or get a fix on our position.

'You'll have to fly the plane while I work on the radio,' he told me.

I had "unofficially" flown planes before, but never a twin-engined one, with a vast panel of instruments. However:

'I have control,' I said and took charge.

I don't know if the film unit in the seats behind me knew what was going on.

The Aztec was pleasant to fly and in truth there was little to do, other than watching the artificial horizon and the turn and bank indicator. Pete tinkered with the radio for a quarter of an hour or so, then a voice crackled in my earphones.

'Hi Pete.'

It was an RAF plane in the air. The pilot conveyed our messages to Newcastle airport and we were out of trouble. Pete, however, was enjoying his rest and was content to leave me to fly the plane. He even had me begin the descent towards Newcastle until I felt the joke had lasted long enough. 'It's all yours,' I said and was not sorry when I heard him say, 'I have control.'

Pete Tunstall was a "swashbuckler" of the vintage World War II breed. His career – and that of Aztec G-ARYG – came to an end a year or two later. His sole passenger, strangely enough, was the owner of a rival airline, Logan Air. Millionaire builder William Logan's own aircraft were unavailable, and Pete was taking him home to Dingwall in Ross-shire. The Aztec hit a hillside on approach to Inverness and Logan was killed in the wreck. Pete got away with broken legs. I don't think he flew professionally again.

Just after Easter, 1966, Mary's father died very suddenly of a heart attack. He was just short of his seventy-first birthday. There was a sombre funeral service in Christ Church Cathedral conducted by the Dean. It was a very trying time. Mary was heavily pregnant, and on June 30th our second son, George, was born.

Two weeks before, *Who Were The British?* was previewed for the press in a small private cinema in Mayfair. A second preview was held on the 16th June in the Odeon Cinema, Haymarket, for members of the archaeological establishment. Glyn Daniel gave a brief address, in which he said that as Hope Taylor was the presenter and Forbes Taylor was the director it was a "tailor-made production". National transmission began on the evening of the 20th June (the northern ITV station, Tyne-Tees, demonstrating its confidence in serious programmes by airing it at twenty to eleven at night!). The programmes won a satisfyingly large audience, even though the national network lost its nerve after the first episode and followed Tyne-Tees' example, consigning the series to the wee small hours.

Despite that, *Who Were The British?* was widely praised, largely due to Brian Hope Taylor's instinctive grasp of the medium. But also because I too had found my natural *metiér*. I was nominated for a Bafta award (though it didn't materialise).

The academic establishment, which to us meant Cambridge, approved of our efforts (somewhat reluctantly, I suspected), and from then on the colleges ceased to be off-limits for our cameras. Glyn Daniel no longer had to smuggle us up to his rooms under cover of darkness.

This was the moment when I could have exploited the notice I was getting, and made a bid for something bigger than a job in a small provincial television company. A return to the film industry, perhaps. In fact, I was approached by the representative of a Hollywood studio, inviting me to go there on a trial basis. I considered my options, but in the end decided that my responsibility to my family made it too risky to make such a radical jump into the unknown.

In the November of 1966, the BBC announced the launch of a second channel, and applications for jobs were invited. I went to Cambridge to meet a BBC Appointments Officer (no "Board" this time), but it seemed I was too senior for anything on offer. It was a pity, because BBC2 went on to produce the sort of programme I was interested in. On the other hand, it relieved me of the problem of re-locating my home and family, with all that implied.

In 1967, the existing ITV franchises expired. Two or three companies lost their licences and new companies took their place. Anglia won a renewal of its contract for the following seven years. It was an occasion for several far reaching changes, including the departure of some of our middle managers, including our programme manager, Arthur Clifford, to more lucrative pastures at the new companies.

Over the years, our North Norfolk farmer, Dick Joice, had become increasingly important. Lord Townshend saw him as someone who had a shrewd finger on the pulse of the local viewers – as quite probably he had. The weekly *Farming Diary* programme had always played a leading role in our schedule, but Dick was interested in more than that. He was fascinated with antique agricultural and household ephemera, and had built up a large collection. "Bygones", he called them. A surprising result of the franchise shake-up was the appointment of Dick as Head of

Local Programmes. Many – perhaps most of us – thought that, whatever his talents as a genial programme presenter, he was not an instinctive manager or organiser. He could hardly be expected to refuse such a flattering prize, of course, but he soon became unhappy and lost some of his *bonhomie.* With it went a serious decline in his health.

There was also a change in my own position. My masters decided that administration was a waste of my time and talents and I should devote myself entirely to production. I was given a new title, Head of Documentaries and Adult Education, and my long-time assistant took over as Head of Films. The change brought to a fore a tension within me, one well known in the senior reaches of television. I enjoyed working in a creative role, but sensed (correctly, I believe) that the only way to achieve status and control one's own destiny was to be in management. It took me many years to resolve this dilemma, and of course, in the end there is no real solution.

I found myself with a new assistant, a charming bluestocking named Jean Burns. I blush to recall how I sounded off to her about Dick Joice's shortcomings as production head, not knowing that she and Dick had "become an item". She became Dick's second wife not long after. Whether she ever told Dick of my remarks I could only guess.

20

WHO WERE The British? had shown that serious subjects could also be entertaining, and reinforced Anglia's reputation for quality production. Brian Hope Taylor and I were encouraged to begin talking about the subjects we would like to work on together. An obvious choice was a sequel series that would take advantage of Brian's specialised knowledge of Anglo-Saxon archaeology. The themes explored in the earlier programmes, the relevance of past events to modern situations, could be re-visited, and the story begun in *Who Were The British?* carried forward into later Romano-British, Saxon, Viking and early Renaissance times – the so-called "Dark Ages".

Before I could embark on such a project another assignment came my way. Aubrey Buxton had developed his wildlife project, *Survival*, into a major success shown regularly throughout the network and indeed the world, including the USA – something rare for British television in those days.

Aubrey's friend, the Duke of Edinburgh, was a leading figure in the World Wildlife Fund, and Aubrey persuaded him to make a first ever television appearance, introducing a programme about the Galapagos Islands. Filming royals was unknown territory in those days, and Aubrey was apprehensive about the way film people would respond to the situation – especially how they would behave when interacting with the prince. For some reason, he had confidence in me, and invited me to direct the sequence. In doing so, he passed over *Survival*'s regular director.

I took the film unit down to the Natural History Museum in South Kensington, where the sequence was to be filmed the following day. As I began to rig the main dinosaur gallery, *Survival*'s producer-editor, Colin Willock, arrived and confronted me. The regular director was upset by my acceptance of the assignment, he told me, and was threatening to resign. I told Colin that I had not put myself forward for the job, and the decision had not been mine.

The *Survival* unit was a very close knit family, used to working with one another over many years, so I sought out Aubrey Buxton and said that although I was honoured to have been chosen, I thought that passing over the regular director in this way would be a blow to the unit's morale. Probably Aubrey had come to the same conclusion. He thanked me for making it easy to put the matter right. The filming with Prince Philip took place the next day, under the regular director, and went off very smoothly and amicably.

The favour I had done Aubrey stood me in good stead. Instead of having to make a detailed pitch to the dreaded Programme Planning Committee to be allowed to embark on a sequel to *Who Were The British?* I was able to make a direct appeal to Aubrey.

'Brian Hope Taylor and I want to make a major series all over Europe and the Middle East,' I said. 'We want to make it in colour, in readiness for the launch of the colour television service. We want to set off immediately on a research trip.'

'Then you'd better go,' Aubrey replied, with a smile.

Brian could only take a limited time away from his lecturing post at Cambridge, so we planned a lightning tour of the sites we intended to film – a round trip, beginning in Istanbul, then travelling to Syria to visit the desert ruins of Palmyra, back to Rome via Cairo, Ravenna for the Byzantine mosaics, Arles and Nîmes in France, then westward to Spain to see Cordoba and Segovia. It was a veritable "grand tour".

Because of Brian's fear of flying I planned the six-week expedition so that we could travel wherever possible by sea, rail or road. The first stage would be on a cruise ship from Venice, down the Adriatic to Greece and Turkey, when the ship's leisurely pace would allow us to work on the scripts.

We spent the night in London prior to joining the boat train to Dover, enjoying a farewell blow-out, on good old British steak-and-kidney pud, in Rule's Restaurant. Next morning we went to Victoria station to find, not one, but two ten-o'clock boat trains – one of them labelled *Golden Arrow*. For some reason we were booked on the other one, which left first. We arrived in Dover and boarded the cross-Channel ferry for Calais, where we were to catch the night sleeper to Venice. We would arrive in Venice the next morning, and have plenty of time to look at some important sites there, before boarding the ship for the evening departure for Greece.

To our consternation the ferry remained firmly tied up at the Dover quayside. Minutes went by. The scheduled departure time came and went. No explanation was forthcoming. It became clear that unless something happened fast, we would miss our connection in Calais. I found a Cook's representative, who explained. The Golden

Arrow had broken down. As it was a prestige train, with important passengers, the ferry would not leave until it arrived.

I pointed to the crowd of frustrated passengers crowding the ferry's deck and asked why we should all be compelled to miss our connections because of an unlucky few. My protest fell on deaf ears.

The Golden Arrow arrived hours later, and when we reached Calais our sleeper train had long since departed. The only alternative was to take a train to Paris, and catch a slow train south from there. This – we hoped – would get us to Venice with about thirty minutes to spare before our ship embarked. No time for sightseeing but better than total disaster. Even then, we were not quite out of the woods. At Venice station we could find no one who knew where our Yugoslav ship was – or, it seemed, had even heard of the departure quay, San Basilio. A water taxi driver agreed to take us in search. The sun was well down as we sped through the canals, and then – without offering much hope – the "speedo" driver decided to draw in at the base of a high wall with a flight of stone steps. I was taking no chances, and told Brian to stay in the boat while I investigated. When I reached the top of the steps, a happy sight greeted my eyes. On the far side of the quay was a gleaming white ship with lights blazing and two immaculately uniformed officers at the foot of the gangway. They waved at me frantically. I shouted down to Brian, and we sprinted for the ship. Only just in time, and the officers hurried us to our cabins as they hauled in the gangway.

It was April, the first cruise of the season, and the leisurely progress southwards, through the pattern of islands off the coast of Dalmatia, was delightful. With no other distractions, we made rapid progress on our scripts.

We disembarked at Patras, and travelled by road to Athens. For Brian, everything was new. He had never been further afield than Scandinavia and had not seen the great monuments of antiquity. We stayed in Greece for a few days so that he could see the Acropolis, Corinth, Mycenae and the theatre at Epidaurus. At Mycenae, our Greek lady guide informed us that we were running late and there would be no time to climb to the top to the palace complex. We took no notice – we had not come all that way to miss out on the reason for being there. We climbed up through the Lion Gate, past the circular burial places to the acropolis, and stood where Agamemnon had planned the expedition to Troy.

We returned to the bus to find a furious guide. She took a look at Brian, and hissed, 'I *hate* blond people!'

The theatre at Epidaurus was famed for its extraordinary acoustics – a whisper, it was said, could be heard at the back of the tiers of stone seats. We had not counted on hearing it put to the test. An enormously fat American tourist took the stage, and gave a rendering of *Show Me The Way To Go Home* in a voice as powerful as Sophie Tucker. It rather spoiled the magic.

From Greece we travelled on a Turkish ship to Istanbul, where – surveying the interior of the great basilica of Sancta Sophia – I wondered how on earth we were going to light such an immense space when we returned to film it.

An important theme of our series was concerned with the expansion of the Roman Empire, and now we followed it eastwards – by air this time – to the Lebanon, en route to view Palmyra, in the Syrian Desert, one of Rome's furthest outposts. Syria was already unpopular with the west. Its socialist military government was allied with even more unpopular Egypt, and was in dispute with Israel over the Golan Heights. We had been warned by the Foreign Office not to go there. We disregarded this, of course.

Lebanon, on the other hand, was for the moment an oasis of peace in the Middle East – a situation that tragically would soon change. Our arrival night in Beirut was disturbed in the small hours by the sound of a loud explosion. We were given no explanation next morning, but there was confusion at the airport and a lengthy delay for our flight to Damascus. We overheard the gossip, and put two and two together. The explosion had been caused by a bomb dropped from an Israeli plane. Perhaps it had been intended for Syria. We presumed it was *pour encourager les autres.* We did not guess, of course, that the start of the so-called Six Day War between Israel and its Arab neighbours was only a week or two away.

We boarded an ancient Russian plane, which immediately spewed a spectacular fountain of sparks from one of its engines. The engines were quickly shut down, and we were led back to the terminal shed while repairs were made. Brian and I looked at each other and wondered whether this was the moment to find somewhere else to go to. Before we could make up our minds, we were shepherded back aboard the obviously doomed aircraft. To our relief, the short flight to Damascus was accomplished without a spectacular nosedive into the desert. That was it, however, as far as flying was concerned. The Syrians were in no mood to take to the air while Israeli air force jets might be lurking overhead, and our planned flight across the desert to Palmyra was "can-sell".

Our complaints were met with the suggestion that we go by taxi, and to our amazement a crowd of taxi drivers gathered, all offering to take us the hundred and fifty miles across the arid desert, as though it was just down the road. We chose a lethargic youth (or he seemed to chose us) with a battered American limousine that seemed barely roadworthy. The price was the equivalent of £60, which seemed reasonable for such a ridiculous journey. The adventure was beginning.

Our Cadillac had only just reached the outskirts of the city when we turned off the road and rolled to a halt between low mud houses. We felt the vehicle rising beneath us, and realised we were being jacked up. The driver made us understand that he wanted good tyres for the harsh desert surface. We could not disagree with that.

Minutes passed, and then we saw through our grimy windows a drama about to be enacted. Two or three men were engaged in a lively discussion over a young goat, one of them testing the blade of a long knife.

'I fear that we're in the middle of a butcher's shop,' I murmured to Brian. He groaned.

All too soon I was proved right. A bargain was struck and knife man proceeded to draw the blade across the throat of the unfortunate animal. Blood spurted everywhere. Then he made an incision in the goat's leg and blew into it, like someone inflating Christmas balloons. The goat appeared to go rigid. More butchering followed, as the creature's entrails were expertly drawn and discarded in the dust. Then, after much shaking of hands and blessings, the men departed, leaving us once more alone. Our driver was nowhere in sight, having presumably gone in search of tyres.

A small dog appeared between two of the houses. It looked carefully round, then made for the goat's entrails. They were obviously too fresh and sinewy to be chewed, so they went down the puppy's throat in one swallow. A moment later, they reappeared. On the second attempt, the offal stayed down. Then, as Shakespeare put it – *Exeunt.* The *dramatis personae* left the stage. The show was over.

Eventually our driver returned, accompanied by a police inspector, who announced that he would be riding with us part of the way. A tyre that looked anything but new was fitted, and we set out on our journey.

We travelled north to Homs, where we saw, on the horizon, the Crusader Castle called the Crac des Chevaliers. There, the policeman left us, and we turned east, to head out into the flat, sun-baked Syrian Desert. It is not the desert of popular imagination, the rolling sand dunes of a Sahara, but a great expanse of rock-hard gravel, strewn with large stones, lethal to car tyres, stretching seemingly limitlessly to the shimmering horizon on every side.

We had driven for about an hour when the first blow-out occurred. We rolled to a standstill, and Brian and I got out, to stand around while our driver jacked the vehicle up again and fitted the spare. We reached Palmyra some four hours later without further mishap, and after a surprisingly good lunch in the dilapidated Zenobia Hotel, we spent the afternoon exploring the spectacular Roman ruins. There were no tourists and we had the place to ourselves, an experience I was to enjoy many a time in those halcyon days.

Our driver did not bother mentioning to us that he had gone in search of a sound tyre to replace what was left of the one that had burst, but had been unsuccessful. Unaware of our hazardous situation, we set off on the long return journey on four patched-up rings of worn-out rubber. No spare, and only God – or Allah – to rely on.

Of course, none of the tyres were up to it. With complete inevitability, another tyre burst when we were about halfway across the desert. We stayed in the car this time as our driver jacked it up to assess the situation. After some minutes' head scratching, during which the light vanished from the sky with that suddenness and seeming finality that is a feature of the desert, he joined us inside the taxi. We would have to wait for a passing traveller to send for assistance, he told us. Brian and I exchanged a glance. We had seen no other vehicle on the road the entire day.

The hours ticked away. On the far distant horizon, a flare soared into the night sky. What it was for, we had no idea. A lone Bedouin appeared out of the darkness and studied us closely, scratching his chin and frowning.

'They like shoes,' I remarked, under my breath, to Brian, in a juvenile attempt to scare him. The aged Bedu gave up and melted into the darkness. Perhaps, we thought, he would fetch help. We put from our minds the thought that he might return with a band of covetous mates after our shoes.

Our driver now confessed that he had been working without break for more than twenty-four hours, and drifted into a deep slumber.

After what seemed an eternity, a twinkling light appeared far down the road. It materialised into a battered lorry, and to our relief it stopped. There was a lengthy discussion between its driver and our gormless youth, probably about money. A hard bargain was being struck! Then the lorry departed with our ruined tyre – *plus the useless spare.* It did not entirely escape us that jacked up with one axle without a wheel, we were totally immobilised, marooned in an inhospitable desert.

By the time another hour had passed, we had made up our minds that the lorry driver had abandoned us. But our fears were fortunately unwarranted. We were overjoyed to see him coming back. Perhaps we would *not* now be discovered, weeks later, with our throats cut and our shoes missing. He brought with him just one, heavily patched tyre. The other was beyond repair. There was no alternative – we would have to resume our journey without a spare.

Dawn was breaking when we saw a little roadhouse a short distance off the carriageway. Our driver was falling asleep at the wheel by this time, and swerving alarmingly from side to side across the sandy track, so we pulled in beside the shack and entered – somewhat apprehensively in view of the warnings we had received from the Foreign Office. But inside it was surprisingly welcoming, with a warm fire, hot sweet coffee and friendly company.

A teenage youth came to sit with us and asked in quite good English why we were there. I explained that we were preparing a film – whereupon he told us, in excited tones, that he was going to film school in Cairo.

'I want to be like your Alfred *Hotchkick*,' he said.

Confounding all our gloomy fears, the replacement tyre survived the remainder of the journey. We had no regrets when we paid off our driver, and watched him resume his place in the airport taxi rank. For us, it was the next available flight to Egypt.

We spent a day in Cairo, when we visited the Pyramids, then boarded the night plane, a sumptuously appointed VC10 of East African Airways, to "civilisation"

– Rome. In the soft blue lighting, we curled up in our airline blankets and slept the sleep of the just.

When we arrived in Rome, however, we were compelled to wonder if it was so civilised. Unlike the welcome we had received two years before filming *Who Were The British?*, now we were faced with cold unwillingness to help. All the government officials we approached for permission to film sites of antiquity seemed to be former *Fascisti*. Most were calculatedly rude, keeping us standing in front of their desks while they argued among themselves whether to allow us to film anything. Fortunately Brian knew the head of the British School (of archaeology) in Rome, and he intervened on our behalf. *Signor Fascisti* accepted that *Dottori* 'ope-Taylor was indeed an archaeologist, and that we intended to make a *documentario culturali*, not a *documentario touristica*. We received permission to film the Imperial Forum and the Coliseum when we returned later in the year.

There was no such harassment when we went on to France. The authorities there welcomed us with open arms. We went to Arles, to see the Roman amphitheatre. But both Brian and I were moved by the thought that we were in Vincent van Gogh's town. We were booked in at the *Hotel Nord Pinus*, in the *Place du Forum*, with its statue of the poet, Frédéric Mistral (when I returned home and told my PA, Anna, that the unit would be staying there, she said, "I'm not staying anywhere called Gnawed Penis"). The ancient hotel had been built into the remains of the Roman Forum, part of which formed one of its corners. Brian and I were the only occupants, and we were conducted to our rooms by an ancient *concierge*. We passed doors marked *La Chambre de Maurice Chevalier* and *La Chambre de*

Charles Trenet. I was deposited in a room labelled, mysteriously, *La Chambre de l'Empereur*. Brian was taken along the passage to *La Chambre de Picasso*.

I was unpacking my bag when Brian appeared at my door.

'I can't open the wardrobe,' he said. 'It appears to be locked.'

'Oh –' I said, '– let's get the old man to open it.'

But the old man was shocked. He held up his hands. 'But *messieurs* – it is full of the clothes of *Monsieur* Picasso...' he explained. I resisted the impulse to investigate what clothes "*l'Empereur*" wore.

Our marathon journey ended in Spain, where we travelled by train to Segovia to see the towering Roman aqueduct – and be offered the nastiest meal either of us had ever experienced, in what was reputed to be the town's internationally celebrated restaurant. It was decorated with portraits of General Franco, and the restaurateur, decked out with a Legion of Honour, came to our table and beamed. We were served what appeared to be boiling oil soup and roast sucking pig that did not look as if it was quite dead. We were too well mannered to throw up in front of the *maestro*.

After a day in Madrid, to order photographs of artworks in the Prado, we left Atocha station on the sleeper to Malaga, which we made our base for researching Moslem Andalusia. In Cordoba, the vast scale of the famous *Mesquita* promised the same photographic problems as Sancta Sophia in Istanbul, but we were delighted that the authorities agreed to put it at our disposal.

During our extended expedition, Brian and I had been aware of something astir in several of the places we visited. In Athens, there had been student demonstrations – they eventually led to a rightist coup by "the Colonels". In France, our travel arrangements had been disrupted by student riots, and in Spain, the frontier was sealed off for a few days. In the Middle East, the Israelis launched the Six-Day War, invading and occupying Arab land, and changing the political landscape. Nineteen sixty-seven was a year when even in America there was student unrest, provoked by the Vietnam War. As a result of all this, we were compelled to fly home from Barcelona, rather than travelling to England by train.

While plans were made for our return odyssey with the film unit the following year, Brian had his university duties to catch up on, and I had other smaller projects to take care of in Norwich. I was glad to be back at White Horse Farm for a while with Mary, Timothy, then aged seven, and baby George.

Brian Hope Taylor and I found ourselves with something else to think about before we could begin filming *The Dark Ages.* A friend telephoned me on Boxing Day, and mentioned, in passing, that Brian was excavating at York Minster. I called Brian to wish him a happy Christmas, and he told me he was standing in the crossing of the Minster, beneath the central lantern tower and that it was about to fall down!

As soon as the Christmas holidays were over I hurried up to York, and Brian took me down a ladder into a large excavation beneath the central lantern tower of the Minster. The tower had shown signs of settlement – and there was the cause, a great crack running across the foundations. The medieval builders had erected the four great columns that supported the tower on an oak "raft". Due to changes in the water table over the centuries, this had dried out, and the columns were effectively "punching" their way through the underlying ground. This central prop supported the entire building – if it collapsed, everything would go with it. The Minster would be no more.

Brian told me that the Dean and Chapter were concerned that hallowed ground would be disturbed when making the necessary repairs, and had consulted the eminent archaeologist, Sir Mortimer Wheeler. Wheeler knew that Brian believed that the remains of a Saxon timber structure lay beneath the Minster, so he recommended him as someone who would oversee the project sensitively.

What followed was more than just a piece of "tele-archaeology". I persuaded Anglia to let me produce a programme recording the entire excavation and subsequent restoration. It became the centrepiece of an appeal to raise the two million pounds needed to rescue the Minster for posterity.

I expanded the theme of *The Fight For York Minster* to highlight the plight of Britain's medieval cathedrals. They were all roughly the same age, and all were suffering the ravages of time – perhaps even reaching the end of their lives. When Brian interviewed the Archbishop of Canterbury, Dr Michael Ramsay, in the programme, however, the archbishop surprised us by expressing an unexpected point of view. He would, he said, be more concerned by the death of one single person than the destruction of a cathedral.

21

LORD TOWNSHEND met The Great Panjandrum during a skiing holiday. I shall not mention his name. He has been long dead now; may he rest in peace. TGP had once enjoyed a position of eminence in television's aristocracy, rivalling the BBC's Richard Dimbleby as anchorman of a flagship ITV current affairs programme. It was said that there had been some sort of falling-out with his producers, resulting in his dismissal, and his star was on the wane. Townshend and he struck up a friendship, and the result was that he came to Anglia as "programme adviser" (*Everyone I meet has two professions – their own and film producer...*)

It soon became evident that he wielded considerable power. He was patronising towards the lesser talents labouring in the halls of what he thought an insignificant provincial TV station, and was not well liked. I got on with him well enough, though I thought him rather overbearing and pompous.

Townshend put him to work reviewing and criticising the local programming, and among his activities he took it upon himself to view film rushes – often before they were seen by their director. (In a film studio that would be regarded as the ultimate breach of professional etiquette.)

To save cost, 16mm film was not printed. The negative was edited, then scanned for transmission in a telecine machine that had been set "reverse-phased" to produce a positive image. So rushes consisted of the entire footage shot, not just takes selected by the director at the time of shooting, as in the film industry.

I fell foul of it. I was in London one morning, filming for a political programme, and had shot a first take of Big Ben, when the assistant cameraman reported a problem with the camera. It was near eleven o'clock, so I broke the unit for a coffee break while the problem was put right. About half an hour later, I was able to resume shooting, with a second shot of Big Ben.

The following morning, while I was still in London, Panjandrum viewed my rushes. His eagle eye homed in on Big Ben's clock face. Horror! In take one, the time by Big Ben was five-to-eleven. In take two, it was twenty-past. Panjandrum submitted a long report for the chairman, claiming that as nearly half an hour had passed between takes one and two, this demonstrated how idle and wasteful film units were. It was not until I returned to Norwich that I was able to put the record straight.

The Great Panjandrum over-reached himself in a hilarious episode. He devised his own programme – a clone of John Freeman's brilliant *Face To Face* – to which he gave the self-important title, *The* [Panjandrum] *Interviews*. Although many of the people he invited to appear were distinguished, he clearly believed that he was more important than them. Interviewing people was all too easy, he seemed to think; it did not require any substantial research by one so adept as himself.

One day, he arrived from London barely in time to record an interview with a Norfolk doctor who was also an authority on diseases in ancient times. The doctor had been on television many times before and had brought along a selection of bones from his collection, arranged on a table before him.

Panjandrum bustled into the studio, and as usual assumed that his guest was a country bumpkin who needed to be nursed along.

'You will see the camera over there has a red light on it,' he said. 'When that comes on, you are being broadcast... et cetera... et cetera...' While this rambled on, the programme director looked anxiously at the clock's sweep hand. Time was running out. '... There is no need to be nervous...' Panjandrum continued, '... I will guide you through... I shall ask you what we can learn from these specimens...'

He picked up a bone.

'This one, for instance...'

The good doctor started to reply, 'Oh – that is an example of arthritis–' when the red light came on. Panjandrum cut him off.

He turned to the camera.

'I have with me Doctor X, who is the nation's foremost expert in ancient diseases...'

He turned to his subject – this time picking up a skull.

'Tell us, doctor – what can we learn from this?'

The doctor responded with enthusiasm.

'That is a particularly interesting specimen,' he replied. 'It is the earliest evidence we have of syphilis.'

Panjandrum looked horrified, and threw down the skull.

'Oh –' he gasped, in a panic '– that should be an example to all of us!'

For the first time in the country's history, Labour governments were being regularly elected. The trade unions were becoming steadily more powerful. This did not please many people who considered it their divine right to decide how things should be run. We, in "the media", heard rumours of a farcical attempt by the proprietor of the *Daily Mirror*, Cecil King, to instigate a *coup d'Etat*. It went unreported by the press, and it was not until the publication of the book *Spycatcher* in the 1980s that the public got to know of it.

What the public *did not* get to hear about was that one or two far-right fanatics, apparently taking encouragement from criticism of the media by a prominent Labour (!) Minister, Lord Chalfont, became convinced that television was riddled with Communist subversives. There was a discreet "witch-hunt" in the BBC and some of the ITV companies, and one sensed an "atmosphere".

I don't know what part, if any, The Great Panjandrum played in this – although in later years he boasted that he had spent "fifteen years as an anti-Communist Trojan horse inside the television fortress".

In any case he was responsible for a shabby piece of deceit.

One Friday afternoon he came to my office.

'Forbes,' he said, 'I believe you to be Anglia's most talented director...' (I could hardly be offended by a beginning like that, and began to warm to a man who demonstrated such impeccable judgement!). He told me that he was going to produce an important series of arts programmes for the network. The first programme would be about Soviet art.

'There is a major exhibition of Soviet art at the Hayward Gallery in London at the moment,' he said, 'and it is just what we need. The problem is, it is due to end after the weekend. Could you possibly take a unit down there before it closes?'

I said I thought it would be possible.

He then said:

'I haven't approached the Hayward Gallery, and I do not want my name associated with the series for the moment. Would you be kind enough to make the request, emphasising how important such an arts programme on ITV will be? – That it will be good PR for them, et cetera...?'

'I'll do my best,' I said.

I got on the phone to the Hayward Gallery. They were not enthusiastic. A Japanese film unit was going in over the weekend, and the Soviet exhibition had to be cleared away by Monday, ready for the next show. I used all my persuasive powers. This was for a major national series. We would ensure that the gallery got maximum publicity. And so on.

The curator gave in. Provided I filmed throughout that night, and was out of the way before the Japanese arrived next morning, he would keep the staff on and put the show at our disposal.

The film unit travelled to London immediately, and we spent a long, exhausting night, filming. Many of the exhibits were historic examples of "Agitprop" – of a high standard artistically, but propaganda pictures, designed to whip up hatred of capitalism.

We left for home with a large footage in the can.

I had other programmes in production or preparation, and put The Great Panjandrum's art project from my mind, assuming I would hear more when it reached a further stage of development. So I was more than a little intrigued when, checking on the production schedule, I heard, from my assistant, mention of a project called *Reds Under The Bed*.

'Oh?' I asked, 'what's that?'

'Panjandrum's programme,' my assistant told me. 'It's about communist subversives in Britain.'

I smelt a large rat.

'Tell me...' I said, '...the Hayward Gallery material?'

'That's in it,' my assistant nodded.

I was furious. It was now blindingly obvious why The Great Panjandrum had wanted his name kept out of it. He had conned me into lying to the Hayward Gallery in order to get the material he wanted by false pretences. He intended to show that the arts establishment was also riddled with Communists – the Hayward Gallery had even sent to Russia for Agitprop material! I went to Lord Townshend and gave him the facts – I had assured the gallery that the film was for an arts programme – I had given my word, and used heavy persuasion. Lord Townshend listened sympathetically. The programme was never made.

One of the results of the 1967 franchise changes was that Rediffusion lost its licence as the London network broadcaster. Its place was taken by London Weekend Television (one of whose principals was David Frost. 'Pity we lorst Frorst,' one of our proprietors was heard to remark). Anglia now no longer had easy access to the network. It meant that we would have to fight for a place for *The Dark Ages*. On the other hand, no producer from London was inflicted on us, this time, and I was in charge as executive producer. We were also no longer compelled to film in 35mm, which made it financially viable to shoot in colour.

I spent the whole of 1968 filming the new series. I treated the eight scripts as a single programme, breaking them down and cross-plotting as I would a feature film production. We planned two lengthy location expeditions, in the spring and autumn, to fit in with Brian's university terms, and in March we set out on the first marathon tour – Jordan, Israel, Istanbul, Athens, Rome, Monte Carlo, Nice, Arles, Nîmes, Segovia, Cordoba, Madrid. A trip that would take about three months.

The Director of Photography was Ian Craig, of course, and my PA was a pretty girl in her mid-twenties named Anna Dickie. She spoke fluent Spanish and could also get by in French. The use of 16mm film meant that the unit could consist of only five members (the BBC and the network companies regularly crewed up with twice this number – without a consequent improvement in quality, as far as I could see).

As our entry point for the Middle East, we flew to Nicosia, in Cyprus. The Six Day War the previous year had changed the map. Syria was now *really* a no-go place, and Palmyra was inaccessible. We substituted the Roman town of Jerash in Jordan.

On our arrival at the Jordanian capital, Amman, a Ministry of Information Under-Secretary named Peter Salah met us at the foot of the aircraft steps.

'Angela Television?' he asked, holding out a hand.

It was the first time I had been called Angela! (Fans of the film *Airplane* may recall the character who said: 'Don't call me Shirley' to understand why I struggled to keep a straight face.)

Had I smiled, however, it would have quickly been dispelled by Peter Salah's next words. An attack by Israel was expected at any minute. He advised us, nevertheless, to go ahead with our agenda.

Instead of putting us in one of the hotels in the better part of town favoured by Western media folk, Thomas Cook had fixed us up in The Philadelphia Hotel, in the heart of the most "Arab" district of the city. We claimed our rooms and had a bite of lunch, and set out across the desert, east of Amman, for an oasis called Qasr Al Asraq (Qasr = Arabic "Castle", Asraq = "blue") to film its bluestone Roman fort. The Jordanian Ministry of Information provided a Land Rover and driver-guide to carry us across the desert.

A mile or two from the city, the metalled road came to an abrupt end. The driver bounced over the edge, and set off across an apparently featureless sea of sandy gravel. How he found his way baffled us. We arrived at the first landmark, a smaller fort called Qasr Al Amra, and broke out the camera. In the distance, we could see a Bedouin camp, which I thought worth filming. Our guide looked worried. He advised us not to hang about, as the Bedouin were unpredictable. We sneaked a few surreptitious shots from behind the vehicle.

Eventually we reached Al Asraq, which had been Lawrence of Arabia's headquarters, where he rested up after the "Dera'a incident" when he was captured and flogged by the Turks. An old Druze custodian led us inside the fort, to a vaulted room without furnishing, which I recognised from an illustration in Lawrence's book, *Seven Pillars Of Wisdom*. A tattered reproduction of Augustus John's portrait of Lawrence fluttered in the draught against one wall. The Druze claimed that he had been Lawrence's servant.

We had only filmed two or three shots of the outside of the fort when our driver drew my attention to some shimmering shapes, floating just above the horizon. Very David Lean, I thought...

Our guide was alarmed. The shapes became a cloud of dust – and then took form as a party of camel riders – racing very purposefully towards us. It was a patrol of the Desert Legion – magnificent in khaki headdress, long coats criss-crossed with ammunition bandoleers, and World War 1 Lee-Enfield rifles. They towered over us on their camels as their commander gave rapid instructions. We were to return to Amman at once. The Israelis had mounted an attack and we were in danger of being mistaken for Israeli spies. We did not argue.

On arriving at our hotel, we found the British Embassy's Head of Chancery, David Crawford (he was subsequently ambassador in several Arab countries) waiting for us. He had alarming news. An Israeli armoured unit had crossed the River Jordan, and fierce fighting was taking place on the east bank. Amman airport was closed, and communication with the outside world had been suspended.

Crawford then drew me aside on my own, and confided that HM Foreign Office was unhappy that the continuing conflicts between Israel and its Arab neighbours was so often depicted from the Israeli point of view, probably because the media preferred the hotels in Tel Aviv. He asked me if I would film the present incident. He would send it to England by RAF plane in the diplomatic bag, to be delivered to ITN.

I pointed out that we were not a news unit, but he stressed the importance of his request. I consulted the unit about going to the scene of fighting. Quite obviously, we could not continue with the archaeology series for the time being, but the unit had not been employed for hazardous assignments of this kind, and had a right to refuse. After a small huddle beyond my hearing, they told me they would do it. It was their duty, Ian Craig – acting as their spokesman – pronounced. Very commendable! (Ian was just the man to have along in a potentially hazardous situation. He had gone through most of World War II as an artillery officer attached to the Army Film and Photographic Unit.) I then mentioned a slight further problem. We had no news correspondent with us. The unit conferred again, and expressed their opinion that I was admirably suited to do the job. Flattering, of course, and quite absurd. But I agreed.

As word of what was happening may have got out at home, I sent a telegram to Anglia, reporting that we were all safe, and that next of kin should be kept informed.

I then went to a briefing from Peter Salah, and was told that an Israeli tank force had crossed the Allenby Bridge, and destroyed some villages on the Jordanian side of the River Jordan. We set off in two taxis for the battle – part of a convoy of vehicles, commandeered by *a rabble* representing some of the world's newspapers.

At the village of Shuna, close to the River Jordan, the air reeked of cordite. An Israeli tank was in the middle of the roadway. It had been "knocked out", and the crew were inside, dead. I did a hastily improvised "into camera" in front of it, while some desperate-looking characters hovered behind Ian Craig, listening to what I was saying, and ominously toting their machine-guns.

I was in the middle of a second piece beside the tank, when we were warned that we were within artillery range!

We moved on to another village, El Kharameh, where a desultory firefight with small arms was still in progress. We moved around, grabbing what shots we could, while our taxis stayed close by, ready to get us out if it became necessary. The whole thing became surreal when I found myself in the ruins of a cinema, with what remained of the previous night's film tangled round my ankles.

Suddenly we were taken by surprise. A number of young men, brandishing Kalashnikovs, burst out of a nearby street and ran towards us. They were not in uniform, and the newspaper reporters looked alarmed – they probably knew of the new underground guerrilla group called "Al Fatah". We didn't.

The sight of us seemed to anger the new arrivals. There was much shouting – which, to our consternation, seemed to be encouraged by a loud-mouthed Italian woman journalist. I spotted our taxis racing to rescue us. As we began to scramble into them, the situation became clear. The young gunmen were on the run, and wanted out too – in our cars! One of them threw open my door, and pushed me over, so that he could share the front seat. Ian Craig was faced with a guerrilla, who thrust a fist holding a grenade through the window of his taxi with his thumb in the ring of the safety pin.

'*You* take me to *Amman*!' he shouted.

Ian looked incensed.

'Have you got permission?' he asked, with withering dignity. A prod from a Kalashnikov supplied the answer, and Ian moved over to make room.

En route at high speed to Amman, my young guerrilla gossiped away in good English.

'We're on your side,' I assured him.

When we arrived in Amman we were relieved when he and his pals dived from the cars and made off down the side streets. The entrance hall of the Philadelphia Hotel was in chaos. I delivered our precious film to David Crawford, and he debriefed me. He pricked up his ears when I told him of the guerrilla fighters. They must be part of the new force in the conflict between Jordan and Israel, he told me. It was called "Al Fatah". Unbeknown to us, Al Fatah was virtually in control of Jordan. It was some years before King Hussein succeeded in ejecting them.

Crawford sent off our film on an RAF plane, and ITN's foreign editor was delighted. My despatch was broadcast in *News At Ten* the next night. Mary allowed eight-year-old Timothy and two-year-old George to stay up late to watch Daddy on television. It must have been a weird experience for her.

The report was a scoop for ITV, and an unprecedented one for a regional station. ITN cabled me to get more material – if possible, an interview with King Hussein. But this was turned down. I heard that the leader of Al Fatah – named Yasser Arafat – might be found somewhere in the neighbourhood of Kharameh, and fired up by my recent experience, I wondered if I might get an interview with him. In the hotel bar I ran into the newly arrived BBC correspondent, Brian Barron, and suggested we pool resources. He told me he thought it would be suicide. So ended my brief career as a war correspondent.

22

THE WAR seemed to be over for the moment, so we got back to our main purpose. One of our programmes was about the cultural influence of Islam during the Dark Ages, and I wanted shots of worshippers at a mosque. Our fat, jolly – but totally incompetent – police "minder", Sergeant Abdullah, took me to check out a coffeehouse that overlooked the main mosque to use as a possible camera position. We picked our way through a throng of not at all friendly customers to an upstairs room from which Abdullah said we could get a good shot.

'But is it all right?' I asked, thinking of the crowd below. I wondered if they might at that very moment be deciding what to do about the "Israeli spy" upstairs.

'You can try,' he answered.

Try? It did not sound very reassuring.

I went back to the hotel and collected the unit. We got as far as the road leading to the mosque. As Ian Craig began to mount the camera on the tripod, a large crowd mobbed us. A grubby-looking villain forced his way to the front and thrust a large dagger under my nose.

'You're a spy!' he screamed. 'You're a Jew! You're a fucking Jew!'

The thought crossed my mind that I didn't *look* very Jewish. I protested vigorously, while hissing to Ian out of the side of my mouth to get the hell out.

I still had to get past that knife, however. The situation looked decidedly dangerous. Then a young man, in a camouflage overall, came running from a side street, brandishing a Kalashnikov. He explained to Sergeant Abdullah that he was an idiot, then turned to me and told me, in English, to get out as fast as possible. I presumed he was one of these mysterious Al Fatah fighters. With increasing anxiety, I watched the unruffleable Ian Craig *ever so slowly* dismantle the Arriflex, methodically wrap the lens in its soft chamois leather, close each side of the camera case, and carefully lift it into the boot of the taxi. Only then did we push our way through the crowd and climb in. I expected at any moment to be shot at, and told Anna to get on the floor. We inched away, amid screams and curses. Again, our luck held out.

One further adventure lay before us, before we left the Middle East. Our next destination was Israel, but direct travel between Jordan and Israel was supposed to be impossible – as a result, we planned to return to Nicosia, and double back to Tel Aviv from there.

When the time came to leave, Jordan's ministry man, Peter Salah, showed surprise when I told him I intended to take such a roundabout route.

'Why not go across the bridge?' he asked.

I laughed at the joke. 'Because it's not possible,' I answered.

'Yes it is,' he replied. 'The King Hussein bridge' [as the Jordanians call the Allenby bridge] 'is there. Go across it.'

I recalled that, only three days earlier, there had been a tank battle on that very bridge, and wondered if he was serious. He was.

As a sometime soldier, I could hardly funk such a challenge.

'OK,' I said. 'We'll give it a try.'

David Crawford was quite taken by the idea, and accompanied us when we set off for the bridge, travelling in two vehicles – one of which was his car. I went with him, along with Brian Hope Taylor. The film crew went in a taxi. I carried all the passports, except for my own, which for some reason Anna Dickie kept with hers. The two cars became separated very soon after we set out.

We had travelled about thirty miles, to a place called Es Salt, when we found the road blocked by a group of armed Al Fatah guerrillas. They demanded to see our passports. Crawford spoke fluent Arabic and got out to talk to them. Brian Hope Taylor and I looked on as an angry argument broke out, with much brandishing of Kalashnikovs. Then the row calmed down, and Crawford returned to the car, whispering that one of the Fatah men was an idiot. Crawford had shown him Ian Craig's passport. Arabic writing is read from right to left, and when the youth had attempted to read Ian's name that way, he had somehow made it out as "Moshe Dayan" – the name of a famous Israeli general. Crawford had eventually managed to convince him that General Dayan was hardly likely to come that way – or to offer his passport to be checked!

We waited for the unit to arrive to join us for the remainder of the journey, but time passed, and there was no sign of the taxi. Then we then heard an ominous clanking and rumbling in the distance. Es Salt stands on a height above the Jordan valley, and below us, we could see the road leading to the bridge. Coming towards us was a column of tanks.

As they got nearer we saw that they were Israeli. But it soon became clear that they were captured ones. Their upper parts were crowded with jubilant Fatah fighters.

Crawford turned to Hope Taylor and me.

'I don't know about you,' he said, 'but I'm orf.' He made a hasty U-turn, and we made off back to Amman. When we got there, there was no sign of the film unit. The Jordanian police and military were out in force, looking for them, and we feared the worst. We waited at the British Embassy until nearly midnight, when Crawford decided that it was possible that they may, somehow, have made it to Israel. He fixed me up with an embassy passport and suggested I travel there by air to investigate. As I got ready to depart, we received welcome news. The unit had been found.

What had happened to them? It was barely believable. The driver of the unit's taxi had been ordered, by his wife, to take a detour to a village where they baked good bread and get her a couple of loaves. The idiot then compounded this lunacy by getting himself lost. It was really rather funny, except that the unit had been in considerable danger. We spent what was left of the night in the Philadelphia Hotel, and – incredibly, I suppose, when one thinks about it now – departed next morning on a fresh attempt to cross the Allenby Bridge. This time the ministry man, Peter Salah, came too.

An intimidating sight awaited us at the bridge. A large Jordanian army force was dug in along the river, with guns trained on the ridge that overlooked it from the opposite bank. That bank – the Israeli one – appeared utterly deserted.

'But they are up there, watching,' Salah said, portentously.

We unloaded our bulky equipment, and stacked it at the end of the metal Bailey bridge.

'Now I have to tell you that you have only one chance,' said Peter Salah. 'You must get all your stuff across in one go. You must not return for a second load, as our men may shoot. Is that understood?'

I said it was.

But it proved impossible to comply. We had just too many boxes. Clearly, there was only one person who could take a chance on a return trip, and that had to be me. Fortunately, the Jordanians were not trigger-happy. It may, perhaps, have been because portly, dignified Peter Salah helped me with the loads as far as the middle of the bridge. Pretty brave of him, I thought. His Arab headdress presented a tempting target for Israeli snipers.

We arrived on the Israeli side, and wondered – what next? There were no Israelis in sight, much less a reception committee. Before us was a deserted track, between high hedges, rising to a ridge. There was nothing for it but to hump our loads up the slope, and see what lay beyond.

After about a hundred yards the bushes opened out, and there, behind the crest of the ridge, was – so it seemed – the entire Israeli army. Artillery – armour – the lot.

A young officer advanced towards us, grinning.

'Welcome to Israel,' he said. 'We've been expecting you.'

He held a rubber stamp over my passport.

"Do you want it?' he asked.

We both knew that the Israeli stamp would make the passport invalid in Arab countries in the future.

'What does it say?' I asked.

'*Allenby Bridge*,' the young officer grinned. 'Rather rare.'

'Stamp it,' I said.

Apart from that encounter, we met no other Israelis all the time we were in the country. Their government ignored us when we filmed Islamic monuments in Jerusalem. Two or three days later we flew out of Tel Aviv for Istanbul.

The government *there* did not ignore us! Although I had agreed a filming itinerary with Turkish representatives in London, their counterparts in Istanbul did everything they could to frustrate us. I was forced to station poor Anna almost permanently at the government offices, waiting for permits to be issued. They were so rude sometimes that she was reduced to tears. A redeeming feature was the presence of kindly taxi driver Kemal, a giant former wrestler, who attached himself to us as general guide and assistant. Somehow we managed to get the tyrannical bureaucrats to allow us into the great basilica of Sancta Sophia, and the underground Roman water cistern (it had featured in a James Bond film, and the Turks were incensed that it had been shown swarming, fictitiously with rats).

The Turkish authorities had a real Catch-22 trick to pull on us. Our unexposed film had been checked in by their customs on arrival. Now – the regulations stated – the same amount must be checked out on departure – also *unexposed*! In other words, although we had permission to film, we must not use film... We dealt with this insane system in the only way possible. We boarded the plane with our exposed film in our personal baggage.

It was a relief to arrive in Italy, though we still had bureaucratic problems to cope with there. We had to deal with the Vatican, as well as the Italian government. The department concerned had the impressive title, *Comisario della Archaeologia Sacre.* Commission for Sacred Archaeology. And that did not have authority over the autonomous custodians of the catacombs, the monks, who we had to persuade to allow us access. I had been forewarned of all this, and had arranged for Anglia's Catholic religious adviser, Father Robert Manley, of Gorleston-on-Sea, to fly out. He was accompanied on the journey by our guest, the distinguished *Daily Telegraph* television correspondent, Leonard Marsland Gander.

While cheerful Father Manley found his way round the Vatican offices, we began filming in the arena of the Coliseum. Marsland Gander was amazed when I dreamed up an impression of Christians being killed by wild animals – from the point of view of the lions. It brought us some excellent publicity when he reported on it in the *Telegraph* on his return home.

After much persuasion, the Brothers who watched over the Catacombs of Saint Sebastian allowed us to film. It had never been allowed before, we were told. It was believed that we would be suffocated by the lack of air in the maze of tunnels underground, and we were directed to film during the night, when the temperature above ground would be cooler, and therefore less likely to draw air out from below.

As the sun went down we assembled above the entrance, with a mobile generator for our lighting and an army of priests and monks gathered to watch over us. I thought that if I died then, I would have had no difficulty with the heavenly entrance formalities.

I now have a very strange story to relate, concerning this filming.

We had begun to set up in an underground chapel carved out of the volcanic rock that form the catacombs – here, persecuted early Christians took refuge, and actually lived out their lives, during the holocaust conducted by the Emperor Diocletian in the third-century AD.

An hour or so's work was required, to hump our equipment down the steps, run out cables, fire up the generator and get the lights in position. While this was going on, I had nothing to do but watch. I felt a touch on my arm. It was a young priest, much taller than me, and wearing a black soutane with a white ruffle around the neck, rather like one sees in Old Master paintings. He asked me if I could spare a moment away from the activity. I might be interested to see something that had only recently been excavated.

I was naturally curious to see something that might be important. Ian Craig was also standing idle, so I asked him to accompany us. With the priest leading the way, we set off down a tunnel, lit by bare light bulbs strung along the walls. Making frequent turns, to left and right, as we came to corners, we eventually arrived at a roped off section, barred with the sign *"PASSARE VIETARE"*. The priest led us through, and we continued quite a way further, until suddenly we came into a small square space that had obviously been a tiny chapel. The walls were decorated with ancient paintings of early Christian symbols: the "Good Shepherd", fishes, the Chi Rho sign. I was moved by the thought that we might be among the first people, in two thousand years, to see these simple, pathetic images.

The lights went out, and we were plunged into velvety darkness!

It was a moment or two before we took the situation in. The lights did not come on again, and I heard the priest say that we should have to make our way back as best we could. He knew the way, he said, and we should hold hands, so that we did not become separated. I took his hand, and Ian took mine, and we shuffled forward in the inky darkness. Although these tunnels had been a place of burial, it did not feel eerie. Rather warm and comfortable, in fact.

After perhaps ten minutes, we had still not reached any light, or our companions. The priest stopped. It would be quicker, he said, if he went ahead alone. We should wait where we were, and he would return for us.

Ian and I stood alone in the darkness. 'Do you mind if we don't hold hands?' I said. 'I don't want to start a rumour...'

We chuckled. It was an absurd situation to be in, though I recalled the legend we had heard, of the party of schoolgirls who in 1915 lost their way in the catacombs, never to be seen again. I wondered if we were to share their eternity, amid the miles of tunnels covering over ten square miles of Rome.

Then I saw – seemingly far away – a twinkling light. It disappeared, and then appeared again, somewhat nearer.

'Guvnor?' came a faint cry.

I recognised electrician Harry Bush's voice.

'Over here, Harry!' I called.

The light got nearer... ever nearer... until at last Harry was beside us. He was holding a battery hand lamp.

'Where have you been?' he asked.

I asked him if he had seen the priest, but he looked mystified.

We arrived back to find a worried crowd of people. Our priestly guide was nowhere to be seen, and the Brothers were anxious to know where we had been.

When I explained, they looked baffled.

'How did you say this man was dressed?' I was asked.

I described the priest's garments.

'No one dresses like that,' said the monk. 'Where is he? Is he here?'

I looked round, but there was no sign of him. And we never saw him again.

23

IT WAS a pleasant surprise to discover that Thelma was in Rome, working on an Italian epic at Cinecita Studios. Paul was staying with her. We all got together for dinner at the *Three Steps* restaurant, near the Trevi Fountain. We were in for a further surprise, when it was discovered that Father Bob Manley had been priest at Radnage, in Buckinghamshire, where Frank Launder and Bernadette lived, and had baptised their daughter, Aesling.

There were far fewer tourists about in those days. We had the Imperial Forum virtually to ourselves. Filming there, a day or two later, as I sat on a fallen column to eat an *al fresco* lunch that Anna and our Sicilian "gofer", Michelangelo, brought from a nearby *trattoria,* I thought, 'I shall remember this as one of the happiest times of my life...' And so I have.

From Rome, we travelled north to Ravenna, where we filmed the gorgeous mosaic decorations in the churches of San Vitale and Sant'Apollinare, and the Mausoleum of Galla Placidia. These monuments were made freely available to us, so we repaid the custodians' generosity by keeping the film lighting on when tourist parties came in, so they could view the mosaics in their full beauty. It was amusing to observe the differing character of the parties. The Japanese seemed silenced with awe – their multiple cameras, for once, stashed away. The Americans *used* their cameras, ignoring their guide's lecture as they frantically snapped away. I assumed the scene only became real when they viewed the pictures later, back at home. The Germans – mostly plump ladies wearing men's hats with feathers in the band – listened closely to their guide's explanation, then asked interminable questions, pulling the poor guide up for some omission, and even taking notes. The Brits merely sighed, complained about their poor feet, and gasped for a nice cup of tea.

There was a further variation on this when we got to Spain. There, the authorities in Cordoba insisted on presenting us with the exclusive use of the *Mezquita*, the Great Mosque. Despite our protestations that we could film quite comfortably with people about, they closed it to tourists (Franco ruled then, remember). We had just lit the magnificent *Mihrab,* the holy niche facing Mecca, when an official approached us, looking embarrassed and apologetic. A very important visitor had arrived, he said – an Italian *Principe* and his wife. They had moored their yacht at Malaga, and made a special journey to see the mosque. Would I make an exception and allow them to come in?

Of course, I said – and that goes for any other visitor.

'No, no – just the *Principe*...'

The elegant young couple duly joined us, *bella figura,* all Armani and Gucci and Calvin Klein. They were polite and charming, as was to be expected. The *Principe* effused over the film lighting, and asked if he might take a photograph. I referred him to Ian Craig for permission.

Ian preened himself. Of course...

The *Principe* turned to his wife.

'Carissima?'

She took up position in front of the exquisite *Mihrab – and he took a close-up of her!*

From Spain we travelled to Nîmes, in southern France, to film a bullfight in the Roman amphitheatre. The authorities were so welcoming that they placed us so close to the action that Ian was splashed with blood – to his indignation.

We returned to Norwich with a mountain of film. Alas, there were disasters. It would be the first time the amazing historic monument, Sancta Sophia in Istanbul, appeared on colour television. It had been impossible to light the great space adequately, so we had used a newly available high-speed colour film. The film laboratory processed the film at the wrong temperature, however, and many of the shots were spoiled. We managed to salvage some of the footage, but the final effect was disappointing.

Another mishap had befallen the footage of Qasr El Azraq, shot with such trouble in Jordan. To our puzzlement, the film came back from the lab completely black. After an exhaustive investigation, we arrived at the explanation. It was standard practice to travel with a full film magazine loaded on to the Arriflex camera – but without the film laced through the camera gate, to prevent the formation of kinks.

In the scramble to grab the clandestine shots of Bedouin, our assistant forgot to complete lacing the film, and it had passed from the front of the magazine to the back without passing behind the lens. We might even have discovered it at the time, had we not broken another golden rule. It was normal practice to reload with a fresh magazine while there was still a foot or two of film left. The assistant would then see his mistake when he removed the lens to inspect the gate for hairs and dust. But wanting as much footage as possible, I had told Ian Craig to run out during the last shot on the roll. It was an expensive lesson.

These mishaps were not uncommon in the past, shooting on film, and are happily unknown in these days of video.

After a few weeks at home to allow Brian to catch up on his university duties, we set out again. This time, the destination was the cold north – Germany and Scandinavia.

The whole enterprise very nearly came to an end in Norway. I chartered a four-seater floatplane to fly us up to the Hardanger Vidda, the ancestral home of the Norsemen. Its owner was also the pilot. His wife was not enthusiastic. Although it was sunny and clear in Oslo, she thought there would be dense cloud in the mountains. He dismissed her fears, arguing that as he flew the hunter rescue service, he was well able to cope with any condition. The truth, of course, was that he wanted the charter fee.

We got into trouble within minutes of taking off. The cloud closed in on us, and however high we climbed, there was no break in it. We roared on through thick fog, knowing that mountains far higher than us were on every side. Pete Tunstall's words came back to me – "You have to be careful in these mountains that you do not run out of space to turn round," he had said. "You would not have the height to fly yourself out over the tops." The thought had hardly entered my head when our pilot yanked the control column violently back and threw it over to put us into a steep bank and turn and a wall of rock passed only a foot or two below our floats. It was only then that he admitted that he did not know where we were. For the next forty-five minutes it was sheer terror.

After roaring on and on through the dense murk, convinced that we were certain to be killed, I suddenly glimpsed a small thinning in the cloud below us, through which we could see barren hillside. I ordered the pilot to put us down on the first piece of water we saw. There was no point continuing the expedition in any case, as it was not clear enough to film. The cloud thinned enough for us to spy a lake below and I breathed a sigh of relief. We might not be killed, after all. The pilot lined up and made a smooth approach, but just as we were touching down the idiot opened the throttle and zoomed skywards again.

'What the hell are you doing?' I demanded.

'It's OK,' he said, 'I know where I am now. If I'd put you down there, you'd be miles from anywhere.'

With that, the cretin put us right back in the fog.

A few minutes later, I noticed that he was looking anxiously at the instrument panel. I followed his gaze, and my heart missed a beat. *Both* fuel-gauges were showing empty.

'It's OK,' he muttered, 'I think there's enough to get home.'

Think!

I can't describe our feelings when we finally broke through the cloud, and saw the seaplane jetty ahead. The pilot's wife came running to meet her husband. We did not stand on ceremony. I gave him his charter fee, and felt lucky that we were still alive.

We were filming in Charlemagne's cathedral in Aachen in Germany a week later when we learned that the BBC had been there a week or two earlier. I made enquiries when I returned to Norwich, and discovered that they had been filming nearly all the same sites as us. It was for a series called *Civilisation*.

We had competition...

The March winds of 1969 brought another kind of windfall for Anglia. ITV provided services to the north of England from the tallest transmitter mast in Europe, at Emley Moor, near Kirklees in West Yorkshire. It was also the most vulnerable, and in March, gales and ice caused it to collapse, potentially depriving several millions of people of a television service. A temporary solution was found by increasing the power of Anglia's mast at Belmont in Lincolnshire. Anglia found itself providing programmes for most of Yorkshire. Our Hull foothold had suddenly become much more important.

The company's production schedule did not allow us to begin editing *The Dark Ages* until the late autumn of '69. During the hiatus, I was invited to join the Royal Television Society. It was not then a widely known society, its membership consisting mainly of engineers. It was now attempting to broaden its membership, by including every sort of practitioner so as to enhance its influence in the industry. I was one of a very few producers who joined, and I was elected to the council. Recalling my early run-ins with the engineers, it was rather ironic.

In March 1970, the society held its first biennial convention, at Churchill College, Cambridge. I was on the organising committee, and got to know many eminent industry figures in the process. For the first time, I mixed with the BBC's top people.

As Cambridge was in Anglia's area, I got Aubrey Buxton interested in the convention (he eventually became the Television Society's president, and it led to his being elevated, by Margaret Thatcher, to the House of Lords, as Lord Buxton of Ailsa. He bowled me over, years later, when he suddenly said that he owed it all to me. A wild exaggeration, of course, but a typically generous remark.).

One of the duties we imposed on Aubrey was to look after the Cabinet Minister responsible for broadcasting, John Stonehouse. Stonehouse and his wife stayed with the Buxtons the night before the convention, and Aubrey told me he had trouble getting him up in the morning. After one of the conferences days, the sly Stonehouse quizzed me over drinks on my *Dark Ages* travel arrangements. Later, that year, he faked suicide, leaving his clothes on a beach to suggest drowning, and absconded with his secretary to Australia. He was eventually discovered, brought home to England, and sent to prison on various charges. It was the tabloid story of the year.

Editing *The Dark Ages* took up the whole of 1970. It had been planned as six fifty-minute programmes, and work was far advanced, when we were told by the network that they would not allocate the slots. Our senior religious advisor, Canon Peter Freeman (who had christened both of our children) saved the day. The series contained a lot about the birth of Christianity and Islam, and he persuaded his counterparts in the network companies to allocate "the God slot" – Sundays at six-thirty p.m. That did not provide the necessary timings, though, and we were compelled to reshape the series so that it could be put across in eight programmes of twenty-six minutes. It meant revising the entire concept, and much cherished footage went into the bin. (In writing this, I find it amazing that archaeology should now be such a popular subject on television. In the early 1950s, a senior BBC manager had decreed that it had no future, and cancelled all the BBC's programmes.)

While editing was going on, I had other work to do. Peter Fairley, the science correspondent for Independent Television News, had written a book called *Project X*, about British inventors throughout history who had failed to get backing for their ideas in Britain, and seen them taken up abroad. Faraday, whose work on optics was developed by German lens manufacturers, Alexander Fleming, whose discovery of penicillin was exploited by the Americans, and Whittle, who could not find a British manufacturer for his jet aircraft engine. It was a sobering object lesson on the lack of British entrepreneurism.

I worked with Peter Fairley on a programme based on his book, and we filmed in many parts of the country, most interestingly at the hovercraft factory on the Isle of Wight, where we interviewed the hovercraft's inventor, Christopher Cockerill.

John Woolf liked what he saw when we showed him the rushes, but entirely missed the point. He decided that he could contribute an idea, too (*Everyone I meet has two professions – their own and film producer* – Korda*)*. He insisted on adding the discovery of radar. This was a rare example of a British invention that *was* exploited at home, and it demolished Fairley's theme. Like so many TV documentaries, the programme lost its impact, and became merely interesting wallpaper.

Through my regular contact with Glyn Daniel and Brian Hope Taylor, I became more and more drawn into the world of archaeology. I also gave much time to the development of the Royal Television Society. Its council met once a month in the early evening, adjourning afterwards for dinner in a private room in Kettners Restaurant, in Soho, to hear a talk from some celebrated guest.

It was on one of these occasions that I witnessed Glyn Daniel in his full glory. I had heard tales of his gargantuan appetite for food and wine, but little suspected what was to follow when I brought him to a council dinner as guest speaker. He had just been elected to Cambridge University's highest position in archaeology, the Disney Professorship. I arranged to meet him before the meal, so as to be there to make introductions, and when I arrived at Kettners, he was already about four large Negroni cocktails ahead. He did not appear too far gone, however, and I briefed him on his fellow diners.

During the meal, I noticed – with considerable misgiving – that he was toying with his food, and consuming heroic quantities of wine. When the time came for him to speak he had almost fallen asleep in his coffee.

I stood up and introduced him, and after a long and uncomfortable moment, he climbed to his feet. I was fairly sure that, by then, he had no idea where he was, or who he was addressing.

'Not long ago...' he began, in a stumbling voice, '...people believed... that the world began... in 4004 BC...'

A long pause.

'Now...' he resumed – to my relief.

Another long pause.

'...largely because of the discovery... of Sumerian cuneiform writing...'

A lengthy silence.

'...a magnificent exhibition of which... is currently on view in The British Museum...'

Another lengthy silence.

'... and which I am sure you have all been to...'

He broke off, and glared round the table – seeming to see his listeners for the first time.

'I presume you *have* all been to see it?'

The listeners, senior television luminaries all, wriggled with embarrassment.

'Well – *who* has been to see it?' demanded Glyn.

No response.

'You're a lot of bums!' Glyn snapped.

'Oh well...'

He swayed a little.

'Not long ago...'

He was beginning again!

'... people believed...'

A long pause.

'...that the world began... in 4004 BC... Now...'

Another pause.

'...we know...'

A longer pause.

'...it has been a lot longer than that.'

He sat down, and returned to the Land of Nod, gently snoring. The address was over.

After the dinner, I saw him off in a taxi.

'That went rather well, didn't it?' he said.

24

As *The Dark Ages* neared completion, John Woolf began to take a close – and tiresome – interest, as he had *with Project X*. It was clear that he understood even less of what our programme was all about than he had with the inventions. Wearing his Hollywood producer hat, he pronounced that the title was too "downbeat". No one, he said, would want to watch something that was "dark". The Programme Planning Committee deferred to him, as the expert. They did not ask Brian and me to decide on a different title, however. Instead, they invited us to submit a list of possibles, from which they would make their choice. It did not occur to my lords and masters that Brian and I might feel just a *teeny bit* insulted. I was naughty, and taking their point that we needed a crowd puller, I sent Dick Joice a list. I headed it with *Excavation Street*, followed by *Sunday Night At The Rome Coliseum*, and *Top Of The Pots*. He was not amused, and (perhaps wisely) declined to present it to the committee. The title they went for was hardly less risible. *The Lost Centuries*, I thought, would be greeted as something to do with cricket.

On Thursday, July 8th 1971, the series was launched, with a lavish reception and preview at the National Film Theatre, on London's South Bank. It was attended by television critics, leading figures in the industry and a number of important archaeologists, including Sir Mortimer Wheeler. Robin Steele had made a brief appearance in one of the episodes as a kilted Scottish Anglophobe, and I invited him and his wife as my personal guests. Transmission began on Sunday, July 18th, at teatime. There was a heat wave, so everyone could confidently be expected to be on the beach.

Nevertheless, the press was unanimously full of praise. *The Times* wrote a gushing review, remarking on my artistry, and there were similar paeans of praise from *The Telegraph*, *The Guardian* and many other publications.

Despite the ruinous slot, the audience figures held up. One person even told me that he and his family regularly came in early from the beach to see it. The only people who seemed unenthusiastic were Anglia's management. Lord Townshend complained about the excessively academic tone. 'Some of us left school at fifteen,' he complained to me (the school he left was Harrow…).

Many of the techniques I employed were ahead of their time, and frightened Anglia's conservative management (it is interesting that when the BBC's *Civilisation* was repeated, after thirty-five years, in 2005, it appeared slow and tedious, its presenter Lord Clarke stiff and ponderous, whereas *The Lost Centuries* still stands up quite well).

One of the real pleasures of my job was receiving letters from appreciative members of the public. I particularly treasured one from an elderly viewer in Woolwich:

"Dear Sir, I was looking at the Telly on Sunday
night on the above date and it was 6-30 The Lost
Centuries about Arthur Well at a place called Carleon

just out side of Newport Mon there is a field and it as got like a big ole in the center of the field and we called it King Arthur's round table I have sat in that ole when I lived in Newport many years ago. I am 82 now. But when I see that on the Telly I just had to send to tell you about it. Trusting these few lines will meet you approval I am yours sincerely (X) P.S. IT WAS ON THE I.T.V"

I always replied personally to such letters, and sometimes an interesting correspondence ensued.

For the time being it was back to the common round of filming for the magazine programmes and an occasional half-hour "special" for me. I enjoyed re-enacting "old time" ploughing, with heavy horses, for *Farming Diary*, which we filmed in a small field at Blythburgh beside the road to Walberswick. I took the elderly retired farm workers to lunch in the White Hart at Blythburgh afterwards and they regaled me with tales of the hardships they had endured during the hungry thirties. When the harvest had been got in, they were sacked, and then had to trudge across England, sleeping rough under hedgerows, to work for a spell turning the barley into beer at Burton on Trent.

I received invitations to give lectures on our work. I went to schools in Lincolnshire, Rotary Clubs in Suffolk, and photographic groups in Norwich, and showed excerpts from films I had made. As a basically shy person I found this public speaking enjoyable, rather to my surprise. The company appreciated the good public relations.

A few years before I had been asked by the Further Education College at Lowestoft to advise them on careers in the media. I was now appointed a governor of the college and attended monthly meetings, under the chairman, Lord Somerleyton. The college had a lively art department, in which one of the lecturers specialised in the oriental art called batik. This had an unexpected outcome. With the children at school, Mary found herself at a loose end. Since we had been in Norfolk she had been in two films, *A Life In Danger* and *The Curse Of The Fly*, and had parts in one or two Anglia dramas, but a return to a serious acting career while not living in London was clearly impractical. She had a childhood talent for painting, so she enrolled at Lowestoft Art School as a mature student. She became "hooked" on batik, and the foundations were laid for what became a highly successful second career.

It seemed to me that the style and character of Anglia was changing. It became increasingly evident that Anglia's "proprietors", as they had taken to calling themselves, had become rather different people from the enthusiastic entrepreneurs of 1959. They had become distant from the production staff. The Programme Planning Committee still met in London and decided what programmes were to be made. As the company created only ten hours of local programming per week, of which the news, and hardy perennials like *Farming Diary*, took the lion's share, inevitably most new programme ideas were rejected. In the ten years or so since we went on the air the staff had grown enormously. Several score producers had been appointed, most of whom had little to do. Talking to many of them, it became apparent to me that job satisfaction was at a low level.

At this time, I was, I suppose, at the height of what powers I possessed as a documentary director and all sorts of assignments came my way. An idea of mine for making half-hour profiles of prominent local people won the planning committee's approval. I began with a portrait of the squire of a small village in mid-Norfolk who had reconstructed "Boadicea's camp", complete with watchtowers, "punishment pits" and sundry live animals. He was delightfully eccentric and perfect television material. I followed with a similar film about a Lincolnshire landowner who had just been appointed sheriff of the county, with responsibility for maintaining a gallows to be used on people who committed the crime of high treason for which the death sentence was still in force (and still is, as far as I know).

These programmes were very popular and fun to make. June 1972 found me filming a profile of the celebrated chef, Robert Carrier. He had bought Hintlesham Hall, a Jacobean stately home near Ipswich, and was turning it into a gourmet restaurant. I had been to Hintlesham before soon after we went on the air when, with Stephen McCormack and musical director Norman Hackforth, I had visited its then owner, Anthony Stokes. Stokes planned to create a music festival, along the lines of Glyndebourne. He was the complete eccentric. Lunch consisted of a crab for each of us, with a pair of nutcrackers. The village gossip had it that he harnessed his wife naked to a Roman chariot, and whipped her round the grounds. I told Robert Carrier this, and was amazed when he took me down to the cellar and showed me a chariot.

Carrier, an openly gay American, was hardly less extraordinary than Stokes. The hall was crowded with his flamboyant friends, including the painter Francis Bacon. I had a great time filming – not least because Carrier whipped up the most delicious lunches for the unit. The restaurant he established was successful for a number of years, until he got bored with it, and retired from public view.

Early in 1972 I drove north through the heart of Lincolnshire, and took the antique ferryboat across the River Humber to Hull. Our newsroom had alerted us to something very big that was about to begin. After many years of planning, several abortive projects, and much political manoeuvring, a massive road bridge across the River Humber was going to be constructed. There was no question that such a major historic undertaking should be recorded, and we decided to set up a long-term project to film every stage of the operation. In the next year or two, I was to travel north every week or so, filming every detail of the fascinating project, as it grew from two holes in the ground on either side of the river, to the erection of four giant towers brooding over Humberside and north Lincolnshire. I was not to complete the assignment. In 1974, the newly created Yorkshire Television Company, based in Leeds, won custodianship of the Belmont transmitter, ending Anglia's northern sphere of interest. (Rather unfairly, North Norfolk now found itself outside Anglia's transmission area for a time.) I don't know what Yorkshire TV did with all the film I had shot. I had too many other interests. The bridge was completed in June 1981.

While I had been in Hull we filmed the maiden crossing of a new North Sea Ferry. One of the VIP passengers who accompanied us was the young local MP, John Prescott. If I had been told he would be Deputy Prime Minister one day I would not have believed it.

In November of 1972, the Royal Television Society began a re-launch campaign, masterminded by the BBC's Chief Engineer, Neville Watson. I was invited to an exclusive luncheon in Television Centre, to discuss plans. It was fascinating to see how the BBC top brass lived. In one of a series of private dining rooms on the top floor, we had a superb three-course meal, with various wines. There was even a printed menu, with a gold tassel. The head of BBC2, David Attenborough, was lunching a party of his high-flyers in the next room.

In December, Brian Hope Taylor came back into my life. He was preparing an excavation of the Devil's Dyke in Cambridgeshire, and Glyn Daniel wanted it recorded. This was another programme that had to be filmed over several months, so I fitted it in with the similar stockpile-filming of the construction of the Humber Bridge. Both projects necessitated lengthy journeys, and I was away from home a great deal.

I had kept in touch with Michael Seligman, the person who had brought me to Anglia, thirteen years before. He now owned a small compact film studio in Holland Park, and had built up a company specialising in industrial and corporate documentaries. In the early summer of 1973, a commission came his way to make a recruiting film for the Shah of Iran's air force, to be shown in every cinema and television channel in that country.

It was a larger project than Michael was used to, and he asked me if I would write and direct it. I had "clocked up" entitlement to several weeks' holiday from Anglia, so I accepted the job, and flew out to Tehran to carry out research on which to base a script.

It was an overnight flight, and I arrived at two a.m. I was taken to the Sheraton Hotel, half asleep, where I was told that a helicopter would arrive at eight, to take me to the military airfield. I had hardly time to change my clothes before the telephone rang, and a voice told me that I was awaited downstairs. I sleepwalked to the lift, and found my way to the hotel car park, where a twin-rotor military helicopter was waiting for me with its blades idly rotating. Inside was my Iranian employer, PR-man Mohsen Tayebi. I climbed in beside him and, in what seemed like a dream, soared across the city, to descend on to the runway of the air force base. It was where I had arrived an hour or two before. The Imperial Iranian Air Force shared Tehran airport with the civilian facility.

I transferred to a four-by-four and we slowly moved off along the perimeter track, in front of what looked like the entire Iranian air force, lined up for my personal inspection. When Mike Seligman had briefed me, I had – rather condescendingly – wondered if the Persian air force flew magic carpets. Now, I saw before me the sixth largest air force in the world. I passed down line after line of F4 *Phantom* fighter-bombers, F5 *Freedom* fighters, C130 *Hercules* transports, helicopters and lighter aircraft. It was an air force that flew – I was told – more hours than any other in the world. I was now introduced to some of the pilots, from whom I should choose my "stars". I decided on a short, chirpy captain named Majid Tabrisi. Like most of the flyers, he had been trained in Texas by the USAF, and spoke perfect English, though with an American accent. In choosing him, I passed over another young pilot, who clearly thought he was a potential Hollywood star. He was not pleased.

After a whirlwind round of research I came home to Norfolk, and Anglia, for a few weeks during which I wrote the script. It told the story of a young pilot, from his first days as a recruit to mastery of a state-of-the-art aircraft.

Looking back – and consulting my diaries – I cannot understand how I fitted so much in during those days. I managed to scale down my travels to Humberside and the Devil's Dyke to every two or three weeks, which allowed me to embark on a new major documentary project.

The removal and destruction in 1962 of the historic Doric arch that stood in front of Euston railway station provoked a great deal of condemnation, inspiring a movement to conserve monuments that were not necessarily ancient. A new academic discipline was born called "Industrial Archaeology". I saw an opportunity.

Dick Joice had become a local "star", with his appearances in a regular studio-based series, called *Bygones*, so I persuaded him to front a filmed series in which we would travel all over the British Isles seeking relics around which we could tell the story of the Industrial Revolution. Although his health had suffered a serious decline he was enthusiastic, and in the late summer of 1973 we set off with the film unit, accompanied by Dick's wife, my former assistant, Jean. We ended up with a fascinating series which we called *Digging For Yesterday*. Mary voiced some of the commentaries and my old friend, Hector Ross, narrated others.

Shortly after we finished filming Dick Joice underwent a major heart operation. It compelled him to put a curb on his enthusiasm and pull his horns in – just a little! – as far as television work was concerned.

I returned to Tehran in November to shoot the Iranian Air Force film, with a small unit from Mike Seligman's company. An Iranian joined the crew as assistant cameraman. "Zandi" was actually a veteran cameraman. He confided to me that Iranian filmmakers were upset that a British company had been appointed to make such an important film. He omitted to say that the Shah did not trust his own countrymen – at that very moment some film people were under arrest for supposedly attempting to assassinate him. When we began filming it quickly became apparent that language, and other technical difficulties, made it more practical for Zandi to take over as cameraman. He was very professional and we worked well together.

It was an interesting film to make, at a key moment in Iran's history. We could not predict, of course, that the Shah's days were numbered, and a revolution, followed by a war with neighbouring Iraq – during which many of the pilots in our film would be killed – was only a few years away. As it happened it was not necessary to wait for that war for tragedy to strike.

As a dramatic finale to the film we flew to Tabriz on the extreme western borders of the country, to film a display by the aerobatic team. It consisted of four F5 fighters. I briefed the pilots before take-off, explaining where our camera would be positioned so that they could fly where we would get the best view of their manoeuvres. The pilots' wives accompanied us when we set up our camera on the edge of the runway.

The opening routine passed directly over our heads, making it hard to follow. I was in communication with the aerobatic team leader through a radio link, so I asked him to move further away across the runway. The four aircraft made a wide sweep and turned towards us again. I saw one of them peel off and cross through the formation and assumed this was part of the routine. But we had not expected it, and the cameraman – his eye to the finder – asked me out of the side of his mouth whether to follow the one or the three.

I made a snap decision. 'The three –'

I had hardly got the words out before the single aircraft flew straight into a block of buildings, with a *crump* and a burst of flame.

'Cut!' I yelled.

Beside me a woman screamed and burst into tears. She knew it was her husband's aircraft.

It was chaos. We were very much surplus to requirements now, and I ordered the unit to wrap and return to our vehicles. Then I walked off alone along the runway, shocked and distraught. Sudden death is difficult to take in. We flew back to Tehran in silence.

There was a lengthy debriefing, during which the film was examined. There had been a flock of birds at the end of the runway, the team leader said, and he had seen one of them smash through the unfortunate pilot's windscreen, killing him instantly.

I wondered… if I hadn't changed their approach line…

General Rabi, the air force commander, saw my distress and tried to comfort me.

'He was doing his best for you, and you were doing your best for the air force,' he said. 'That's life…'

'It's not much of a life when that happens,' I replied.

The general's kind words helped when I passed through the crew-room afterwards. The unpleasant pilot I had not chosen for the leading part sneered at me.

'You couldn't get through without killing *somebody*!' he said.

It was just what I needed.

I returned to Tehran to find a telegram awaiting me at the hotel telling me that my father had died. As I stood in my hotel room contemplating this run of awful luck, the floor suddenly raced towards me and smashed into my face. I recovered consciousness lying beside the bed. I had fainted like that before when I was in a high-altitude place but in later years I have wondered if this was a precursor of the heart attack I would one day suffer.

Before we flew home I got hold of the English-language newspaper. It reported that the aircraft had "damaged a building". It did not report that the apartment block had been demolished, killing about a hundred people.

Another, and perhaps even more awful tragedy was in store for most of the people who made the film with me. Following the fall of the Shah nearly all the air force's top commanders, including General Rabi, were executed. And I wonder what happened to boisterous little Majid Tabrisi in the devastating war with Iraq that followed.

I never got to my father's funeral. I returned to England two or three days before, but there was a petrol-station strike on the day. Mary and I set out for London and were immobilised in a massive traffic jam on the approach road. We arrived after the cremation was over. I was not sorry. I knew the ceremony would be drab and perfunctory, and I preferred to remember my father in his young days as the unorthodox and interesting person he had been then.

25

IN 1974 Anglia's broadcasting licence expired for a second time. There were no rival bidders when the franchise came up for renewal, but Anglia's board thought it advisable to make their application as persuasive as possible. I was given the task of compiling a presentation, made up of excerpts from the best programmes. It was an ironic assignment in view of what was to happen six years later, when the contract came up for renewal again.

At the beginning of the year I had a visit from Michael Satow, the former managing director of ICI in India. While there his hobby had been "rescuing" ancient steam locomotives he found abandoned and rotting in the Indian jungle, and in his retirement he occupied himself bringing them to England, to be restored by youngsters on a government apprentice training scheme in the north of England. He had an ambitious project to propose. Britain's oldest steam locomotive, George Stephenson's *Locomotion*, was exhibited on the platform of Darlington railway station. Satow wanted to build an exact working replica, to be installed at the soon-to-be-created "North of England Open Air Museum" at Beamish, County Durham – would Anglia sponsor the exercise? I put his plan to Dick Joice and Dick enthusiastically agreed.

We spent February and March making the film. The trainee apprentices made a superb job of the replica, and it was "fired up" for the first time in the marshalling yards at ICI's Billingham works. It was a scary hour or two – we remembered tales of boilers on early locomotives exploding. However *Locomotion II* made steam properly and we had a thrilling maiden run, with the unit and me perched on top of the coal tender.

Early 1974 saw the completion of the Devil's Dyke film. It was my last association with Brian Hope Taylor, and – as it happened – his last excavation. Soon afterwards he began to suffer various complaints rooted, it seemed, in some sort of depressive condition. He resigned his university lectureship and began a steady decline. It was a genuine tragedy.

My fortunes, on the other hand, were still in the ascendant. The phone rang when I was in bed one night and I was surprised to receive a call from a BBC man I did not know. He was head of a unit in Bristol specialising in wildlife and archaeology programmes. He confided to me that he was about to resign to take up a job in America. I had been "noticed" he said – if I wanted to apply for the vacant position he was sure I would get it. Mary and I gave it a lot of thought over the next few days, but in the end I decided not to apply. It would have meant disrupting the boys' schooling, at a sensitive moment for them. So life continued at White Horse Farm.

Another interesting phone call came from marine archaeologist Sidney Wignall. From studying ancient charts and the topography near Panama he claimed to have identified the exact spot in the ocean where Sir Francis Drake was buried in 1596. Drake, he said, was likely to have been buried in a lead coffin – there was every chance that his body would be largely intact. It could be brought back to England for a state burial in Westminster Abbey.

It sounded like an important project, of worldwide interest, and I took the proposal to Aubrey Buxton. He was excited, and we began preparations, but then Aubrey told me he had discussed the idea with his friend, the Duke of Edinburgh, who ruled that a sea burial must not be disturbed. So the world never knew whether Wignall had found Sir Francis Drake.

The celebrated novelist Kingsley Amis called at Anglia one day to offer us an idea for a documentary that he wanted to write and present. He was fascinated with science fiction at the time, and what he described sounded like the basis for a very interesting programme. Most people, Amis told us, assumed that the inventor of rocket propulsion was the German scientist Werner von Braun, who had developed the V2 missile for the Nazis during World War II. Von Braun had been taken to the USA after the war and under his guidance the Americans had initiated the space industry.

Kingsley Amis said that this was an entirely wrong reading of history. There were two pioneers of rocketry, and neither was von Braun. One was Russian, a man named Konstantin Tsiolkovsky and the other American, Robert H. Goddard. They had pursued their experiments in the early 1930s, unwittingly beginning what became an ongoing "space race" between the USA and Soviet Russia, of prime importance in the *Cold War* which was at its height when Kingsley called on us.

The Programme Planning Committee asked me to collaborate with Kingsley on a programme that would follow the story of *"The Race For Space"* from its earliest days to the current exciting developments in space exploration. We began our research with a visit to the Soviet Embassy in Kensington Palace Gardens, to gain details of Tsiolkovsky's life and work. We received an enthusiastic reception from the Cultural Counsellor, who treated us to a slap-up lunch in a nearby expensive restaurant. Over a jovial alcoholic meal I asked him about his background. He told me he had studied at Moscow's Film Academy to become a director, but the authorities had decided he should do his present job.

I must have looked surprised. 'But are you happy with that?' I asked him.

He looked at me with a sardonic expression.

'You don't understand us at all, do you?' he grinned. 'We are judged by people who know better than ourselves what our potential is. We don't spend our lives eating our hearts out, wanting something we do not have the talent for. We accept what we are given. That's the recipe for a happy life.'

I don't know what Kingsley made of that – whether it chimed with his political views of the time, which apparently veered from extreme left to extreme right. In any case, he got tired of the project and it was eventually dropped. It was a pity, because it could have been an important programme, and I got to like Kingsley (a sentiment that I understand is not universally shared).

The current sensation in the world of archaeology was the discovery in northern Kenya of a fossilised skull that seemed to set the beginning of humankind earlier by a million or so years.

In the 1950s and '60s, an anthropologist named Louis Leakey and his wife, Mary, had discovered in East Africa's Great Rift Valley the oldest remains of a forerunner of humans. Now their son Richard, exploring further north around the eastern banks of Lake Rudolph (since renamed Lake Turkana), had discovered the fossil fragments of a skull that appeared to be similar to the one found by his father but much older. Newly developed scientific dating of the volcanic rock in which it was found suggested that the creature lived around two and a half million years ago. Leakey gave his discovery the museum catalogue number 1470, and the creature had come to be known as "1470 man".

The Leakey's were friends of Glyn Daniel. He had introduced them to Aubrey Buxton, and on the strength of *Survival*'s reputation, Aubrey got Richard Leakey's agreement to make a film about his discovery. Aubrey asked me down to London. 'This is obviously your film,' he said to me – which, in Anglia terms, indeed it was. I was excited by the prospect of making such a film. It would be a high point in the many years I had spent developing archaeology as a subject for television.

I did not guess that the assignment would have less pleasant, and even more important, consequences for me.

Aubrey and *Survival*'s editor, Colin Willock, told me that they hoped the film would sell in America. It would therefore be co-produced with an American who understood the transatlantic market. John H lived in Kenya, and was a friend of Richard Leakey. One or two teeny-weeny details were omitted from this briefing, as I would find out. I was informed that the American had already carried out the research with Leakey and would therefore be responsible for the script. I was rather surprised, and not too happy about this, as I was used to preparing my own script.

John was waiting outside the door and he was invited in to meet me. He greeted me with great charm, as was to be expected of an Ivy League man. 'I shall learn a lot from you, Forbes,' he flattered me. We went to lunch at a Mayfair restaurant, accompanied by Colin Willock and a burly "white hunter" from Kenya, who was to manage the expedition. The latter habitually hailed my new American colleague as "Sunshine", a hint that he knew where his interests lay. Politics reared its ugly head straight away. John told me he was an old acquaintance of Richard Leakey. He warned me that we were likely to have trouble persuading him to cooperate with some of the things required of a television production.

I was given a copy of a "script". It was no more than an outline of the subject matter – a thumbnail sketch of the human evolution story, a CV of Richard Leakey, and a brief description of the discovery of skull 1470. John said that he was working on a scenario, which he would give me when we arrived in Africa.

Colin Willock then had two surprises for me. The first was that he had engaged a film unit from outside the company. 'We don't want any union interference,' he explained. I was sorry that I would not have my old friend, Ian Craig, along and asked about the chosen cameraman's experience. The answer was vague. It seemed as though the man had only made amateur films.

The second surprise was that I was to direct some other filming while in Kenya. *Survival*'s leading wildlife filmmaker, Alan Root, had shot film of a hot-air balloon flight over Mount Kilimanjaro. A programme was being assembled from it and I was to direct sequences in which Root and his wife acted in front of the camera.

At the end of July I left for Nairobi with my unfamiliar unit. On the evening of my arrival I had dinner with Richard Leakey and one or two of his academic team in a Japanese restaurant. We sat cross-legged on the floor while African girls dressed as geishas fed us *sushi* titbits. Contrary to what I had been led to expect, I liked Richard Leakey. He treated me as an academic equal (as indeed I probably was, for Leakey was self-taught and like me had not been to university). As we were leaving he drew me aside.

'How well do you know John?' he asked.

I replied that I did not know him at all.

'Well I do,' Leakey said, 'I've known him for years. As far as I'm aware, he has no experience as a television producer. We are relying on you.'

The misunderstanding was now complete. I was bewildered, and began to wonder what of earth I had found myself involved in.

I then went to see Alan Root to make arrangements for the balloon filming. He and his wife, Joan, lived in a house on the shore of Lake Naivasha. They were a brilliant wildlife photography team who had created their own small wildlife reserve which they used in making their films. When I arrived, Alan was on his way to visit Minnie, his pet Striped Hyena. He invited me to accompany him, and assuming that he would not deliberately endanger my life, I followed him into the animal's enclosure. The enormous beast raced towards me, and I found myself staring into two mad-looking yellow eyes. They were level with mine, for the hyena was a good four feet tall at the shoulder.

Root gave it a playful wallop in the side with his fist, and it rolled away, delighted. Almost immediately, however, it returned to stare me down.

At that moment, Alan's wife, Joan, appeared at the gate.

'Alan! What on earth are you doing with Forbes in there?' she shouted.

To which Root grinned and replied, 'Well, I didn't ask him to come in.'

By this time the hyena was making up its mind that I was well down the animal order of precedence. I backed to the gate, while Alan diverted its attention by engaging it in a boxing match. I was to learn that Alan was a famous practical joker and sometimes irresponsible, even with his own life. Showing off one day in front of a party of tourists by "milking" a deadly puff adder of its venom, the snake had bitten his hand. As a result he lost three fingers – and very nearly his life because of an allergy to the anti-venine. On another occasion he was attacked by a hippopotamus while swimming with a herd of the brutes, and nearly had his stomach ripped out.

Before we flew up to Lake Rudolph to begin the serious business that had taken me to Africa, Alan Root, an assortment of "white hunters" and an American millionairess who had just returned from shooting crocodiles on the borders of the Sudan, got together to whoop it up in a Nairobi nightclub in the basement of the New Stanley Hotel. Richard Leakey did not come. Alan announced that he intended to fly his hot air balloon by blowing flame from his mouth in the manner of a circus fire-eater. He then demonstrated by taking a mouthful of paraffin from the table light and spitting a roaring swirl of fire across the adjoining table, to the understandable consternation of its diners.

He took no notice of their protests, and followed up with another spectacular conflagration, and one of the white hunters, very drunk, said, 'I say – I'd like to try that.'

I was probably the most sober person at the table and had no desire to see the idiot burn his face off so I made a hasty trip to the loo. When I returned the deed was over. The hunter looked a little less cheerful, and his face was streaked with soot. Alan seized the lamp again and blew an even more impressive tongue of flame.

This brought the hotel manager, who said, with quiet dignity, 'Mister Root, would you kindly cease blowing fire?'

Alan took no notice of him, so the manager sat down beside me and helped himself to a drink. The affair was pure *Boy's Own Paper* stuff and, I am told, typical of the white inhabitants of Kenya in those days.

John and I flew north to Leakey's camp on the eastern side of Lake Rudolph in a four-seater single-engined Cessna, my co-producer spending the entire time writing away furiously on a yellow A4 pad. Leaving behind the "White Highlands", the home of the Happy Valley set of expatriate farmers, we eventually came upon a chain of small extinct volcanoes, around which stretched the desolate, arid landscape I was to live in for the next eight weeks.

The plane bounced and yawed as it approached the shore of a vast lake, and landed fighting a violent crosswind blowing off the water. We had arrived at a "non-place" called Koobi Fora, on the eastern shore of Lake Rudolph, where Richard Leakey's expedition was based. We climbed out of the plane, battling to stand up against the violent gusts. The tents lined up along the beach were flapping and straining at their guy-ropes. The wind did not drop for the entire period of our stay, and more than once a tent was blown into the lake.

I looked around at a terrain that relatively few Europeans have seen. Austrian explorer Count Teleki discovered the lake in 1888 and named it after the heir to the Austro-Hungarian throne, Crown Prince Rudolph, who shot himself a year later. Other people call it "the Jade Sea", which gives a deceptively attractive picture. It is utterly hostile, the water teeming with crocodiles, the surrounding land infested with scorpions and Carpet Vipers, one of the deadliest known snakes.

It has been said that more people have died by the lake in proportion to the number who had ever been there than anywhere else on earth.

The landscape was certainly like nothing on earth. Smashed and thrown about, time after time, by tectonic activity over the ages, it is a parched wilderness littered with thorny scrub, rocky outcrops, and ridges stratified at crazy angles. Only the cones of the two active volcanoes Shin and Derati break the otherwise flat horizon. One can easily imagine a primeval world in which our remote ancestors struggled to cling to existence.

The expedition's mission was to place Richard Leakey's discovery in the fossil record of human evolution. It was also to acquire as much knowledge as possible of the environment in which the owner of the 1470 skull had lived more than two million years ago, so as to build a picture of the creature's lifestyle. All this was designed to throw light on the most fascinating question of all – at what point did the ancestral creature become "human", and what features made it so? It was a dauntingly complex subject to make understandable in a fifty-minute television programme.

As I had anticipated, John shared a tent with the white hunter. I moved in with the sound recordist, Keith Desmond, who was the most agreeable member of the film team. A few hundred yards along the beach, Leakey and his associates were accommodated in *bandas* – more substantial wooden buildings with openings for windows and doorways.

Most of the expedition's scientists were "Physical Anthropologists" (as distinct from "social" anthropologists). Their interests lay in the study of external human characteristics rather than cultural ones. The majority were American, from the University of California campuses at Berkeley (pronounced "Burkly"), Stamford and Santa Cruz. The principal archaeologist, Glyn Isaac, was also at Berkeley, but was Welsh.

Richard Leakey was accompanied by his anthropologist wife, Meave, and their two small children. Bob Campbell, the *National Geographic* magazine photographer, had brought his wife, Heather, who was a vet. Although the Leakeys seemed to think it a suitable place to bring small children, there were serious dangers apart from the wild animals. Somali bandits, "the shifta" from the north, had more than once carried out a raid, and a guard with loaded gun was always on standby.

Leakey had brought a party of ten or twelve homeless hunter-gatherers to the camp to observe how humans supported life in such an environment. They were probably part of the "Dosanech" community in the north, but they called themselves "Shankilla Molo". An odd choice for them. "Shankilla" is a derogatory term, roughly meaning "nigger". They clearly had a low opinion of themselves. They went naked, and appeared to be totally wild, living on roots – and crocodile when they were lucky enough to kill one with their spears. They spoke a language of their own, and it was only possible to communicate with them through a blind man who lived with them, who spoke Swahili.

I liked my American colleague at first, but as the days passed I grew more and more concerned and baffled. It seemed that he and I had a fundamentally different view over how the film's content should be presented. John's script evolved day by day and reached me in instalments, so that I was never able to get a handle on his overall concept. This also left me with no opportunity to make contributions, which was especially frustrating, as I was used to doing the research and writing a script myself. Having made so many similar documentaries, it did not take me long to form ideas on how such a subject should be approached. I thought it essential to capture a sense of *place* – convey "atmosphere", conjure up a vision of what it was like to be one of those most ancient of creatures. We were in "the Garden of Eden", after all. It was all there before our eyes. It immediately became apparent that my co-producer had no intention of boring the American viewers with anything like that. Perhaps Americans really do insist on furious action in every shot. I just did not believe that such an approach was compatible with the subject we were engaged upon.

My attempts at directing the kind of film I was used to ran into trouble almost immediately. Especially with documentary, it is vital that the director and cameraman have a good rapport. I just couldn't get the measure of this young chap. Each time I turned to him to indicate what I wanted to film, I found that he had wandered off to shoot something else that caught his eye. After the first day or two, I thought I saw glances pass between him and my co-producer, which aroused my suspicion that there was an "understanding" between them. A further irritant was that "Sunshine's" every pronouncement was greeted by a congratulatory slap on the back by the white hunter.

Directing became almost impossible. John had a totally different view from mine about the way every shot should be handled. One morning, I observed an amazing scene – the naked Shankilla Molo were sauntering with their spears through a herd of Grevy's Zebra and topi, and the animals were taking no notice of them. It was a vivid picture of nature in equilibrium. John frustrated my attempt to film it. As soon as I called "action", he dashed towards the zebra shouting, so that they stampeded. We had a heated discussion and eventually agreed that once the herd had settled down, I would be allowed my version as well as his. However, when the moment came, he could not resist stampeding the animals again. I began to feel a deep depression – a totally new experience for me when filming.

The project passed inexorably beyond any control I could impose. By now, John was encouraging the cameraman – who had very definite ideas of his own – to expose miles of film on scenes that had taken his eye, but which had little to do with the subject. It was obvious that there were three "directors" on the case. That evening, I insisted that we had a private talk, away from either the white hunter or the cameraman. Then John told me the truth. *He* had brought the project to Anglia, and it had been made clear by the *Survival* people that he was in charge. It was unnecessary to add that I was only there to meet British trade union requirements. All the talk of it being "obviously my film" and John learning from me was cynical baloney.

26

RICHARD LEAKEY was also unhappy about the way the thing was going. I was in a difficult position. At any other time or place I would have told John to stay away from the camera when I was directing or walked out of the production. But we were a thousand miles from base with almost non-existent communications (no mobile phones then). I would have liked to consult Aubrey Buxton, but that was impossible. I was at the sharp end of a very expensive and supposedly important project. The last thing needed was for me to wreck the thing. I decided that all that mattered was to get the film done – recriminations could wait for another time. I had to face the reality, however, that what had promised to be the climax of my career as a producer of archaeology documentaries was now going to become a fiasco.

Another obsession we have American television to thank for is the use of "reconstructions", without which no documentary is acceptable nowadays. John wanted to fake a scene showing Leakey and his wife stumbling upon the famous skull, which had been virtually in one piece lying in a dried riverbed. John's script required the Leakey's to gush words like, 'Gosh – look at that!' 'I've never seen anything like it before!' et cetera, when they saw it. Not *too* hammy, perhaps, but my co-producer wanted me to place the camera with the skull in the foreground and the Leakey's seen in the distance approaching it. In effect, the viewers would be "discovering" the thing before the discoverers! An entire nonsense. At this point I gave up and told John to direct the scene himself. To my annoyance, he did.

Our differences were temporarily forgotten when my birthday – my forty-eighth – was celebrated with a feast of roast oryx and a liberal supply of champagne flown up from Niarobi. My presents consisted of a safari hat with a poisoned arrow stuck through the crown, a supply of aspirin from camp doctor Hazel, and a worked chert scraper, dated to 2.3m million years BP, from University of California anthropologist Dianne Gifford. She had covered every millimetre with an inscription in Indian ink announcing that it was "unsullied by any pedestrian catalogue number". This was a reference to a gaff I had committed soon after my arrival, when I told Leakey that I hoped he didn't deface any of his finds with indelible numbers, as was the practice in many museums. He had bristled and declared that of course he did.

It is amazing to look at that tiny piece of material today and realise that it was fashioned by hands that were not "human".

If I had not had the frustrating situation with John to cope with, being in a remote part of Africa with an expedition like Leakey's would have been the experience of a lifetime. Life beside the lake was amazing. One could never be unconscious of the proximity of dangerous wildlife. At night we heard the curious "coughing" sounds of nearby lions. Hippos roamed the shores of the lake. We were astounded at first to see that everyone used the lake as a bath. It reputedly had the highest concentration of crocodiles in all of Africa, and seemed like madness. But we, too, caught the madness. It was heaven to laze in the warm alkali softness of the water after the heat, dust, and burning wind of the working day. We discussed why we were not attacked by the crocs, and could only assume that the enormous quantity of fish in the lake made attacks on human prey unnecessary. We would sit in front of the tents after dinner and hold torches level with our eyes, aiming the beams across the water. Pairs of glowing coals, reflections from the crocodiles' retinas, revealed them cruising to and fro hunting for fish.

The *National Geographic* magazine's photographer, Bob Campbell, was an interesting companion. He is portrayed by the Australian actor Bryan Brown in the film *Gorillas In The Mist* about "the gorilla lady", Diane Fossey. When we were not shooting, Bob took me into the bush in his specially fitted-out Land Rover. He had inherited it from the veteran wildlife photography team, Armand and Michaela Denis, from whom he had learned his trade. On one occasion we spotted a full-size male lion not far ahead. Bob climbed down from the Land Rover and walked towards it. I followed. The lion watched us for a few moments and then took to its heels. If we had been in a wildlife park it would have attacked us, Bob told me. 'They know when you're not allowed to shoot them.'

The Kenya police had lent us a helicopter, piloted by what I was told was "the best pilot in Africa". He was a former RAF officer and was known as "Punch", because of his prominent Roman nose. I was astonished to see that he had only one hand. He strapped the aircraft's control column to the stump where the other one had been. For a moment I wondered what the *worst* pilot in Africa would be like! He flew the helicopter expertly however and I had some thrilling rides, especially when we zoomed low over herds of elephants, zebra and topi.

We were all very surprised one evening when two white girls walked into the camp. They were French and studying at the Sorbonne. They told us that they had been living among the primitive Merilli people north of the lake, and were making their way back to Nairobi. They asked to stay the night in the camp and were overjoyed when our pilot, who happened to have arrived that day with supplies, agreed to take them back with him. Walking along the beach with one of them after dinner, I voiced my surprise at seeing girls there – alone in such a wild place. My companion, named Elizabeth, laughed. 'There are a lot of white girls around,' she said. 'They work as prostitutes in the tribal villages!' What one might call a conversation stopper! The girls slept in the open beside the lake that night. When morning came hippo tracks were found all around them.

Another evening I walked along the shore to the Shankilla Molo hunter-gatherers' "camp". It was nothing but a scooped-out hollow in the sand. They were boiling pieces of crocodile in a margarine can, and a clawed foot was hanging over the side. The rest of the reptile bubbled away in a foam of white slime. Not an appetising sight and I declined their invitation to dinner.

I visited them again when one was bitten by a snake. Our camp doctor administered aspirin and I sat holding the patient's hand while he stared at me with a pathetic expression and we waited to see if the bite was from a Carpet Viper, when he would have died, or a cobra, when he would probably emerge with nothing worse than a massive headache. It proved to be the cobra. The other Shankilla insisted on having some of the "magic" pills too.

Richard Leakey owned a seven-seater Cessna, in which he piloted us from location to location. Often we were so heavily loaded (even probably overloaded) that being the lightest of the cargo I had to wedge myself in the rear of the plane, lying prone with my feet up against the tail. I was in a more comfortable seat, however, when we took off to get a shot of Richard at the controls. The cameraman needed to be in the seat alongside him so I took the seat behind and between them. Unfortunately, however we tried, the wide-angle lens included my knees in the frame. Richard circled around until he saw a large enough clearing in the trees and landed. I got out. It was arranged that I would be picked up after the other two had flown around and taken the shots.

I walked over to the shade of some euphorbia shrubs and watched the plane take off. As the sound of the engine died away there was absolute silence. I was alone, totally vulnerable to any dangerous animal that might get my scent or stumble upon my presence. All around out there, I knew, were lions, as well as hyenas and sundry other unwelcoming inhabitants. I felt wonderful. I was, in the purest sense, "part of the ecology" and did not care if I was attacked or not. I suppose it was what some people would call "a spiritual experience". I am sorry that everyone cannot have one like it. After the best part of an hour, Richard's aircraft came back and picked me up. It was all too soon.

One of the lines of research was whether our remotest ancestors were hunters in their own right – or simply scavengers, taking their place in the pecking order for carrion alongside prehistoric vulture- or hyena-like creatures. It was necessary to discover whether virtually unarmed men were *capable* of hunting down and killing their food. An injured oryx, a large member of the antelope family with long sabre-like antlers, was discovered not far away. It had been attacked and crippled during the night by a lion, and was lying on its haunches unable to move away, awaiting the predator to return to finish it off.

The lion returned just as we set up the camera and I was amazed to see the Shankilla, armed only with crude spears and stones, chase it off.

They then turned to the wounded oryx.

I took no part in the discussion that followed between John and Richard Leakey. They agreed that the Shankilla should attempt to kill the animal. As its lethal horns made it virtually impossible to get close enough to use spears, that meant throwing stones. The Africans proceeded to hurl their missiles as the poor beast sat there, sweeping its great sabres in circles and doing its best to dodge the stones. An eye was dashed out. After nearly three quarters of an hour the animal was still very much alive. The filmmakers were unmoved, concentrating on the footage we were getting – which I guessed (rightly as it turned out) would be unusable on public television. I was nauseated – and to my surprise, so was one of the Shankilla. A boy, who I took to be in his teens, was in tears.

Finally Leakey called a halt. The oryx was exhausted and feeble enough for the Shankilla to go in with their spears to put the unfortunate beast out of its agonies. It seemed to me that a madness seemed to take hold of people at Lake Rudolph.

The climax of our filming was to have been a scavenger experiment to reveal how far humans would go to chase dangerous animals like lions off their prey.

Early one morning our white hunter reported that he had spotted a lion, lying low in a dried riverbed nearby. We could now discover if the Shankilla tribesman would attempt to flush the beast from its cover.

I don't know how I could have been persuaded to take such an insane risk to get a dramatic shot. We set up the camera on short tripod legs behind a low bush, and the film crew and I took up position around it. The lion would be driven towards us – and with luck (!) – it would leap over us in its rush to escape. It would be a thrilling, *unique* shot! (The incident is described by Leakey in his autobiography, *One Life*.)

It is hardly necessary to say that everything went wildly wrong. As the cameraman, the assistant, and I lay behind the camera in the dust of the riverbed, waiting to get our momentous shot, we could see, in the distance, the Shankilla advancing.

Suddenly Richard Leakey appeared behind me.

'Get out – and get our fast!' he shouted.

We did not waste time. The white hunter's "solitary" lion had turned out to be a pride of at least five lions, including cubs. Had the lioness been disturbed she would have taken out as many humans as possible. The hunter had a rifle, of course, but in whatever direction he aimed he had to endanger someone – us or the Shankilla. We were lucky to get off so lightly from that bit of insanity.

On my last evening at Lake Rudolph I took a final dip in the lake. The local game warden came to say farewell, and he and I sat in the lake with our heads just out of the deliciously cool water, watching the sun go down.

Usually, remembering the crocs, it was considered advisable to get out rather before that time.

'I'm going home tomorrow,' I said, 'and it looks as though my luck is going to hold. You're staying, and presumably going on doing this. Do you think you'll always get away with it?'

He looked at me, and said, 'You know – every time you have been inching towards to the shore, I have been inching a little closer...'

Back to Nairobi and civilisation. Mary and my PA, Valerie, arrived, and we travelled to Alan Root's home on Lake Naivasha, moving into one of the *bandas* belonging to the small hotel nearby.

The Roots were just as eccentric as on my earlier visit. They had adopted a baby hippopotamus, and were keeping it in their house. It was too young to have teeth, but snapped at our camera assistant's legs. The Roots were forced to release it into the lake when it grew large enough to try to kill everything in sight. Alan kicked off the proceedings in characteristic fashion. While we were preparing to film he came up behind me and said, 'Here – hold this.' He handed me a bright green snake. Assuming that it was harmless I took it. 'What is it?' I asked. Alan shrugged. 'I think it's a Tree Snake – not poisonous, of course.'

Throwing myself into the spirit of the thing, I crept up on Mary and Valerie, and laughed heartily at their shrieks of terror. Then the thought slowly came to me. What if the joke was on me? What if the snake was *not* harmless? Alan had been known to pull gags like that before. I carefully put the creature down and watched it slither away. Some days later, Mary and I went to the Nairobi snake park. There in a cage was a non-venomous African Tree Snake. It looked very like the one at Naivasha. But then we saw the cage beside it – containing a very poisonous Green Mamba. You could not tell the difference...

I got down to filming scenes of Alan flying his hot-air balloon. A favourite antic was to fly out over the lake, then descend until the basket was just touching the surface, when Alan would lean over and scoop up crayfish. He would then land on the shore, boil the crayfish over the balloon's burners, and everyone would have a delicious breakfast.

On our first morning it went wrong. Joan Root, Mary and I were watching as the balloon sailed far away across the hippo-infested water. Suddenly, Joan reacted.

'The balloon's lost its shape!' she gasped. When that happens a balloon spills the hot air and it collapses.

We watched the craft settle in the water. I wanted to send help, but Joan refused. It might be intentional, she said. Alan would be cross if we interfered. So we delayed, and it very nearly became a tragedy.

Eventually Joan agreed that something must be done, and a neighbour with a powerboat went to the rescue. By the time he got there Alan and the camera crew had been in the water for about forty-five minutes. The cameraman had been smothered by the collapsing balloon and was only saved when Alan slashed it away with a knife.

I did not meet the Roots again after this filming. They separated a year or two later. In 2006, Joan was murdered in the house beside Lake Naivasha. Her killers have never been discovered.

At the end of my prolonged stay in Africa I was rewarded by the *Survival* people with a tour of the Masai Mara game reserve on the border of Tanzania. Mary and I lodged in a wooden *banda*, and Mary was terrified by the sound of buffalo rubbing themselves against the wall behind our heads as we lay in bed at night.

When I returned to England I went to see Aubrey Buxton and gave my opinion that the Leakey film was unlikely to be as good as he had expected. Aubrey said he was grateful to me for holding the thing together, but I suspected that I was not taken seriously.

I was more frank with *Survival*'s producer, Colin Willock. I said that I was upset that I had been prevented from using my talents to make a much better film.

Colin shocked me by replying, 'Come on, Forbes – it's only television...'

I began to wonder if I had been at Anglia too long.

My confidence was restored when *The Lost Centuries* was repeated in October 1975, at the more reasonable time of ten thirty p.m. Once again it got record audiences and much critical acclaim. However, largely due to the philistine behaviour of the network companies, Anglia made no more nationally shown documentary series. In any case, the expense of making programmes like *The Lost Centuries* was escalating. Museums and ancient monuments had got wise and introduced fees, that quickly soared. Gone were the days when I got everything for nothing!

27

BY 1975 the gap had widened between the proprietors and the creative staff in Norwich. Much of the problem stemmed from the board's stubborn determination to run things through the Programme Planning Committee. Committees always decide to do what most of its members dislike least! Almost all the other ITV companies had a Programme Controller who was a professional programme maker. Harlech TV in Wales had the brilliant Pat Dromgoole and Granada in Manchester the visionary David Plowright.

In flattering themselves on their imagined broadcasting expertise (*Korda*: *Everyone I meet has two professions – their own and film producer*), and cushioned from the real commercial world by the immense profits ITV enjoyed, Anglia's owners lost confidence in their employees. Lord Townshend was even heard to remark (I hope unthinkingly) – "No one with real talent would leave London to work in Norwich".

Compared with Anglia's bravura beginnings, everything we were doing seemed smaller and more trivial. The company seemed to me to have lost its initial distinctive sense of adventure. There was a perennial diet of safe formulae; a programme about ephemera of past times, *Farming Diary*, a shallow nightly magazine programme, a quiz show called *Sale Of The Century*. Even John Woolf's early full-length blockbuster dramas had shrunk to half-hour *Tales Of The Unexpected* (they were so predictable that they came to be called *Tales Of The Expected*).

Endless suggestions for programmes were submitted by the programme producers and turned down by the committee without apparent awareness that it might discourage creativity. As a result, many members of the large work force that Anglia had managed to amass over the years had little to do. One producer told me he contributed only one half-hour of programming *per year*. No wonder morale was low.

The Lake Rudolph affair reared its head again. The material had lain in the company's London cutting rooms for nearly a year, awaiting assembly. During this time it never entered the *Survival* people's heads to invite me even to view the rushes. I told Colin Willock that I did not want my name in the credits as director. Aubrey Buxton was cross and tried to pressure me, but I said it was my prerogative to decide whether my name appeared. Work on completion, overseen by John, eventually began just before Christmas.

I went over the details in my mind and could not see how the programme could be anything but a disaster. However, 'No doubt I shall be proved wrong,' I said gloomily to Mary.

'You've been at it far too long to be wrong,' she replied.

In March the following year I received an alarming phone call from Paul and Thelma's daughter, Stephanie, telling me that her mother had been taken ill while working on the James Bond film, *You Only Live Twice*, in Japan. I asked how serious it was and was shocked when Stephanie said it was terminal lung cancer. Poor Thelma had only weeks to live. She and Paul had bought part of a villa, next to Frank and Bernadette Launder's, overlooking the sea at Cap d'Ail, beside Monaco. I flew out to see Thelma and found Bernadette lovingly nursing her long-time friend. I spent several hours with Thelma talking of old and better times and never saw her again. She died a month later.

Back at Anglia things were changing, and not for the better. There was a muddled reorganisation of departments, resulting in an illogical chain of command and insensitive duplication resulting in squabbles and feuds.

In concentrating on my programme-making ambitions I had failed to safeguard my own interests regarding my status in the company. I had stayed out of the infighting that went on among the executives, and had consequently lost out in the scramble for management preferment. (I remembered talking about it once with David Attenborough – he, too, had been compelled to make the choice between his natural history programme-making and nursing his career as head of BBC2. 'You only have status if you are a manager,' he had said. Like me, he had chosen the creative path.)

The catch, however, is that without status you do not have the power to decide what programmes are made – and following that, the power to decide how you are able to employ your talent. I decided that I must at least try to remedy the situation, play my part in influencing the direction in which I thought Anglia was going. Although Aubrey Buxton had a pet fish to fry, the promotion of his *Survival* project, I knew that he was not happy with the situation either. He set up a boardroom lunch with himself, Anglia's managing director, and me to discuss my ideas for reorganisation. I put in some work before the occasion and seemed to get an interested reception.

A few days later, Glyn Daniel phoned me and asked for an outline of what I had proposed. That was the last I heard of it.

I was reminded of my unhappiness with the way the company was going when the Lake Rudolph programme was broadcast in April 1976, with the absurdly cute title, *Bones Of Contention* (I would have had something to say about that).

During all the time it had been in the cutting rooms I had not been invited to view any of the film or contribute opinion, but even I did not predict the raspberries the programme would receive from the press when it was broadcast.

Richard Leakey damned it with faint praise, writing in his autobiography that it was obviously made by a committee. He had the Anglia style just about right.

The programme was indeed pretty dreadful, as I had feared, and did nothing to enhance Anglia's reputation in the USA. (I notice that it is not to be found in the record of *Survival*'s productions.) A year or two after it was made, the BBC's *Horizon* unit made a film with Richard Leakey. It was everything that Anglia's fiasco failed to be.

Thankfully, the Rudolph affair had not harmed *my* reputation. Early in 1977 I received a clandestine approach from a member of the BBC's "Chronicle" archaeology unit, asking me to meet him in London. Over lunch there, he told me that the staff of the unit were unhappy with its current head. I was widely admired, the BBC man said, and would be supported if I applied for the post. It was a flattering offer, but once again I decided that I was past the age to begin a career at the BBC.

Aubrey Buxton clearly had a bad conscience about me and invited me to lunch to meet Bernard Campbell, a wealthy North Norfolk landowner, who was also an "adjunct" professor of anthropology at the University of California Los Angeles, and a leading authority on human evolution. Campbell pulled no punches in criticising *Bones Of Contention*. The discussion ended with Aubrey suggesting that he and I should collaborate on a programme.

Campbell invited Mary and me to dinner in his Regency home, Sedgeford Hall, to discuss ideas. I had thought that the main interest in the Leakey project was whether "proto-man" was a hunter or a scavenger, and we decided to investigate making a programme about that. There were various areas that could be researched – the last surviving social hunter-gatherers, the Kalahari Bushmen – animal behaviour, et cetera. Most of the academic work was being done in the USA, Bernard said, and we agreed that I should go there, with a list he would provide of people to be interviewed.

In April I flew to Seattle where an anthropology seminar was being held. My hotel was at the top of a skyscraper looking out across Puget Sound and the view was breathtaking. It was my first trip across the Atlantic and I was curious to see if my preconceptions proved correct. I was not disappointed on that score. Buying a coffee in a nearby deli I was touched when the assistant said, 'Have a nice day'.

'Thank you,' I replied.

She glared. 'Tryin' to be funny?' she demanded.

At the conference I made several useful contacts and renewed acquaintance with two Britons who had been on the Leakey expedition. Archaeologist Glyn Isaac, who was at Berkeley, invited me to stay with him and his family when I was in San Francisco, and anatomist Alan Walker, who was at Harvard, offered to put me up when I got to Boston.

The stay with Glyn Isaac, his wife, Barbara, and two little girls, turned out to be a delight. They took me north to Marin County to camp beside the Pacific at Drake's Bay. It did not seem to matter that the San Andreas Fault was directly below us. The air was balmy, and I slept on the grass under the stars. Poor Glyn, a young and brilliant academic, died suddenly a year or two later, from a mystery infection picked up in China.

From San Francisco, I travelled south to Los Angeles, stopping off at the University of Santa Cruz on Monterey Bay to interview Dianne Gifford – the anthropologist who had given me the chert scraper at Lake Rudolph.

Bernard Campbell had advised that I would need a car in Los Angeles and said I could borrow his, which he left with friends. I phoned ahead to the Travises and arranged to pick it up. Mrs Travis asked me where I would be staying and I sought her advice on hotels. The only one I had heard of was the Beverley Hills.

'You're staying with us,' she announced.

I protested, but she insisted. 'We'll pick you up at the airport.' Thus began a long and affectionate friendship with two wonderfully generous people.

Joan and Arnold Travis's home was a large, comfortable ranch-type house in the exclusive suburb of

Westwood, on the edge of the University of California Los Angeles campus. The Travises also had a ranch at Blyth on the Colorado River, complete with its own railway marshalling yard for transporting the cattle to market in Chicago. Joan was heavily involved in human evolution research. Louis Leakey had been a frequent house guest, and she was chairing the international Leakey Foundation.

I was taken to meet people Joan thought might advance my "hunting man" research, including the film star James Stewart, who lived nearby with his wife Gloria. At UCLA I talked to anthropologists Clark Howell, Sherwood Washburn and Irv DeVore (these American names!) who all had views to offer on "the hunting hypothesis". I began to realise what a difficult subject I had taken on. Joan also whisked me round Los Angeles and I saw the La Brea tar pits, with the life-size model of a mammoth drowning in the oil bubbling at the surface. We stopped off at the gate of the 20th Century Fox film studio – my first sight, after thirty years in the film business, of your actual Hollywood. I paused to think of the turns of fate during those years that had led to my standing outside that "dream factory" and not inside. Not many years later, though, I was to work in Hollywood.

I then made my way eastwards across America to consult more of the people on Bernard Campbell's list, stopping off at Las Vegas on the way to see the Grand Canyon. I went on the sightseeing flight with a dozen fellow tourists in a light aircraft. It was a hair-raising experience. We dived below the rim of the canyon and circled, on a wing tip, above towering pillars of rock, the hot air updraft buffeting and tossing us crazily. Not long afterwards this flight was forbidden following an accident.

I went to Cambridge, Massachusetts, to see Alan Walker, then on to Yale University to talk to Bob Trivers, an authority on Neanderthals. In New York I visited Columbia University in the dangerous black district of Harlem. The name of the anthropologist I interviewed there now escapes me. He had a human skeleton standing beside his desk and told me that a mugger had once burst in on him and threatened him with a knife. 'That's what you're gonna look like!' he threatened, indicating the skeleton. The professor's life was saved by security men.

Finally I went to New York to take the plane home, staying overnight at the venerable Biltmore Hotel which then stood close to Grand Central railroad station. My itinerary had been too rushed to give much thought to presents to bring home and I needed to buy some little souvenirs for the boys. I went out into the station concourse to see what was available, but all I could find was a selection of what the Americans call "candy" bars at the sales kiosk. There was an enormous selection, all with wrappers unfamiliar back home, and I bought around thirty.

When I arrived at White Horse Farm, to a heart-warming welcome from Mary, Timothy and George, I produced the candy bars. The boys' eyes gleamed. But it was supper time, and Mary said they could have only one bar each that evening. They lined up the "candy bars" along the kitchen working surfaces and made their choice. The following morning – disaster! Our lurcher, Fly, was creeping around the room with a distended stomach – all that remained of the candy bars was ones or two torn wrappers. At least the boys saw the funny side but poor Fly had to have an enema.

It was obvious that if we were to do justice to the "Hunting Man" subject many more months of research would be needed. The production would call for large resources, and for the time being the *Survival* people decided to put the project on hold.

The decision was less discouraging for me because Glyn Daniel had been elected to the chair of archaeology at Cambridge and was bombarding the Programme Planning Committee with proposals for programmes he wanted me to produce. Glyn told me he had been giving thought to an idea I had put to him several times over the years. His book, *150 Years of Archaeology*, had established him as a foremost authority on the history of the discipline and I had proposed making a film about him and his work. He had declined for a number of reasons. Now, however, he was writing his autobiography and thought a television programme reviewing the progress of archaeology during his lifetime would be appropriate.

I went to work right away.

Glyn also played a part in our lives in another way. He had taken a liking to our sons Timothy and George, and declared that both should come up to Cambridge to become archaeologists. That was far into the future for George of course, but Timothy was coming up to his A-levels. He did well, and was accepted at St John's College to read archaeology and anthropology.

Glyn's history of archaeology programme was obviously a long-term project and I busied myself with one or two more modest programmes as well. One was about two of our neighbours at White Horse Farm. Lady Margaret Barry was a daughter of the Earl of Radnor and had been brought up at the turn of the century in a castle with forty servants. Mrs Gertrude Smith was a brewer's drayman's daughter who had been in service all her life. The two ladies became unlikely but firm friends through providing "meals on wheels" to the local old and infirm. They devised a joint talk about their contrasting backgrounds and gave it to Women's Institutes and church get-togethers. It was called *Above And Below The Salt*.

I was enchanted by the novel situation and we filmed their presentation, interspersing it with family photographs and other relevant scenes to make it visually interesting. This involved visiting Lord Radnor's home, Longford Castle near Salisbury. While I was waiting in a turret room to meet its owner I was astonished to see Holbein's *Erasmus* on the wall. I was even more amazed when I turned and saw a matching Holbein, which I did not recognise, on the opposite wall.

My little film was well received, and Lady Margaret, Mary and I travelled to Longford to show it to the family. Afterwards we sat round a large table for lunch of shepherd's pie and Brussels sprouts. At the head sat Lord Radnor, a very nice man who had been dwarfed through childhood polio. Sundry Rembrandts, Velasquez's and Durers looked down on us. We stayed in touch with Margaret Barry throughout her long life, until she died in her Cotswold home in her late nineties, blind but somehow still writing us letters.

I was Anglia's "history man" and when the Imperial War Museum opened its Air Museum at the former RAF station at Duxford, near Cambridge, I took a unit down to record the event. We were promised an interview with the famous fighter ace Douglas Bader. Another interview, however, proved almost more fascinating. The frightfully *refined* lady who had been in the wartime WAAF as manager of the officers' mess, came along from her stately home nearby to stand in the ruins of RAF Duxford's once gracious dining room. I conducted the interview from behind the camera.

'I joined the WAAF at the beginning of the war hoping to be taught to fly a Spitfire,' the lady told us. 'Instead, they said I should be a cook. I had never done anything like that so I went home and asked cook to show me how.'

'What is your most vivid memory of this room?' I asked.

'Oh...' She thought. 'That would be when Dougie Bader –' She blushed. '– I mean *Group Captain* Bader – came into the mess brandishing a pistol. "Oh sir," I said, "why have you got that gun?" "I've been listening to the wireless," he replied. "Hermann Goering speaking. He says that when the Germans have conquered Britain, all the blue-eyed English girls will be taken to Germany and given to SS men to produce babies for the Reich. Before I allow that to happen I've got a bullet in this bloody gun – " *Group Captain Bader spoke like that* " – for each of you girls."'

I could not resist it.

'You don't know what you missed,' I said.

The lady looked at me for a moment with a puzzled expression then burst into peals of laughter. 'I never thought of that!' she said.

Word reached us that Douglas Bader was in his aircraft on final approach to the airfield, so I hurriedly set up the unit in front of one of the hangars. It was nearly twenty years since I had met Bader when we were making *Battle Formation* and I did not expect him to remember me.

The small white plane made a smooth landing and I saw Bader swing his artificial legs over the side of the cockpit. He came stumping across the grass towards me shouting, 'Why don't you comb your hair?'

'Because I'm not going to be in front of the camera like you, Douglas,' I answered.

He grinned and slapped me on the shoulder. 'At least lend me your comb,' he said.

After we finished filming I took him to lunch down the road in the Red Lion at Whittlesford. It is the "Battle of Britain pub" and the room fell silent as the very recognisable Bader entered the room. We had a hilarious meal regaling each other with stories of our "naughty boy" escapades in the services. As I saw him off in his car afterwards he wound down the window.

'Let's keep in touch, old Forbes,' he said. 'The evenings are lengthening and there's not a lot of time left.'

But sad to say I never saw him again. He died five years later, in 1982.

28

IT WAS then that my life was turned upside down. Feeling rather "down" and becoming more and more convinced that I should make a change, I went to London to attend a Television Society meeting. On my way from the station I ran into Jack Sheppard of United Motion Pictures. We went to lunch and he told me that he was suffering from an incurable blood disease and had only a limited time to live. He wanted to retire and enjoy his remaining time with his wife Anne and family. He had built United Motion Pictures into a moderately successful company by industrial film making standards, employing fifty or so people. Now he needed someone to whom he could hand over the helm.

'The only person I would consider is you,' he told me.

I thought I saw what might be a way out of my Anglia dilemma. Although the prospect of returning to UMP's kind of activity was not an exciting one, it offered a chance of becoming my own boss. In any case the invitation was flattering. Someone at least valued me. But Sheppard had a problem. UMP was still partly owned by the person in South Africa who had created it years before. He had initially lost interest in it, but now the company had become successful he was taking advantage of Jack's situation in an attempt to recover his investment. The position had to be resolved before Jack could make any firm offer to me. We agreed that Jack would keep me informed.

It never rains but it pours, and only a week or two later another tempting offer came my way. The Royal Television Society held an Awards Ball at the Dorchester Hotel in May each year and Anglia always took a table. During a break in the proceedings while the tables were being cleared for dancing I was approached by a "head hunter", who asked if I was interested in a job in a new television service in the south of the Arab state of Oman. I would be Director of Production, with a tax-free salary. The approach was at least worth investigating and I accepted an invitation to meet the bizarrely named "Buzz" Bowen, who was head of Personnel & Electronics, the company that had won a contract to run Southern Oman's studio and transmission system and train the Omanis to eventually do the job themselves. The tax-free salary he offered was much larger than my Anglia one.

Mary and I thought long and hard about it for the next two or three days. We also asked the boys for their opinion. What was proposed would mean a disruption in our happy family life and a less certain future. In the end we agreed that I should accept the offer.

It was a full moon the night before...

I rather enjoyed breaking the news to the Anglia management. I had been offered a senior appointment, and the clear implication was that I was undervalued by them. They got the message and asked if my mind was made up. Aubrey Buxton, though, took me by surprise. He was excited for me and said I was doing the right thing to be adventurous – he would do the same in my position.

They say things go in threes, and I was in for yet another surprise a few days later. At the Royal Television Society council dinner it was announced that I had been elected a Fellow. It had been rare for a producer to be honoured in this way. The citation, signed by the President, the Duke of Kent, said it had been awarded for my contribution to the arts and sciences of television. As an "encore" I was invited to join the committee of the prestigious International Broadcasting Convention.

I was due to take up my Oman appointment in November, when my predecessor left for home. In the meantime I shot some footage for the Glyn Daniel biography, and tried to work out a scenario for the "hunting man" programme so as to leave these projects in good shape for my successor. Glyn told me that the production of archaeology programmes would not come to an end.

During my last few days with Anglia I was asked to cover for a director who was sick, and went with the film unit and a pretty presenter named Jane Probyn to Tring in Hertfordshire to shoot a short programme about the antique specialist, John Bly. We filmed in his shop, which I found fascinating. On the other hand, I discovered – to my surprise and consternation – that the filming process had begun to bore me.

Bored with "the train set"? That was something I never expected to happen!

When the time came for me to leave, Aubrey Buxton and other board members gave me a farewell lunch in the boardroom. I was amazed when I received an enormous greetings card, measuring nineteen inches by thirteen, made by the graphics department and signed – with numerous ribald suggestions for my future – by a hundred and fifty members of the staff. Most of them crowded into Studio A to see me presented with a leaving present, of a sumptuous pigskin briefcase, to which they had subscribed. Aubrey and Dick Joice made speeches, and I replied, saying it was like being cut adrift from one's family. As indeed a family is what Anglia had become in the eighteen years since that day when the words I had written put the station on the air. Lord Townshend wrote a nice letter, saying he hoped we would see each other again. Even the Great Panjandrum sought me out and wished me *bon voyage*. I thanked him politely. Perhaps his advancing years had caused his antenna to pick up unreliable signals – he must have thought I was becoming important...

Brian Hope Taylor gave me more genuine pleasure by emerging from his reclusion and coming over from Cambridge to my farewell thrash in the company social club. I was to see him only one further time.

Just before I departed for Oman there was a curious little incident. My very old friend, Robin Steele – he of the Covenanters' Inn, Aberfoyle, and provider of horses for *Proud Heritage* – had sold the hotel and moved to England some years before. We had kept in touch and visited each other from time to time. He was now in the process of selling his house at Henley-on-Thames – and the buyer was none other than Anglia's director, Sir John Woolf!

Robin mentioned my name, saying he regretted my departure abroad. To which, Woolf replied, 'Yes – but one can never keep these people...'

I wonder what he meant by that...

29

I WAS now past fifty – high time to be making the move into management. Film direction is a youngster's game, and in any case I had lost "that careless rapture". And so began a new, interesting and varied ten years in my life (during which I still found myself from time to time reluctantly directing film).

The stay in Oman was short. The Omanis were well capable of running the television service, without the supervision of "white eyes", as they called us behind our backs. The job proved to be rather pointless, though it did give me some management experience. It also gave me a rare privilege – the chance to experience one of the last surviving parts of old Arabia before it became corrupted by tourism.

When my initial year's contract came to an end I was invited to renew but decided against it. Instead of flying straight back to England I stopped off to spend a few days with Frank and Bernadette, in their villa at Cap d'Ail. Mary flew out and met me at Nice. Frank was his usual warm-hearted host and Bernadette looked as glamorous as ever. Paul Connell had re-married. His wife, Virginia, was an artist and they lived on the other side of Monaco. The Launders had them over to dinner, and Paul drank too much and became very "Oirish". It was wonderful, and more than a little poignant, to be together with the old gang again after so many years.

Frank and I exchanged remembrances of our early careers. He reminisced about his own first day on a film set in 1929. He had been working as a "back-room boy", writing titles for silent films. When sound came in, he had the job of writing the spoken dialogue. On the first day of shooting one of the first "talkies", Thomas Hardy's *Under The Greenwood Tree*, the equipment was so primitive that it was impossible to get a microphone close enough to the leading man and woman to capture the sound when they kissed. Frank was ordered to stand in front of another microphone on the other side of the studio, and loudly kiss the back of his hand at the right moment. It was his first and only film acting role!

Although Frank was seventy-three he had no intention of retiring. He gave me the screenplay for a new St Trinians film to read. It was called *Wildcats Of St Trinians*. I did not say that I thought the St Trinians' joke had rather had its day. In any case the script did not seem as funny as the earlier films. (*Wildcats* went into production the following summer at Bray studio on the River Thames, and Mary got a part as one of the St Trinians' schoolmistresses. Bernadette had a small part too, and they both enjoyed being back in greasepaint after so many years. As I had feared, the film was not a great success. Frank never made another film, though he went on nursing dreams.)

After the heat and dust of Oman it seemed strange to be back at White Horse Farm, in the heart of the Norfolk countryside. It was Christmas time, and I called in at Anglia and had turkey with Aubrey Buxton.

I now had to decide how to spend the remainder of my professional life. From almost the moment I arrived in Oman I had received letters from Glyn Daniel trying to persuade me to return to Anglia. It was flattering, of course, but I politely refused. I did not believe in retracing steps. Now that I'm older and wiser I think I should at least have investigated what Anglia had in mind. A series of letters also arrived from Jack Sheppard, telling me that the complex financial situation at United Motion Pictures was at last being sorted out, and he looked forward to my taking over from him.

I more or less drifted into accepting the offer to manage United Motion Pictures. It was a disastrous decision. Although Jack had used much energy fighting off the attempted takeover of his company and bombarding me with letters urging me to hurry back from Oman, he had not thought it necessary to inform the two or three employees he had appointed as directors of his intentions. When at last he broke the news they rebelled. Jack was now critically ill and in no condition to impose his authority, and I had no choice but to accept the situation. I visited Jack in hospital, and he was apologetic, but the consequences for me of his actions did not seem to occur to him. I had declined a renewal of my contract in Oman and refused a lucrative job at Anglia and now, it seemed, I was to be thrown to the wolves. All he could do was sigh. The only course left was for me to sue.

It was the last time I was to see Jack. I had known him since the very beginning of my career, when making *Proud Heritage*, and it was a sad occasion. UMP muddled along for a year or two, before disappearing. It had been very much Jack's personal operation and had, as it turned out, never been more than a subsistence enterprise.

I was now without the comfortable shelter of the regular salaries I had enjoyed from Anglia Television, and Personnel & Electronics, and had to find another source of income to support the family.

I had kept in touch with Bernard Campbell, and over lunch at Sedgeford Hall one day in June I chanced to remark that Anglia Television's broadcasting licence was due to expire the following year, 1980. It would have held the East of England franchise for twenty-one years, and had enjoyed three renewals while other regions had changed hands. Due to the conversion to UHF the transmission area had become larger and more profitable than the one Anglia had originally won in 1959. All in all the "proprietors" had been extremely lucky.

The sole fly in the ointment was that Norwich was no longer in the centre of the enlarged broadcast area. All sorts of demographic changes had put it out on the fringe. Cambridge, on the other hand, was right in the middle.

Bernard and I pondered these thoughts during lunch. I had been struck by a quotation from the Television Act:

"...contracts have a finite term. The Authority can never be in the position where, once an appointment has been made, the company concerned has a more or less automatic right to reappointment..."

It seemed to me that new people might make a rival bid when Anglia applied this time for renewal, and they might have a fair chance of succeeding. Bernard remarked that it would be a pity if that happened and incomers to the region took over. Why shouldn't he and I put in an application – proposing a new service, broadcasting from Cambridge?

What began as a pipe dream became a serious proposition. A few days later, I mentioned the idea to an old friend, who introduced me to a firm of merchant bankers in the City of London. They offered to support an application, if Bernard and I decided to make one. I was being swept along by a momentum that seemed to control its own destiny.

It has been suggested that, in initiating this enterprise, I was disloyal to former employers (a curiously Victorian notion), but nothing was further from the truth. I had severed my connections with Anglia some time before and had my own future to think about, as they had theirs. It was a commercial proposition in which sentiment played no part. However, if the Authority could arrange things so that Anglia and my group could both have licences I would have been delighted. And as far as my former colleagues were concerned we pledged that no one would lose their employment if we were successful.

A more momentous portent for the country was the election in a landslide of a Conservative government. Britain got its first woman Prime Minister, Margaret Thatcher. She was from the extreme right of the party and a process began in which the country (and also television) would be transformed – not entirely for the better.

If Bernard and I were to make a serious bid, we needed to form a "consortium" – get together a distinguished group of people with East Anglian connections who could represent a variety of cultural, entertainment and business interests. The group I assembled seemed to appear by magic. For a start, I had only to look among my friends. I had met Viscount Norwich, better known as broadcaster

John Julius Norwich, some time before, when he visited the city that shared his name – he is the son of pre-war cabinet minister Duff Cooper and the famous beauty, Lady Diana Cooper. Frederic Raphael is a celebrated author and Oscar-winning screenwriter. Peter Fairley had been ITN's Science Editor, with whom I had made the *Project-X* programme. I had not met the most lustrous name I aimed for. Sir Peter Hall, the director of the National Theatre, had Suffolk and Cambridge roots and would give our bid enormous leverage. He needed no persuasion to join us. Bernard brought in an academic colleague, the Principal of Newnham College Cambridge, Jean Floud, who strengthened our credentials as far as serious programmes were concerned.

A very old friend who asked to be included was Michael Seligman. At first I was doubtful, as I feared that we might be portrayed as an Anglia dissident group. But in the end I was glad to have him aboard, and he offered his Holland Park studio as a base. He immediately proved his value by introducing a prominent public relations expert and political lobbyist named Michael Rice.

Bernard brought in a young investment banker named Andrew Obolensky. He was a qualified accountant and we appointed him finance director. Through him I met Lord Aldenham of the Anthony Gibbs merchant banking family. He owned a farm in Harlow, Essex, and therefore had East Anglian *bona fides*. He joined our board of directors with enthusiasm. All members of the group contributed to a £10,000 sinking fund to pay the day-to-day expenses.

An essential requirement was a chairman who was an eminent figure to match Anglia's Marquess Townshend. I approached one or two members of the East Anglian aristocracy and also visited the House of Lords to sound out the young Lord Melchett, who farmed in North Norfolk. I had met him some years before when filming his father for Anglia's *Farming Diary*. Peter Melchett declined, on the grounds that he had enough on his plate as Labour's Northern Ireland Secretary. Nothing came of these efforts, so Bernard assumed the position of Chairman. As a university professor and substantial East Anglian landowner he was well qualified for the post.

The most difficult problem we faced was finding a prospective Programme Controller who would impress the IBA. The best candidates were already in employment, many at the BBC, and were not about to risk their jobs coming out publicly as part of a bid that might well fail. In the end we were forced to decide on the risky policy of going to the IBA without one, making the best of it by saying we would recruit a person of the highest possible standard after our contract had been awarded.

I persuaded Paul Connell's daughter Stephanie to be my secretary/PA. She was excellent. Another piece of nepotism was an invitation to Mary's godfather, former director of the Royal College of Music, Sir Keith Falkner, to become our Music Advisor. The group was certainly looking impressive.

We formed ourselves into a limited company called East of England Television, and Michael Rice offered us space in his palatial offices in Kensington. I spent the following months working closely with Michael, mapping out a strategy for our bid. We needed serious corporate backing, and the merchant bank I had spoken to introduced me to a firm of stockbrokers, who put me in touch with an East Anglian concern they thought might invest in us.

Colne Shipping was the last of the big North Sea fishing-fleet owners in Lowestoft. Its owner, Gordon Claridge, saw an opportunity to exert influence on the government to halt the decline of his industry. We appointed him to our board of directors, but he did not have time to participate personally and nominated his legal advisor as an alternative, a solicitor named David Crome. We now had a lawyer as well as financial specialists.

The final, and as we judged essential, link in the chain was the participation of a powerful media group, preferably a newspaper. Our research led us to a Peterborough organisation, East Midlands Allied Press (EMAP), which did not have an involvement in television. I approached the head of the Winfrey family, which owned the company, and he invited our group to Peterborough to make a presentation to his board. It was a tense experience, as so much depended on its outcome. We were submitted to a searching cross-examination about our competence to run a television service and the chances of our submission being successful. They were especially interested in my proposal to centre our operation in Cambridge. At the end of the morning, Richard Winfrey suggested we left for lunch. We should return afterwards to hear his decision. This would quite likely be the moment when our enterprise would either go forward or come to an end, and we had little appetite for our beer and sandwiches in Peterborough railway station buffet.

At two o'clock we filed back into EMAP's boardroom – to hear Winfrey say that his company had decided to come aboard. We were now seriously on our way.

30

IT WAS February, and the awards of the new contracts were to be announced on the last day of the year, 1980. Detailed applications had to be drafted for submission to the Independent Broadcasting Authority on May 9th. On March 4th I went to the IBA headquarters in Knightsbridge and told David Glencross, the Deputy Director-General, that we were going to put in a bid. The IBA Secretary gave me the application forms and told me that subject to Parliamentary approval the term of the contract was going to be extended to eight years.

The establishment of an ITV service in Cambridge was the central feature of our proposal and we visited possible sites on the outskirts of the city for a place to build a studio. Leading architect John Ware was commissioned to design it. He had built a studio for Yorkshire Television in Leeds, and the new IBA headquarters in Surrey, so we were going for the highest credentials.

Michael Rice and I also went on the road to canvass advice and support from influential people and bodies. We visited all the local authorities in the cities and towns of the East Midlands and East Anglia, and were surprised by the number who welcomed our intention to establish a new television headquarters nearer to the heart of the region. The leaders of Milton Keynes were forthright in their complaints that although it was easy for members of the public living in the furthest point east in Lowestoft, or north in King's Lynn, to take part in political audience participation programmes in Norwich, it was out of the question for those in the far west, in Bedford, or even south along the Thames.

We also wrote to or met all the region's MPs, including the Defence Minister, Francis Pym. Most were polite, some were supportive, and only two ran up their colours as shareholders and cheerleaders of Anglia.

In June – about halfway through the campaign – the IBA called a public meeting in Norwich's historic Blackfriar's Hall. The opposing factions – Anglia and Eastern England Television – were placed on opposite sides of the room, like families at a wedding or funeral, while the IBA "great and good" were seated on the stage, above the plebs. An Authority grandee, the Marchioness of Anglesey, presided.

I had to climb to my feet on several occasion to field questions from members of the public. Generally speaking, I thought we did rather well against a weak showing from the Anglia team. It was evident that they thought they had the thing in the bag in any case, and didn't think it needed a lot of effort on their part. Ladbrokes were giving odds of one-to-five on in their favour, and three-to-one against for us.

As we left the hall I came face to face with Lord Townshend. To my surprise and confusion he greeted me like a long lost son and assumed that I would join the Anglia crowd across the road for dinner. I had to explain that I was committed to entertain my own team. We parted on excellent terms. (I have always wondered what would have happened if I had accepted Townshend's invitation.)

It became evident that not everyone connected with Anglia was so benign. The first omen came when Peter Hall phoned me from New York, where he was producing *Amadeus* on Broadway. His deputy was running the National Theatre in his absence and had caused a rumpus by putting on a play called *The Romans In Britain*, which contained scenes of naked men. Peter had taken part of the flak and been accused of neglecting his duties, even though his contract with the National allowed him to do other work. He was given an ultimatum – give up all his other activities *including taking part in a television consortium* or risk his future at the National. I told Peter that of course he must not take that risk. He replied that he would not give in entirely, because he suspected there was more to the affair than *The Romans In Britain* scandal. He would stay with us on an "arm's length" basis and review the position when we got the contract. We agreed that this would remain a secret between us.

It was a surprise, then, when I read a brief account of what had taken place in one of the "posh Sundays". I suspected that the story had emanated in some way from Anglia's press office. I recalled Peter Hall's suspicions. The chairman of the National Theatre was the millionaire Lord Rayne, and I knew him to be a friend of Anglia's John Woolf (I did not spot at the time that Lady Plowden, Chair of the IBA, was also a governor of the National). Clearly "the gloves were off".

Our response was a glossy booklet, prepared by Michael Rice's art studio, which explained how we intended to be better than Anglia. We believed we had strength in one especial direction. Anglia Television, with no local Programme Controller, and controlled as it was by John Woolf and the London-based Programme Planning Committee, was – ultimately – not a true regional operation. Its two most important programme strands, *Survival* and the dramas, were, indeed, produced in London by London-based staff. No other regional station worked that way, and we did not intend to either. We would be truly regional. Our comments provoked anger in Anglia's London offices in Brook House, Park Lane – they were not used to being criticised.

Rice's studio also prepared our application document, a massive hundred-page tome setting out our programme ideas in all areas, biographies of our personnel, details of our technical facilities including maps and diagrams, and a full disclosure of our finance and business plan. By the time it had been written, printed and bound in hard covers, and the requisite fifty copies had been delivered to the IBA, our spending had climbed to over £50,000.

The merchant bank I first approached had decided to support a second group bidding for a different region and seemed to be putting more effort into that enterprise, so our stockbrokers arranged for us to transfer to a larger and more powerful bank, Standard Chartered. Their board took us on with alacrity, agreeing to underwrite our project to a level of £14 million. As we came away from the meeting with them, Andrew Obolensky asked me, 'Has anyone ever given you fourteen million before?' In the words of Eric Morecambe, there was no answer to that.

The climax of the campaign was a face-to-face interview in November with the IBA. We were warned off to attend at 3.50 p.m. for a quizzing that would take around an hour and a quarter. I ran into Anglia's CEO on the London Underground one day, and learned that Anglia were to precede us in the morning of the same day.

We did not know what to expect, and thought it prudent to have some kind of rehearsal. Peter Melchett agreed to act as the IBA's "chairman", and we rustled up two or three other worthies to be IBA "members". It was a worthwhile exercise.

On the afternoon before the real interview I received a phone call from the IBA, asking for CVs and photographs of my team so that the Authority members would know who they were facing. It occurred to me that we should do the same, and I spent the following hour or two doing some research. Imagine my astonishment when I discovered that among the members of the Authority was a director and chairman of the pension fund of a large public company, which owned shares in Anglia Television. Not only that, the fund had increased its holding in the preceding months. It seemed to me an obvious conflict of interest.

I rang the IBA to ask for clarification, and one of its officers adopted a superior tone, saying I must be mistaken. I referred him to company records, where the facts were clear for all to see. A while later he called me back to assure me that all would be correct at the interview. I took that to mean that the gentleman concerned would not be present. Of course he *was* present, although he gave no sign that he was aware of his compromising position. He took a leading and aggressive part in the questioning.

It seemed clear, from the moment the interview began, that Anglia had concentrated their pitch on a personal attack on me – our application was an act of spite for some supposed discontent while I was at Anglia. The IBA's chairwoman, Lady Plowden, had obviously swallowed it. We had hardly taken our seats when, ignoring the other members of my group, she directed a graceless query at me, demanding to know what I had against Anglia Television. 'Why had I not got on with them?'

Had I been prepared for the question I would have replied that the question was scandalous and out of order. Instead, I merely said that as far as I was aware, Anglia and I were on good terms. How anyone who was not totally naïve could imagine that a group of people would mount a detailed and expensive business operation out of spite is hard to comprehend.

The good lady's next – artfully innocent – enquiry was why Peter Hall was not present. I refrained from replying that she probably knew better than me, as she was one of the National Theatre's governors. She did not disguise her annoyance when I replied that Peter was still part of our group.

We came away from the interview fuming at the way it had been conducted, and I lost no time in phoning the Authority to complain about the presence and contribution of the compromised member. The IBA officer astounded me by replying that it had occurred to him that one of our group, John Julius Norwich, was a cousin of IBA member Lady Anglesey, and he considered that balanced the situation! He then dropped his voice and said, 'You don't need to do anything. Do you understand me? *You do not need to do anything.*'

That seemed to me to mean only one thing – the contest had gone in our favour. On that basis, we decided to take no further action.

I was therefore surprised when John Julius phoned me next morning to say that a *Sunday Times* journalist had been on to him, asking him to comment on "the conflict of interest business". I rang the newspaperman and stonewalled. It was evident, however, that he had full knowledge of what had gone on. A brief account appeared in *The Daily Express* next day. It provoked a call from Lady Plowden, accusing me of mischief. I kept my temper. I told her that no member of our group was responsible for leaking the story. The only other possibility was that someone from the IBA itself leaked it, and I believe that is indeed what occurred. We had friends there – people of integrity who would not have approved of what had taken place.

All we had to do now was wait for the result.

It could not have been worse. On Sunday, December 28th, Bernard Campbell, as chairman, was summoned to the IBA headquarters to hear our fate. We were informed, in cold official terms, that the contract had been awarded once again to Anglia, with not even the suggestion that they might invite us to join them in some sort of merger.

We had hardly begun to discuss the result when our solicitors in Cambridge phoned, advising that we must apply to the High Court for a writ of *certiorari,* on the grounds that there had been a breach of the Television Act. This would have the effect of freezing the award (and consequently all the other awards the IBA had made) while the case was pending. Perhaps it would take Independent Television off the air. I called a board meeting to consider this dramatic turn of events. Peter Fairley and John Julius were apprehensive. Even if we won our case, they thought, we were up against forces that were too powerful. In some way or other we would not be allowed to win the battle, and we could say goodbye to any further activity in television. We decided for the moment to make a strong protest to the IBA, and see what came out of that. I have since come to the opinion that this was the wrong decision, and that I failed in my duty to bring the facts out into the open.

Mary was becoming successful as a batik artist and had been invited to have a "one man" exhibition in Boston, USA. Sadly, she was unable to travel out to be present, as I suddenly developed alarming symptoms. I was seeing flashes of brightly coloured light in each eye. My father had lost the sight in one of his eyes due to a detached retina, so fearing the disorder might be hereditary, I went to the doctor. He rushed me into hospital and both of my eyes were operated on. I recovered consciousness with a pounding headache, and a vision of two bottles of chilled vintage champagne beside my bed. It was a present from Michael Rice. In fact my retinas had not been detached, but the surgeon had carried out reinforcements to lessen the risk in future.

The IBA invited us to a meeting where its new Chairman, Lord Thompson, lightly dismissed our complaint. I went back to the office and got out the 1954 Television Act. The lines leapt off the page. *No one should be appointed to the IBA if he or she had a connection with an ITV company. All members should annually review their status to ensure that they were still eligible. Everyone must check yet again, prior to a franchise round.* The IBA seemed to be in breach of the Act three times over! The regulations made it clear that the ultimate person responsible was the Home Secretary. We had got nowhere with Lord

Thompson, so I wrote to William Whitelaw. Months went by, and then I received a reply – of course, from a junior functionary. Yes. We were right. It was not proposed to take any further action.

It had taken me fifty-five years to learn a valuable lesson on the way Britain works.

Another small bombshell exploded a year or so later, when I was going through the files to throw out the dross. I came across a memo sent to me by Michael Rice early in the application year. It informed me that he had received a personal letter from a friend who was an advisor to Mrs Thatcher on media matters, warning Rice that we would not get the licence. The only franchises that would change were ATV in Birmingham, Southern Television in Southampton and Westward in Plymouth. And sure enough, nine months later these were the companies that lost their licences! One might *just* believe that the entire process had been a charade (an expensive one for us).

I have been told recently that an authorised history of ITV records that we lost the franchise because we criticised Anglia. If this is true, it was an even more scandalous decision by the IBA grandees. But was it their decision? I have a vision of a self-important Lady Plowden presenting herself to Margaret Thatcher with her decisions, and the Prime Minister thanking her with a sweet smile and replying, 'Thank you. How interesting. Now I will tell you what will be done.'

Fantasy, no doubt. I was told rather later by Anthony Pragnell, the IBA's deputy Director-General, that the decision was the most difficult the Authority ever had to make, and went against us by the narrowest margin in its history. I do not know if the Anglia "proprietors" ever learned how close they came to losing the licence.

So Anglia continued for a few more years. It adopted some of our ideas, including appointing new people to their board (though not, for several years, from among their own producers). Shares were made available to the staff. I was surprised when a large programme of enlargement of their Norwich premises was embarked upon, rather than the establishment of new presences in, for example, Cambridge. The advent of Channel Four had also heralded a shift to production away from studios by independents, working from their own bases.

My franchise group, with one exception, decided to stay together and make programmes as independent producers, initially for the new Channel Four. We made an archaeology series, *The Blood Of The British* for the new service and became drawn into developing projects for Anglo-American co-production. I even got to work in Hollywood, but that story is for another occasion.

When our two sons left home to begin their own careers, Mary and I decided that the time had come to leave White Horse Farm. We had loved the house and it was a wrench, but the surroundings were changing and it was no longer the rural paradise we had discovered in 1959. We found a house close to the sea at Walberswick. It was a lovely place to retire to (as many media people have also since found).

Not long after we moved I heard sad news of Brian Hope-Taylor. He had been dead for some days when his body was discovered amid a sordid pile of junk. He had stored valuable papers and records in an outhouse and they were badly decayed. We had still heard from him once a year at Christmas, when he sent elaborate hand-drawn cards protesting undying love, but he had always been "too ill at the moment" to come and see us. After his death his major contribution to archaeology was recognised, and the papers he left are being restored and conserved for the nation.

I was too busy to take more than a passing interest in Anglia's later history. John Woolf's retirement in 1983 must have brought about a radical sea change, and I heard that the management focus was moving from London to Norwich. Five years after Anglia won the contest with my consortium, Lord Townshend stood down and Aubrey Buxton took his place as Chairman. Then – after another five years – the franchise came up for renewal yet again.

I could not envisage revisiting that scene. In any event, inspired by Mrs Thatcher there was a complete remodelling of the licence system, allowing money rather than good intentions to be the deciding factor in the ownerships of ITV companies. Anglia bought back its licence, but in 1994 it sold out to a broadcaster from another region for £292 million. "Managers" were brought in and the output shrank until it consisted only of a celebrity-dominated audience participation show. Gone were the starry dramas, the network wildlife programmes and the archaeology series. In effect Anglia Television – the old, brave, visionary Anglia that we once all loved and admired – died.

I believe that had we won the franchise in 1980 a good regional service would have continued much longer.

I kept in touch with my oldest friends – Paul Connell and Frank and Bernadette Launder. In his late eighties,

Frank suffered a series of strokes that left him virtually helpless and confined to a wheelchair. Bernadette nursed him devotedly during the last ten years of his life. He spent most of his days watching videos of his films, recorded by his daughter Aesling and others when they were repeated on television.

His most ambitious, and favourite film, *The Blue Lagoon*, had disappeared. It had been re-made in Hollywood in 1980, and it was believed that in the process the negative of Frank's version had been destroyed. I discovered that this was not true. The Technicolor three-strip negative had been preserved in Britain's National Film Archive, though no print existed. I persuaded the archive to approach the owners of the copyright, 20th Century-Fox, and they generously paid for a print to be struck just for Frank. He was delighted. He died in 1997 at the age of ninety-one. Mary and I were about to depart on a trip abroad, and I was unable to get to his funeral, or his memorial service which I arranged at St James's Piccadilly, when the address was given by John Boulting. I did, however, attend a very moving funeral service only eighteen months later in Monte Carlo. It was tragic that Bernadette should follow Frank so soon. She succumbed to cancer. She was nearly the same age as me and was the first person I had known as a youngster to die in old age. I had loved her and Frank dearly and it hit me hard.

The fiftieth year of "commercial" television was celebrated in 2004, and I was asked to take part in a programme, made by "ITV Anglia", reminiscing about Anglia's earliest days. It was fun to recall the opening programme, when I had flown across East Anglia in a helicopter, and to hear once more the words I had written declaring that Anglia Television had begun. The programme, however, was a disappointment, concentrating on the trivial output and ignoring Anglia's achievements in the realms of archaeology and natural history.

A month or two later I was invited by the Lord Mayor and City Council to Norwich again, this time for the presentation to Anglia of the Freedom of the City.

The occasion angered me. The feathered tricorn hats, wrinkled stockings and Oyez Oyez – "Merrie England" at its most absurd – was to be expected. What *wasn't* expected was the honour being accepted, without a blush, by the current faceless "managers" who had inherited the ashes of Anglia and presided over the demise of its unique character. There was *no mention whatever* of the founders of the company, Lord Townshend and Lord (Aubrey) Buxton, whose ideals had contributed so much to the reason for the award. I wrote a letter to the local paper saying as much, and received a warm, grateful response from Aubrey from his retirement home in North Norfolk.

I do not expect to have any further connection with films or television, though I have been made a Life Fellow of The Royal Television Society. Looking back on my life, what strikes me is how much that seemed extraordinary at the time appears so *ordinary* by today's standards. Fifty years ago nobody dreamed of being a film director – you could count on the fingers of one hand the number of people who could call themselves that. Today, every youngster I meet seems to have directed a film or television show (even if their careers seem rather brief). It is not even unusual for the army to start people on a film career – serving soldiers are employed as combat director-cameramen nowadays. The Korda principle has become a prophecy.

I don't think I'd like to work in television today. Trying to do something creative in a business dominated by "managers", slick schedulers, "marketing" experts, and City speculators and take-over wizards, makes me shudder, and the thought of being assigned to direct one of these "reality" shows gives me nightmares.

I wouldn't even want to be in films nowadays. I look at the end credits of films like *Lord Of The Rings* and *Harry Potter* listing the vast army of technicians they use nowadays, and my heart drops. I was always a "one man band", or as nearly as I could be.

I think back on the distant days in the cutting rooms learning how to make *Proud Heritage* into some sort of film, with all that has since happened to me still in the unknown and scary future, and reflect that I have been extraordinarily lucky. I have enjoyed countless varied and interesting experiences; been happy far more times than I have been downcast. The blissful moments in the Rome Imperial Forum filming *The Lost Centuries* outshine the despondent ones at Lake Rudolph. I have had a happy marriage, which has lasted. That says a lot in these times.

'What if?' comes to mind quite often these days.

What if I had not been sent to the Highland Light Infantry in 1948? If I had not been there when Colonel Malcolm walked into the Maryhill Barracks mess?

If Roddy Leckie Ewing had not made that remark that led to my making *Proud Heritage*?

If I had not run into an actor friend outside that Kensington coffee bar and not met Mary?

And that decision to make the move from film to television? Had I stayed at the Film Producer's Guild, I was due to direct a film about a new steelworks at Port Talbot in Wales. The director who replaced me was David Villiers, and he was present, along with the unit, when the Bessemer converter exploded during the first pour of steel. David and the electrician were hit by molten metal and killed. That might have been me.

What if? What if?

So many of the people who were with me in Toy Town all those years ago are, alas, no more. Jolly farmer Dick Joice's plastic heart finally gave out on him in 1999, and practically the whole of Norfolk packed the village church at his funeral. Mary and I had visited him and Jean on his "retirement" farm in North Norfolk from time to time and the reunion was always joyful. He was a big-hearted, straight-talking man, and I was very fond of him.

At the time of writing, Mike Seligman is still happily in the land of the living, he and his charming wife, Gabby, dividing their time between homes in Switzerland, the south of France and London. He still spends more time, as he always has done, in airport departure halls than sitting with his feet up at home. I shall always be grateful to him for marking my thirty-third birthday half a century ago with the present of eighteen years' lucrative employment in a beautiful part of the country.

Harry Aldous was nearly eighty when he went into hospital for knee replacements. Sadly, he suffered a heart attack and a stroke during the operation. I visited him during the few days left to him, and he said, 'I had the best of the film business and the best of television, and I'll settle for that.'

I can't think of a better way of putting it.